for the book

Coach D Nicole taps into the very core of encouragement. In fact, she helps you tap into what is inside you. The truth of the matter is, every now and again, we need someone or something to help us focus on what's important: God, family and nurturing ourselves while helping others.

While brief, her daily affirmations are truly heartfelt and offer nuggets for how to cope and encourage yourself. **No matter whether it's you, a child, a friend or a stranger, Coach D Nicole's book has something for you. She helps you reaffirm what God has already promised.**

— Dr. Eric L Ellis
Founder and Pastor of Philippian Community Church of NC
President of Philippian Community College of Theology

Not your typical daily affirmations book! **Coach D Nicole provides the reader with stimulating, thought provoking affirmations that encourage you to take an introspective look into your own beliefs and values.** Definitely the positive motivation one needs to get the day started!

— Jennifer Rosa, MAOM
Higher Education Executive

Expertly written and penned with a level of conviction and passion that will inspire readers to grow, this book contains timeless wisdom delivered firmly, yet lovingly. **D Nicole Williams leaves no stone unturned as she challenges us all to confront the mental, emotional, psychological and spiritual stumbling blocks that have caused so many people to live beneath their purpose. Bravo!**

— NoNa Jones, MBA
Chief External Affairs Officer at Pace Center for Girls, Inc.
Author and Billboard Charting Independent Artist

The message in this book is quite simple: love and be loved. The author wraps up each chapter with affirmations and "homework" to get the reader thinking in a more positive light. I appreciated the simple, yet powerful theme behind each chapter. **This book inspires readers to take a hard look at themselves and their life and take a step towards making changes in their lives by saturating their perspectives with positivity.**

— CAROLLAINE GARCIA, PH.D
Industrial/Organizational Psychology Consultant

The message contained within this book is one of love, acceptance, and peace. It is a message more of us need to embrace within our lives, but don't know how to. **What is refreshing about this text is that is easily consumable. It is direct, but firm. Don't just go through the motions. Say the affirmations, do the activities, and let change into your life.**

— ELIZABETH SCHMIDLIN, PH.D
Human Factors Consultant

As a fellow Professional Life Coach, we are fully persuaded that we must believe in people. As I read through each affirmation, I witnessed Coach D Nicole's passionate and loving desire to see God's greatest creation—man and woman—walking in the state of wholeness as God so desires for us all.

This book is filled with thought-provoking topics which encourages the reader to do better in order to be better. It is an excellent resource which ministers encouragement, motivation, inspiration and admonishment. I can clearly see book clubs and small groups dissecting this one.

Job well done Coach D! I love it!

— COACH J DIANNE TRIBBLE
Certified Professional Christian Life Coach, Trainer & Speaker
At the Table Life Coaching & Motivational Speaking Services LLC

CHANGE YOUR POSTURE!
CHANGE YOUR *Life!*

The PASSION *Fruit* of Purposed PURSUIT

D NICOLE WILLIAMS

WITH EDITS BY
YOLANDA M MITCHELL
REGINA N ROBERTS

Change Your Posture! Change Your LIFE!

Copyright © 2014 by D Nicole Williams.

All rights reserved. No portion of this publication may be reproduced, distributed, or transmitted in any form or by any means, including photocopying, recording, or other electronic or mechanical methods, without the prior written permission of the publisher, except in the case of brief quotations embodied in critical reviews and certain other noncommercial uses permitted by copyright law.

For permission requests, write to the publisher, addressed "ATTN: Permissions" at the following:

Sh'Shares NETWORK, LLC
1601-1 N Main Street 13202
Jacksonville, FL 32206-0202
www.ShShares.com

Bulk discounts are available on quantity purchases by associations, corporations, and others for business, educational and ministry use. For details, contact the publisher at the address above.

Library of Congress Control Number: 2014921826

ISBN: 978-1-942650-00-3 (Paperback)
ISBN: 978-1-942650-26-3 (eBook)

Printed in the United States of America
First Edition

To God, The Father:
For your kingdom, my life is forever yours.
Use me as you will to do great work for this world.
All Glory, Thanks, Honor and Praise is due to You.

To The Loves of My Life:
Adriana, Arielle, Kiara & Terrell
I love you more than you will ever know.
You inspire me daily.
Keep being the great women that you are,
and I will continually be the best that I can be for each of you.

To My Mother and Grandmother:
I could not have asked for a better combination of... ME!
All that I am, and all that I will ever be, is a lovely
(frank, direct and outspoken!!!)
product of YOU!
I thank God for the two of you to model myself after!

fruits of completion

Acknowledgments

Introduction

Posture 01. The Purpose of GOD
- 01. Faithfulness
- 02. Joy
- 03. Peace
- 04. Wisdom

Posture 02. SELF Pursuits
- 05. Diligence
- 06. Self-Control
- 07. Goodness
- 08. Patience

Posture 03. Passion for OTHERS
- 09. Gentleness
- 10. Humility
- 11. Kindness
- 12. Love

acknowledgments

FIRST AND FOREMOST...

I thank my manager, publisher Regina Roberts, without whom none of this would be possible. Thank you for always supporting me, always believing in me and always encouraging me. Thank you for loving me on a level that I have never experienced before and for thusly elevating my awareness of love. You and your family have blessed me beyond measure. For that, I am EVER grateful! Thanks for being so welcoming and angelic!

Thank you to my editor, Yolanda Mitchell!!! I do not envy you the task of reading my words. You helped me *(and the WORLD!!!)* to make sense of them. Thank you for your guidance, tips and TIME!!! Send your parents and our pretty little yogi my love!!!

TO LOLO AND RUTHIE...

Mother, you have been the BEST example of womanhood that I have EVER seen!!! The older that I get, that truth becomes more solid for me. I am BLESSED to be yours! Thank you for your resolute character and maturity! At my age, you had already conquered the WORLD! With your support, I aspire to do the same!

My Angelic Ruthie Mae, no words can sufficiently express my love for you. I am humbled by your love and honored to call you mine. No grandmother around suits me better than you! Thanks for your spunk! I accept my own for seeing how you widely embrace yours. Thank you for that. I always needed to know that it was absolutely OK to be ME! I admire you. Your accomplishments are too many to count, but always know that your family appreciates the bar that you have set for us. Each of us is GREAT because of you!

To My Family...

Trust that you all have NO CLUE how much you mean to me. You are my WORLD, my ROCK, my INSPIRATION!

Jess, Aaliyah and Audrey, my heart is yours.

Gideon, I am a coach because of you. Thank you for EVERYTHING!!! You're... EV'RE! (Did I say it right? lol ☺)

To My Besties...

Adrian Plummer, Ashlle Norwood, Erika Harp, Ebony Wilkins, Elise Gross and Brittany Whigham, for being SO patient during my book-writing shut-in. Each time I leave and return, you all love me just the same!

Tangela, Lord knows how much I pray for blessings simply so I can bless YOU for all you have been to everyone you have EVER loved. We are blessed INDEED to have you as our love and as our friend.

Alicia Bertine, words cannot express how impactful you have been to everyone who has been blessed to know you.

Gator, Thank you for teaching me how to love. I will forever appreciate the lessons you taught. You blessed me.

To My Nameless Muses...

While you will here remain nameless, you and your love will forever remain etched in my memory. Thank you for blessing me with the great fortune of connecting with the world on an emotional level. You taught me the power of love, humility, passion and endurance. For teaching me peace, resilience, fun and flexibility, I heart you. I still have a ways to go to arrive at "dainty," but I could never have made it this far along that path without your help. Thank you.

OH! Darrell Mills... you deserve mention.

THERE IS NO WAY TO CATEGORIZE YOU...

Kari Hicks, for being my guardian angel here on earth! I love you like no other. Thanks for being a GREAT sister!!! I appreciate you for sharing MySon ☺ with me! You give me your heart and I appreciate that from the bottom of mine.

Monte Hicks, thanks for sharing so much without uttering a single word. You teach me SO much about life and love.

Bishop Eric Ellis, for your encouragement and timeless support. Thank you Lady Corranda Baker for your honesty, humility, and service. You both are to be emulated!

Ralonda Nesbitt, for your future!!! I join you on your path toward effortless success! Thank you for setting the stage.

Rory "N" LaShina Gibbons, Thank you for starting me on my way. As a unit, you have been a priceless jewel.

Followers, Friends and Fans, Your engagement means the world to me! Thanks for blazing this trail together with me!

TO TRAILBLAZERS LIKE...

Jarvis Love, for helping me clear this path! Eric Mayers, for allowing me to sit in the chair of a millionaire! John Carter; Candice Stephens; Antonyo Denard Sanders; Adrian Gentry and Livi Anderson; Pastor Vaughn and Lady Angela Brown; Veronda Ford; Jermel Jones, "Cobie" Nesbitt, Virgil Jones, Jr. and Victor Blackshear; Cheikh Mboup; Troy McNair, Sr; Khalil Aziz; Monique Carter; Kavoris Fruster & Gloria Williams; Farris Long; Liltera Williams and Christine Wilson; Carissa Glanton; THE Parker Bryant; BrayZil; Lady NoNa Jones; Darlene Smith; Takia Dickens; Ivory Orr; Quincy Harp; Shay Clemons; Olabode "Odd Rod" Borisade; Moses West; Anthony Heard; Taryn Wharwood; Lady Shay Brown; Angell Davis; LeeKenielle Whetstone and most certainly Coach Christie Speights... Each of you has written a paragraph *(or more!!!)* in my outlook on life.

Thank you for your GREATNESS!!! ☆☆☆

If you're looking for your name, and don't see it... I ran out of space!!! I bet you'll read acknowledgment pages now! ☺

introduction

A dear friend of mine once told me that alignment determines assignment meaning that we can only vie for ranks if we *first* get ourselves in line. Well, Mr. Leonard Chatman, Jr., I beg to differ! Swap positions and we end up with: *assignment* **facilitates** *alignment*.

Our assignments are predetermined for us. Providence handles alignment. Based on our God-given purpose in life, we embark on journeys that strategically *lead* us down the path BEST suited to our final destination. Leaders proactively participate in this process by COMMANDING what is rightfully ours! We don't simply lie in wait, contending with others for things that are already ours—we STAND UP and CLAIM what we will have!

Of course, such *noble* actions don't come without... rigor.

God places us in seasons that reinforce our personal visions and dreams. We are presented with trials that answer the question: ***How bad do you want it?*** In finding the answer to this question, we learn that we are willing to face a great many things in order to see our dreams revealed: We optimistically journey through challenges. We take advantage of powerful opportunities, *and* we shed ourselves of empty negativity to arrive at our purpose with the least amount of resistance that we can manage! At every juncture, experiences find us in the best place to receive all that we will have. So, what will *you* have? What is *your* purpose? What is *your* dream? *How bad do you want it?*

Find answers to these questions through engaging with the contents of this life-affirming series!

Why I Wrote This Book...

Change Your Posture! Change Your LIFE!

This mantra came as a result of my personal endeavor to reposition my*self* and my *mind*. Years before starting this project, I found myself in a frustratingly looooooong valley of STAGNATION! I was at a numbing standstill—mentally, emotionally, spiritually, physically and otherwise. I had lost my mojo! It was COMPLETELY gone, and it apparently did NOT want to be found!!! Eeeek!

Increasingly, I became tired! I was tired of *being* tired, and all of that made me even *more* tired! As much as I *thought* I was doing, from the looks of it all, it seemed that I was doing absolutely NOTHING! Seemingly, I was making NO progress at all! My encouragement was that I KNEW I had somewhere I wanted to be in life, and I knew that I couldn't embark on a "casual" journey to get there. My lofty dreams required effort, inspiration and ACTION that matched the weight of my purpose. In effect, I had to change my own posture to change my own life!

That is EXACTLY what I am urging each of you to do with this series of books: **Change Your Posture! Change Your LIFE!** Be a firm believer in passionate pursuit of purpose! Take the time needed to CREATE the life of your dreams using ALL that you've been given! Commit yourself to your future RIGHT NOW letting no excuse stand in the way of attainment. By everything that has been instilled within you, you owe it to yourself to be GREAT! JUST DO IT! Don't wait another day.

I wrote this book to start YOU on a journey toward **passionate** pursuit of purpose!

How to Get the MOST Out of This Book...

Now, this book makes it reeeeeeeeallly really easy for you to follow along and clearly affirm, decree AND declare each day's statements.

To start from the beginning I'll answer the question: *What is an affirmation?*

- Affirmations are positive statements made audibly so that the soul can hear. Consider affirmations a practice of mind-bending. With the goal of directing your mind to new thought and your body to new action, you affirm aloud for practical communication with your spirit man.
- The spirit of a man controls his destiny, so affirmers don't make these statements casually. Each declaration calls for passionate conviction and mental commitment to the chosen affirmation. No empty statements here!!! State your affirmations in FULL belief of their TRUTH!
- Following audible recitation of the affirmations, participate in the journal entries and occasional task lists to fully vest yourself in the chosen declaration.
- You'll get the MOST out of this book by following closely along in your journal since you will increase your self-awareness along the way.

Self-help is truly what it says it is: *Self*. Help. Self-helps calls into question the things that you are willing to do for yourself. Even with a formal life coach, inspirational audio-visuals and all of the leadership books in the world, it is ALL for naught if you won't help yourself! Commit yourself to each moment, and no matter what happens, don't you EVER quit!

Don't STOP! GET IT! GET IT!

Change Your Posture! Change Your LIFE!

Faithfulness

January

> ## I Will Work on FAITHFULNESS!

With every new year comes an opportunity to approach life differently. We're given the chance to revamp our focus, to renew ourselves and to create habits that lead us toward better actions and bigger achievements. *In* come the dreaded RESOLUTIONS! Yaaaaayyyyy!!! (*Or NOT!!!*) The dread associated with resolutions is optional—the resolutions themselves, on the other hand, are not. Resolutions are only associated with negative connotations for those who aren't faithful—those who lose their commitment along the way.

Faithfulness Affirmation *(Repeat this aloud)*
Faithfulness is a personal resolution of commitment to my*self*, to some*thing* or to some*one* other than myself. Faithfulness is also my personal commitment of, or *to*, divine persuasion.

Throughout January, we review faithfulness to ourselves, faithfulness to concepts, and faithfulness to others. More importantly, we review our faithfulness to The Creator while highlighting His faithfulness to us!

Say Aloud: I Will Work on Faithfulness!!!

January

" I Will Get Out of My Own Way! "

Much of the blockage that we experience in life is caused by ourselves. Us. Self. No one other than you and me. We participate in activities and behaviors that lead us toward a desired end, and when we arrive, we are stomped. On other occasions, we are stomped *within* the process because some aspect of the development requires us to change—or it requires us to be introspective enough to objectively evaluate situations in *any* given moment. We get STUCK!

Affirmation Journal
- ★ **In which areas am I most stuck?**
- ★ **What is the common theme within each of these areas?**
- ★ **What core adjustments can I make to become unstuck?**

GET OUT OF OUR OWN WAY! This is an unceasing, ever-evolving process. Be proactive about making gains in this area. Commit yourself *to* YOURSELF! Don't be the blockage in your own life!

Before committing to anyone else, develop the habit of committing to SELF! Before you commit to yourself, you must first GET OUT OF THE WAY!

> *It takes considerable knowledge just to realize the extent of your own ignorance.*
>
> THOMAS SOWELL

January 3

"

GOD is Just!

"

To say that God is just is to say that He is fair. God is impartial. As God is not a respecter of persons. Every man is measured by God equally according to his own doings. God judges between right and wrong according to *His* principals. In the administration of His authority, God doesn't subject us to the standards, views or laws of man. We're fortunate that God doesn't measure us according to the doctrines of man. Man-made sanctions are often much more harsh and harder to live up to than those of The Creator.

To say that God is our judge is to say that He is our Savior. Faith secures our salvation. Good works secure our rewards. God is sovereign and true, and He renders to each of us all that we are due.

God keeps his promises to us because He is Just.

Say Aloud: **God is Just! I Am Judged By Standards of Grace.**

Affirmation Journal
- ★ **What does it mean to be judged by God?**
- ★ **Why are God's judgments more lenient than man's?**
- ★ **How has God personally shown me that He is just?**
- ★ **How can I be more just in my own assessments?**

January

" GOD is Faithful! "

The awesomeness of God comes through knowledge that He is faithful! God is an ever-present adversary in our time of trouble! He never leaves nor will He ever forsake us.

Knowledge of these facts is POWERFUL information to have during times when we feel our faith is being challenged or when our backs are pressed against a wall. Sometimes, the *only* thing we need to know is that *someone* has our back! We need to be reminded that we're not alone in life and that someone understands what we're *growing* through.

God knows ALL that we're facing at ALL moments in time. He knows *and* He cares! When we feel the need to give up, God shows us His precious hand and reminds us of His companionship. Just by acknowledging and accepting His presence, we are able to keep ourselves encouraged throughout life's journey.

Find comfort in knowing that God is *always* present, even in uncomfortable situations. By putting faith in God, you'll find that He *always* comes through. He is faithful! He is God!

Say Aloud: God is Faithful! He is ALWAYS Present!

But God doesn't call us to be comfortable.
He calls us to trust Him so completely that we are unafraid
to put ourselves in situations where we will be in trouble if
He doesn't come through.

FRANCIS CHAN

January 5

I Will Uphold a GREAT Standard!

Be proud of all that you are and all you have to give! Be proud of what you bring to the table. There isn't a single person who could do life the way that YOU do it. There isn't another person who could share with life the gifts you have to share!

You are your own standard! Uphold a GREAT standard! Exemplify a measure of greatness that YOU can be proud of. Share your light with the world in ways that only YOU can and don't be afraid to make mistakes along the way!

Cherish the lessons gained from your hang ups. Standards aren't about perfection. Standards are about facing the world through a clear lens while showing pride for who you are. Your moral character, values, visions, goals and dreams will be the guiding frameworks that define the standards you create. Create a foundation that will make you proud and don't be afraid to share your brilliance with others!

Affirmation Journal
- ★ **What great standards have I created?**
- ★ **How well am I doing at maintaining them?**
- ★ **What do my great standards afford me in life?**

Say Aloud: I Will Uphold a Great Standard! I Am Brilliant!

January

" I Will COMMIT! "

In focusing on faithfulness and commitment, it's often easier for us to commit to others than it is for us to commit to ourselves. Odd, huh? NO—Not at all! We all show up—*and show OUT*—for others more frequently and persuasively than we will for ourselves. Why is that? It's because the person we have the *hardest* time committing to is SELF!

When it comes to commitment, self is exactly where it starts. Commit to yourself first and foremost, *then* you can effectively commit to all others. That focus starts with trust, so TRUST YOURSELF! **Believe** that you CAN and **know** that you WILL!

Affirmation Journal
- **Where is MY commitment?**
- **What am I doing to develop my ability to depend on ME?**
- **How will I demonstrate that I trust my thoughts and experiences to lead me into a marvelous life?**

Let's COMMIT to ourselves this year and never look back!

Say Aloud: **I Will Commit! I Will Be Faithful to Myself!**

Unless commitment is made,
there are only promises and hopes; but no plans.

PETER F. DRUCKER

January 7

> **My Life is BLESSED!**

It's often said that situations are either blessings or lessons. All in all, every situation is both. There is *always* something to be gained from an experience, and within each of these lessons, there is a worthwhile blessing.

Interactions present us with the opportunity to bless *on*, or to be blessed *by* others. We miss the entire lesson *and* the blessing whenever we're overly focused on what may be the problem while not seeking to find the lessons we've been tasked with learning.

> *"We are all faced with a series of great opportunities brilliantly disguised as impossible situations."*
> —CHARLES SWINDOLL

Instead of focusing on the problem, we should focus more on the likely lesson.

> *"Don't wish it was easier—wish you were better.*
> *Don't wish for less problems—wish for more skills.*
> *Don't wish for less challenge—wish for more wisdom."*
> —JIM ROHN

The faster we learn the lesson, the faster we can move on. Consider yourself and your life blessed by ALL that you encounter daily!

January

" I Am LIVING! "

What is life without its joy and what is joy without its experience? There is a new experience with every moment that passes and within each breath that you take. There's always something to do, something to share in, something to enjoy! The question is: **Are you *living*?**

Are you doing what it takes to create experiences that make you feel ALIVE?! Are you getting the BEST out of each moment? Are there vivid memories that you share recalling the experiences you've created for yourself?

Life is empty without worthwhile experiences and enjoyment! You have NOTHING without adventures and the journeys you take.

Take the time to invest in your LIFE by creating experiences that make you feel ALIVE!

Affirmation Journal
- ★ **What experiences have I created that make me feel alive?**
- ★ **How can I get the BEST out of each moment?**
- ★ **What vivid memories do I recall of the experiences that I've had?**

You've gotta dance like there's nobody watching,
Love like you'll never be hurt,
Sing like there's nobody listening,
And live like it's heaven on earth.

WILLIAM W. PURKEY

January 9

I Will Honor GOD!

The gift of our talents is God's way of endowing us with the tools we need to competently fulfill our purpose in life. Our gift back to God is humbly embracing ALL that He has given us through passionate expression of those gifts. That's how we show God the honor that's due Him.

God believes in us. He believes in our skills, in our talents, in our abilities. He has given us all that we need to effectively carry out and accomplish everything that we desire to. We honor Him by placing COMPLETE trust in His masterfulness and by embarking on the journey toward fulfillment of our purpose.

Affirmation Journal
- ★ What gifts do I have?
- ★ How do my gifts contribute to my purpose?
- ★ How do I honor God with my gifts?

If someone who believed in you *more* than you believe in yourself told you that you could do it, would you do it?

God tells us this daily.

Honor Him with your gifts. Honor Him with your passionate pursuit of purpose!

Say Aloud: I Will Honor God! I Will Honor God with My Gifts!

January

"

I Will Listen to GOD!

"

We often find ourselves in a world of trouble when we lose sight of God. God's involvement within our lives keeps us on a golden track of full appreciation for all that life brings our way. Navigation along the journey is much more impactful and less troublesome when we bring God with us. To do this, we must listen—we must learn to hear God's voice.

God speaks to us in a great many ways. The challenge is learning to still our spirit and to quiet our own voices long enough to listen. We make listening to God a complicated task since we're often challenged with *how* to hear Him. We are concerned that we don't know what God's voice sounds like, so we think we miss opportunities to listen. His voice is often the sound of our own voices or the words of friends, family members, and primarily, our spiritual counselors.

Say Aloud: **I Will Quiet Myself! I Will Listen to God!**

You will often find God within your thoughts and dreams. He shows Himself through signs and messages that you come across. No matter His methods, be sure that you're always still enough to listen.

Prayer is when you talk to God;
Meditation is when you listen to God.

DIANA ROBINSON

January 11

> ## My Prayers Are POWERFUL!

When I was a young girl, my grandmother taught me the practice of prayer. Every single day, she would wake before dawn to praise and pray to God. Daily, my grandmother wakes up with the same practice—singing, dancing, and praising Him! Honoring Him! Glorifying Him! And I THANK HER for embedding those images, those behaviors and those *values* into me! My grandmother's *fine* example taught me to pray for myself!

We must be taught the act of praying with POWER when life takes us to depths that threaten both our mental livelihood and our emotional dexterity. For me, during such times, my prayers change from being those of supplication to NOTHING but praise and worship! You see, finding the POWER in prayer means learning to listen—learning to quiet our thoughts and pleas long enough to stand still and acknowledge the grace of Our Provider and the power we've been given to control ourselves. This helps us to control our lives.

Effective praying is learning to shift from supplication with shaky supposition to prayers of COMMAND and POWER with much praise!!!

Say Aloud: **My Prayers are Powerful! *I* Am Powerful!**

January

There is NOTHING Too Hard!

Say Aloud: There is NOTHING Too Hard!

That affirmation is likely one that we should start *and* end EVERY day with! Such an affirmation removes the limits within our minds—self-imposed and otherwise. We just *have* to know that there's greater to be had, that there's greater to be achieved, that there's greater to be done. Removing limits makes those things possible!

Affirmation Journal
- ★ **What self-imposed limits have I constructed?**
- ★ **Which self-imposed limits do I cling to most?**
- ★ **Which self-imposed limits would be easiest to remove?**
- ★ **What is *Too Hard* for me to do?** *(Answer = NOTHING!)*

Take record of your successes to remind yourself of all that you've done thus far and all you have remaining to do. Periodically review this Listing of Accolades and Accomplishments. Recall the tasks you thought were impossible until you completed them. Remind yourself frequently that there is ***NOTHING*** too hard!!!

> *Faith enables persons to be persons*
> *because it lets God be God.*
>
> CARTER LINDBERG

January

I Will Take a RISK!

Faithfulness requires us to take risks. Through risk-taking, we demonstrate our willingness to believe and be committed to the outcome. How can we show our commitment and faithfulness to ourselves without being willing to take risks for the sake of our futures?

Commitment allows us to endure. Through the good and through the bad, we show that we are bound to our decision by our willingness to persist in faithfulness. Sometimes, the risks we take are so extreme that if things didn't work in our favor, we could lose EVERYTHING for the sake of our faith. *That* is EXACTLY the type of faith that gets us leaps and bounds beyond the steps that others are taking!

Affirmation Journal
- ★ **What risks of mine show demonstrations of my faith?**
- ★ **What is the biggest risk I have taken?**
- ★ **What did I learn?**
- ★ **If reward is measured based on risk, how big would my reward typically be?**

Say Aloud: **I Will Take a Risk! My Reward Will Be GREAT!**

January

> **I Will Be FAITHFUL!**

Fear of Commitment. At various points in life, many of us have struggled with this grossly overused practice. We don't want to commit to a person, to a schedule, to someone else's job or to our own lives! We don't want to commit to much of *anything* yet we still do it and we do it often! What sets you and I apart is that we've realized there is a problem! We have been aware of the issue for some time now—hence our indulgence in coaching measures—and we're no longer OK with the sense of *dis-ease* we feel at the thought of having to commit to any*thing* or any*one*.

Make a commitment NOW to be **FAITHFUL**! Faithfulness is a practice that builds character, integrity, accountability and dependability. Without faithfulness, your affirmations, resolutions and plans will never prosper. If those things don't prosper, YOU never prosper!

Affirmation Journal
- ★ **In what areas do I need to be more faithful?**

Start this year off differently—by being faithful—*first* to yourself, *then* to others!

If you're walking down the right path and you're willing to keep walking, eventually you'll make progress.

BARACK OBAMA

January 15

> ## I Will Make a Faith Move!

Demonstrations of faith require ACTION! We can't show faith through begging and pleading and whining and waiting. Faith is met with courage through ACTION! Action creates the framework where faith can be *manifested* within our lives. Without progressive action, there is no measure of working faith and there is no resulting victory.

If we are to show faith, we *have* to take ACTION. We have to take consistent actions in the direction of our desires. There must be discipline in our efforts since the definition of faith outlines that we're believing in what we can't see. That being the case, lack of visible results shouldn't easily impede the progressive action we take.

Say Aloud: **I Will Make a Faith Move!!!**

A sufficient way to measure faith in action is to assess whether you're literally preparing for what you're seeking. If you're seeking a job, are you applying? If you want a home, are you searching? Are you reviewing financing options? Are you saving? If you are desiring to accomplish some grand feat in life, are you studying and training yourself?

Without matching your actions with your desires, you are simply wasting time. You must ACT upon what you are looking for so that you're aptly prepared for its receipt.

Say Aloud: **I Will Make a Faith Move! I Am *Acting* on Faith!**

January

"

GOD is Able!

"

To believe in God is to also believe in His supreme POWER. Though we might understand this concept on a basic level, these same realizations lack vivid clarity in the midst of our trials. When we're struggling in life or encountering trouble, our faith in God's abilities ebbs and flows.

There is great peace and comfort in knowing that God has it ALL under control. An adequate measure of our faithfulness toward ourselves and toward God is gauging how committed we are to Him during troublesome times. Steadfastness in faith creates a situation that shields us from our own negative thoughts and also from the negativity in the trials we face. Trust in God's abilities is much more favorable than maintaining a shaky countenance at *any* sign of struggle.

We should always remind ourselves to get out of the way so that God can do what He does best! God's abilities are best demonstrated when we remove ourselves from the situation.

Say Aloud: **God is Able! I Trust God!**

*All I have seen teaches me to
trust the Creator for all I have not seen.*

RALPH WALDO EMERSON

January 17

GOD is Mighty!

God is Mighty! God is Strong!

When we are weak, God is our strength! He keeps us pushing when we would otherwise give up. Accepting faith in God means believing in that which is greater than ourselves. It means tapping into a deeper dimension where we are opened up to the greatness of outward comforts and inner peace. God's might is strengthened in our weakness because it is during those times when we succumb to the FULLNESS of His power. We then understand that we can't *grow* through life alone. We awaken to the joy that we've NEVER been alone because we know we have everlasting help in God.

Affirmation Journal
- ★ How has God shown his power in my life?
- ★ In which weaknesses of mine has God been *strongest*?
- ★ How might I find my own strength in God's might?

Say Aloud: **God is Mighty! God is Strong! God is My Strength!**

January

"

GOD is Masterful!

"

The masterfulness of God is demonstrated by His prowess in caring for all things. God is master of all that concerns us and He cares for us in ways that we can't even begin to imagine. His power is even further demonstrated in the way that He imbues us with usage of that same power. In His supreme mastery, God extends control to us. By faith, coupled with action, we have the power to master a great many things! That is how much God loves us!

When we *allow* Him to be, God is present in our lives. Without our *acceptance* of Him, God is STILL our ever-present help. It's up to us to take control of the power we've been given by honoring God's supremacy.

God is utmost.

Affirmation Journal
* ★ Where is God's presence apparent in my life?
* ★ How has God shown Himself masterful in my life?
* ★ How do I use the power that God has given me?

Say Aloud: **God is Masterful! God is Willing and He is Able!**

Knock, And He'll open the door
Vanish, And He'll make you shine like the sun
Fall, And He'll raise you to the heavens
Become nothing, And He'll turn you into everything.

RUMI

January 19

"
I Am Full of FAITH!
"

In accomplishing GRAND feats in life, it's required for us to get outside of ourselves. We *have* to exist outside of our comfort zones to test the limits of our desires. We must operate within frameworks that challenge us to live outside the spectrum of the "typical". If we are to see our grandest visions come to fruition, we must dream bigger than we ever have, leap farther than we ever have and go where we've never gone—mentally, physically and otherwise. Through such devotion we will have the fruits of our labor and the desires of our hearts.

Without the tenant of faith, we go nowhere. We MUST believe in the things that we're working toward—THAT is essential toward achievement! There can be no greatness without great faith! If we hope to fly, we must have faith that we *can*, for it is through faith that we're able to see that which has not *been* but will *be*. Through faith, we're blessed with a new set of eyes that clearly see the end result without being blinded by temporary defeat.

Faith recharges us time and time again. Faith renews us. Faith helps us to believe! Faith lets us know that we're ready—it's our time!

It's time for us to FLY! The wind can't get underneath our wings until we JUMP!

Take a leap of FAITH!

January

" GOD is Love! "

Love is SUCH an amazing concept once we wrap our heads around it, yet we spend SO much time trying to define that which is without definition, essentially attempting to contain that which is without containment!

Outside of GOD, there is *no* definition, *no* understanding, and *no* utterance that can accurately quantify the full breadth of love. Think on that for a bit. We could be done with this discussion for today, but we're not! ☺ Simply put:

God is Love. God is EVERYWHERE—in ALL things!

Affirmation Journal
- ★ **What is Love?**
- ★ **How does God fit?**

Do you allow love in your life? Do you allow God in your life? If you find that you have love issues, start by resolving your God issues. Love is found in God. God is love.

To find the balance you want, this is what you must become. You must keep your feet grounded so firmly on the earth that it's like you have 4 legs instead of 2. That way, you can stay in the world. But you must stop looking at the world through your head. You must look through your heart, instead. That way, you will know God.

ELIZABETH GILBERT

January

> **I Will Value My VOICE!**

You've been blessed with eyes to see and ears to hear. You've also been blessed with a voice. Use it! There are too many methods of expression, so why choose *not* to express yourself? There are too many worthy causes and reasons to express, so why choose *not* to be vocal. Why have a voice if you won't use it? Why have thoughts to share if you don't put value behind them?

Believe in the value of your voice. Trust the value of yourself. Know that there is substance behind the thoughts that you think and the emotions that you feel. Don't ever shy away from expressing yourself in a productive manner. Place value in the wealth of your own self-expression. Share your thoughts, feelings and experiences with others and LIVE! Allow others to live through the feedback that you have to give. Be a proponent of positive self-expression!

Affirmation Journal
- ★ **In what areas of life am I overdue for self-expression?**
- ★ **In what areas of life have I been afraid to use my voice?**
- ★ **Why is it important to value my voice?**
- ★ **How can I ensure that I value my voice well into the future?**

Say Aloud: **I Will Value My Voice! I Will Express Myself!**

January

> **I Am Greater Than My BELIEFS!**

Don't ever limit yourself according to your beliefs. If your belief systems create limits for you, CHANGE THEM! Get out of your own way!!! Move the mountain of your mind so you can reach higher heights, span greater passages and dig deeper depths. Know that you have the power to control *and remove* any limit that you perceive. YOU have that power—USE IT! YOU have that control—TAKE IT! Remove the limits of YOU! You are even GREATER than what you perceive! Test out this fact and watch your life change immensely!

Affirmation Journal
- ★ Which belief systems limit my potential?
- ★ Which belief systems do I have the power to change?
- ★ What is standing in the way of my GREATNESS?

Say Aloud: **I Am Greater Than My Beliefs!**

Do not overestimate the competition
and underestimate yourself.
You are better than you think.

TIMOTHY FERRISS

January 23

"

I Am BETTER!

"

Think back on the person you were ten years ago. Do you remember the feelings you once felt? The reactions you had? The conclusions you normally drew? Think back to a year ago, same questions. Recall where you were in life just a month ago. You have made such GRAND progress over time! Kudos to you!!! No matter what it looks or feels like, you are making PROGRESS!!! You are getting BETTER! Steps in a forward direction are positively progressive steps. With progress comes betterment. There are always new learning experiences to be had with each new day. There are always new insights to be gained with each new question and answer. There are always new depths with each new discovery and we find blessed NEWNESS in each day! Each day, we are getting better. We have more to share and more reasons to live. Our past teaches us that our progress is not in vain. Realization of where we've come from reminds us that we have so much further to go. We are constantly assured that we can get there with time because we are *better* with time.

> Say Aloud: **I am SO much Better than I used to be! I am SO much better than where I came from! I am SO much better than the old me! I am progressing!**
>
> **I AM BETTER!**

January

" I Am SAVED! "

To be saved is to be found, no longer lost. To be saved is to be uplifted, no longer in despair. To be saved is to be fruitful, no longer fruitless. To be saved is to find purpose and clarity in life, a new dimension.

> *"A mind stretched to a new idea can never return to its original form."*
> —ALBERT EINSTEIN

Salvation entails removing oneself from the *common* and transcending to a heightened level of existence based on revitalized awareness of the life we've been given. Once an advanced level of consciousness has been obtained, we can't revert back to our original frameworks. We've then been elevated to a point of no return to the former. We've thusly saved ourselves from past reactions, activities and behaviors. Our BEST self is found along this thriving path. We now know what to do. Salvation helps us to do it.

Say Aloud: I Am Saved! I Know What to Do! I Am Doing It!

> *Three things are necessary for the salvation of man:*
> *to know what he ought to believe;*
> *to know what he ought to desire;*
> *and to know what he ought to do.*
>
> THOMAS AQUINAS

January

I Am BLESSED As I Come! I Am BLESSED As I Go!

Blessings abound in our daily lives. Life itself is an immeasurable blessing, the benefits of which we see daily. Each obstacle that we encounter, good or bad, is a blessing because these challenges show us that we're still alive. Obstacles remind us that there's still much more to learn. Obstacles are our opportunity to be better!

We often disregard crucial facts of life that would help us to be ever-grateful. Relationships, for example, play a major role in creating blessed lives for us. In their own right, friends are essential to our longevity in happiness for the role they play in ushering joy into our existence over extended periods of time. Our family members show us that we are loved no matter what. Kinship is such a benefit because we see the dedication of our family members over decades. Through the good, bad and downright HIDEOUS, our family will always be present in our lives (*so long as we open our hearts and welcome them in*).

Life is a blessing that we can't deny. Whenever we find ourselves complaining about what we lack, we should remember that we're blessed to have life in the first place.

YES! We are indeed blessed!

Say Aloud: I Am Blessed As I Come! I Am Blessed As I Go!

January

"I Am BLESSED By My Enemies!"

When we do good by our enemies, we honor God. It's in our best interest to treat our enemies with the utmost respect and integrity. It's in this level of humility that we are blessed. Kinship toward enemies builds character. We learn how to remove ourselves and our negative emotions from the situation and practice love in pure form—not because of what we may receive in return, but simply because we desire to treat others well. We treat others well because this is how we want them to treat us. We treat others well because of the good feeling we receive by being inherently good.

With all our enemies do to harm us, showing a GREAT example of love, kindness and gentleness will thwart their attempts at causing us grief. The blessings in being good despite how others treat us include a clear conscious, cool countenance and cheerful comfort! We treat others well, not based on how it makes *them* feel, but because of how it makes *us* feel.

Say Aloud: **I Am Blessed by My Enemies!**

The Lord loveth a cheerful giver.
He also accepteth from a grouch.

CATHERINE HALL

January

> ## I Will Value My WORTH!

Don't look to find your value in all the wrong places. If you're looking for your sense of worth, the place you need to search is *within*. YOU determine the value that you bring to life based on what you will, and will not accept. What do you accept about yourself? What don't you accept? What value do you bring?

When you value who you are and what you have to offer, you're able to make better decisions that will keep you going in a positive direction. If you know who you are, it is quickly perceived by those around you. As you increase the value of your own worth, others will do the same.

Affirmation Journal
- ★ What do I accept about myself?
- ★ What don't I accept about myself?
- ★ What value do I offer?
- ★ How do I value my worth?
- ★ How do I *show* that value?

Say Aloud: **I Will Value My Worth! Others Will Do the Same!**

January

"

I Will Value My IDENTITY!

"

Affirmation Journal
- ★ Who am I?
- ★ How do I feel about myself?
- ★ What type of value do I bring?

Do you know who you are? Do you know who you want to be? Have you accepted where you've come from? Do you embrace your heritage, your family, your position? What do you have to offer? Why are you here? Ask yourself these questions to gain deep understanding of your identity. You will find the answers to these questions to be evolutionary—they will change over time. They are supposed to!

As you grow, so too, will awareness of your identity. You will become more in tune with who you are, more accepting of what you've experienced and more clear on where you'd like to go!

Ask yourself these questions on a regular basis. Define the person you'd like to be!

Say Aloud: I Will Value My Identity! I Will Make Myself Great!

*Try not to become a man of success.
Rather become a man of value.*

ALBERT EINSTEIN

January 29

I Trust the Ground I Stand On!

Each step you take in the direction of your dreams requires faith. It takes faith to walk toward what you can't see. It takes faith to keep you grounded. It takes faith to keep you feeling secure in your desires and related work efforts. Do you trust the steps you're taking and the moves that you're making? Do you trust the ground on which you stand?

In order to take next steps in awareness and confidence, you must first accept your current situation. It's hard to get to the next point without fully acknowledging your present state. If you close out awareness of your place in life, you miss the learning experience meant to be gained and you'll find yourself in the same spot again.

The ideal brand of progress is progress that won't find you going in circles. Progression simply means to go from one point to the next—it is not directional which means that the next step you take could be a positive *or* negative one. A succession of poor steps will find you repeating yourself or going backward. Too many left turns will have you going in circles, wasting time.

Trust the ground you stand on and move forward!

Affirmation Journal
- ★ How do I feel about my current place in life?
- ★ What lesson am I learning within my current situation?
- ★ What positive steps will I make in the coming month?

January

I Am FAITHFUL!

Faith gives us power. Faithfulness is a demonstration of said power. Commitment is seen in faithfulness, so are traits of wisdom, peace and resilience. Through faith, we're able to withstand a great many things with pride in the knowledge that we are not our own salvation. We put our faith in what is greater than us. We put our faith in God.

Through the struggles we face, our faithfulness to God and our commitment to ourselves helps us proceed with a sound mind. Life is a struggle when we have all kinds of burdens clouding our thoughts. We change the scenery by focusing on our desired end—we focus on the promises of God! These practices are motivational. The peace that we discover inspires us to stay the path without giving up. We are then further inspired to be faithful—to hope *and* persevere!

Affirmation Journal
- ★ How committed am I to God?
- ★ How committed am I to myself?
- ★ How can I show more faithfulness to God?
- ★ How can I show more faithfulness to myself?

Faith is putting all your eggs in God's basket,
then counting your blessings before they hatch.

RAMONA C. CARROLL

January

> ## I Am Committed to Living My Life FREE in My Truth!

Life, love and success are all about acceptance of self! Self-acceptance means discarding negative thoughts that control us. That freedom means removing thoughts and viewpoints that limit your potential for GREATNESS! No matter what you strive for in life, the goal is to be GREAT at it!

Life isn't to be taken for granted. Love yourself for EXACTLY who you are with NO apologies or explanations. Live life to the fullest in YOUR truth. Commit and be ALL that YOU can be!

You can *be* and *do* great things once you learn to live in the flow of self-acceptance, freedom and love!

Affirmation Journal
- ★ Who am I?
- ★ What truths do I allow to control me?
- ★ What truths about me do I attempt to disregard?
- ★ Have I truly accepted who I am without apology?
- ★ Am I committed to living life FREE in MY truth?
- ★ How can I increase my self-acceptance and freedom?

As your faith is strengthened you will find that there is no longer the need to have a sense of control, that things will flow as they will, and that you will flow with them, to your great delight and benefit.

EMMANUEL TENEY

Joy

2

February 1

"

Today is a GREAT Day!

"

Each waking day grants us another chance on this earth to evoke change within ourselves and within those around us. Every *great* days starts with a smile on our faces and joy in our hearts!

Say Aloud: **Today is a GREAT Day!**

Make a practice of prefacing every other affirmation with today's affirmation to acknowledge the perfection of life and the brilliance of each opportunity to embrace *new* opportunity.

During times where doubts, problems and obstacles stand in the way of your clarity, don't hesitate to remind yourself as often as needed: **Today is a GREAT Day!**

Joy Affirmation *(Repeat this aloud)*
Joy is divine grace. Joy is my awareness of God's grace and supernatural favor. It flourishes best in hard times. Joy is my strength!

During the month of February, we reflect on our understanding of joy. With this month's affirmations, we embrace a deeper awareness and appreciation for the grace of God.

Say Aloud: ***Every*day is a Great Day! I Will Be Joyful Within!**

February

"

I Will Be POSITIVE!

"

Positivism is a method of changing our internal frameworks so that our external environment will be more pleasing to us. We change what we have control over: that which is within us. Our world then appears brighter because we are viewing it—not with different eyes—but from a better angle.

That is the brilliance of being positive. The world doesn't change, but your faith does. Your environment doesn't change, but your tools do. Your purpose doesn't change, but your journey does. Your identity doesn't change, but your awareness does—all because of a revitalized outlook.

Affirmation Journal
- ★ **How do I practice positivism?**
- ★ **How have my views changed since I became positive?**
- ★ **Why is positivity SO essential to success?**

Positive thinking is simple. If your world appears ugly, change your perspective. Look again, through a positive looking glass. The new outlook will change your LIFE!

Change Your Posture! Change Your LIFE!

Happiness is not something ready made.
It comes from your own actions.

DALAI LAMA XIV

February

I Am Saved By GRACE!

Grace is our salvation! Through grace, we are able to live past our mistakes including the portions of our past that could have broken us. Through grace, we are able to see better and brighter tomorrows. By grace, we have faith that allows us to push past the limits of circumstance. It is ALL by grace. Without grace, there could be no peace, no calm and no comfort within calamity. There could be no positive outlook within negativity. Grace allows us to operate outside of our immediate awareness. It places us within a realm of peacefulness within our spirit. Through grace, we WIN!

Say Aloud: **I Am Saved By Grace! Grace in My Salvation!**

Grace is an often overlooked concept, yet it is the selfsame concept that allows us to enact formidable change and embrace it. Grace makes us better. Grace makes life all the more positive. Our acknowledgment and actualization of joy comes by way of our acceptance and understanding of grace.

Affirmation Journal
- ★ What does it mean to be saved by grace?
- ★ How does grace make me better?
- ★ How can I win with grace?

Say Aloud: **I Am Saved By Grace! Grace in My Salvation!**

February

"

I Am HAPPY!

"

Happiness is a choice. We aren't happy "just because." We aren't positive based on "general principle." We are happy and positive because we *choose* to be!

Happiness is optional, and it is actually not that difficult. You can turn happiness on. You can turn happiness off. The difficult part is allowing the happiness *in*—removing yourself from the dark entanglement of trapped emotions long enough to welcome in the light of positive feelings.

Affirmation Journal
- ★ How happy do I want to be?
- ★ How am I making that happen?
- ★ How can I ensure lasting happiness well into the future?

Happiness lies in your ability to choose. The power of choice is where you will find your identity! Choose to find the joy in happiness! Choose to *be* the joy *of* happiness!

Say Aloud: I Will Be Happy! I Will Be Joyful! I Will Share Joy!

> *Folks are usually about as happy as they make their minds up to be.*
>
> ABRAHAM LINCOLN

February

" I Am RENEWED! "

Stop.

For a few moments in time, slowly inhale. Relax. Then Exhale. Slowly. Allow your mind to be free of all problems for five short minutes and breathe. Empty yourself of all pain, all woes, all headaches, heartbreaks and toothaches! Just breathe. Be carefree for these five minutes in time. Relax. Be empty for this period and enjoy it. You deserve it!

Regular periods of peaceful rejuvenation are essential to maintaining a spirit of calm living in peace and joy. Periods empty of burdens and worries free you of thoughts which shake your comfort. They provide you with quick, effortless renewal to restore positivity within your mind.

Renewal periods are created by shifting your focus to a carefree state of existence. Repetition of these meditative practices center your state of being. Over extended periods of time, they allow for better enjoyment of life including the simple pleasures it has to offer.

Allow yourself to LIVE by participating in renewal practices frequently. Leave everything behind for a few moments each day and just *be*.

Be free—free of the baggage you've acquired over the years and the problems currently pressing your mind.

Just breathe. Renew yourself and be revived!

Say Aloud: **I Am Renewed! I Am Joyously Refreshed!**

February

I Am REVIVED!

Create REVIVAL in life by taking off EVERYTHING that keeps you down! Be FREE of strife, agony and defeat by removing the thoughts, worries and concerns that trouble you. Learn to be carefree without ever leaving town! Worry about yourself for a change—no thoughts of friends, family, parents, siblings, bosses, coworkers or others! Focus only on YOU. Prioritize your own internal and external happiness! Relish in the freedom that only solitude can bring and watch your heart and mind be revived time and time again!

Once you master REVIVAL in your life, don't pick up the same burdens ever again! Some things just have to be left where you leave them! Do whatever it takes to feel and *be* revived!

Affirmation Journal
- What does the term *revival* cause me to think of?
- How can I create revival in my life?
- Why is revival essential to my longevity and well-being?

Say Aloud: I Am Revived! I Create Revival in My Life!

No medicine cures what happiness cannot.

GABRIEL GARCÍA MÁRQUEZ

February 7

> ## I Am THRIVING!

After you have mastered practices of renewal and created REVIVAL within your life, you will find that your life begins to thrive. Growth, progress and moments of enlightenment will come to you much more frequently and with much more clarity. The advancements in your state of life at this point are a direct result of having a thriving mind, body and soul! In this context you begin to find peace within yourself—you will be SO **full** that life's blows will have a hard time getting you down.

When we thrive, we are always at the cusp of being further enlightened and more deeply aware. This broadens our understanding that life is exactly what we make it, and we grow even the more!

Those who are thriving *expect* GREATNESS from life, and that is exactly what they get!

Affirmation Journal
- ★ **What is my view of life?**
- ★ **What am I getting out of life?**
- ★ **How am I thriving?**
- ★ **How can I create and maintain a culture within my life that causes me to continually thrive?**

Say Aloud: **I Have Shifted into Fullness! I Am Thriving!**

February

"

I Am ALIVE!

"

A thriving life is a life that you ENJOY living! It is a life that you get the BEST out of—a life that you put your BEST *into*! A thriving lifestyle makes you *feel* ALIVE!

Others see the joy of your life by how you carry yourself, how you are laughing and how FUN seems to just follow you wherever you go! Your life, to them, is the picture of perfection—not because that is your reality but because of the way that you seem to be LIVING while others are just floating through life without purpose, without goals and without freedom to enjoy what they've created for themselves. Strive, thrive and show that you're alive!

Today's To-Do's...
- ★ List out 5 activities that make you feel ALIVE!
- ★ For the next 3 months, formally schedule a date and time to complete each activity within each month.
- ★ Take pictures of your experiences!
- ★ Create an album of your activities for your friends and family to share in the FUN with you.
- ★ Cherish these moments FOREVER!

Do not take life too seriously.
You will never get out of it alive.

ELBERT HUBBARD

February 9

> ## I Am FULL of ABUNDANCE!

You Have an ABUNDANT Life!

This is true!

It is true only if you believe it to be, so BELIEVE IT! You have treasures residing within you that are just WAITING to unfold! Your future depends on YOU to go the extra mile and tap into resources that you don't even **realize** you have at your disposal.

What are you waiting for?!!!

Your abundant life is a product of abundance in your dreams, goals, thoughts, prayers and ACTIONS! Take actions that are in line with masterful ABUNDANCE in life! Create plans of FULLNESS and **no** lack! Don't be afraid to LEAP for your dreams! You will land in a place of peace, contentment and gain!

Affirmation Journal
- ★ Where does abundance reside in my life personally?
- ★ Where does *lack* reside in my life?
- ★ How do thoughts of lack or abundance impact my actions?
- ★ How can thoughts of abundance guide my actions?

Say Aloud: I Am Full of Abundance! My Life is Abundant!

February

I Am RICH!

Riches aren't found in material objects. *True* richness resides WITHIN! Positive character traits determine richness.

What variety of riches do YOU possess?

Affirmation Journal
- ★ **What are my riches?**
- ★ **How do my riches play into my life?**
- ★ **What riches might I like to add to my bounty?**

Awareness of the riches that we boast gives us much pride and dictates not only how we carry ourselves, but it also determines how we approach life and how we engage with others. When we are well aware of who we are and the qualities that we possess, we are less likely to partake in activities that diminish our value.

Understand that you are IMMENSELY valuable and that there is NOTHING in this world worth diminishing your value for! Pride yourself on your richness and lead a life demonstrative of the value that you possess!

Knowing others is intelligence;
Knowing yourself is true wisdom.
Mastering others is strength;
Mastering yourself is true power.
If you realize that you have enough, you are truly rich.

LAO TZU

February 11

"

My Life is WONDERFUL!

"

How wonderful is your life, really? How wonderful are all of the blessings that you have experienced up until this point? How wonderful is everything that you are looking forward to within the future? Is your life *truly* wonderful?

The picture that we have of our lives will never be a perfect one. There will always be blemishes, darks spots and moments that distort our vision. Do these developments make our lives any less wonderful? Absolutely not! Taking life in its totality makes the capture all the more realistic and pleasing to the trained eye. Without lessons, we have no learning. Without messes, we have no lessons. Taking every troublesome burden into full view, we learn to appreciate how wonderful life is. We are STILL here!!!

If nothing else is wonderful, life itself is BEYOND wonderful! Appreciate all that life has given you by way of opportunity, experience and time. Take these gifts and create the perfection you seek using viewpoints that allow for blurred angles every now and then.

Create a WONDERFUL life!

Say Aloud: **My Life is Wonderful! It is a Gift! It is All MINE!**

February

"

My Life is GREAT!

"

What is your outlook on life? When you wake up everyday, are your thoughts predominantly positive OR are they mostly negative? What is guiding your thought processes on a daily basis? If it is negative, what are you doing to change that outlook?

Don't struggle through life just *barely* allowing a regular smile on your face. Your life is as GREAT as you *make* it, so what are you *making* of yours? What levels of greatness are you *producing*? More importantly than that, what levels of greatness are you *feeling*? Are you creating a culture within your life that yearns for greatness? Are the pleasantries that you provide enough to create an ABUNDANCE of joy within your environment? What are you doing to create a joyful life that you can be grateful for?

Is your life GREAT?!

Today's To-Do's...
★ **Ponder on these questions and journal your responses.**

Say Aloud: **My Life is Great! I Am Joyful Within!**

It's your outlook on life that counts.
If you take yourself lightly and don't take yourself too seriously, pretty soon you can find the humor in our everyday lives. And sometimes it can be a lifesaver.

BETTY WHITE

February 13

> **My Life is a MIRACLE!**

Looking back over our lives and the stories we've heard from our friends, strangers or historians, it's a wonder that *any* of us are still here! It's a marvel that we've survived past broken families, burdened lives and societal upheavals that compose the make up of our existence. Our lives are a miracle! Our character is developed through the miraculous bearing of unbearable pain, our tolerance of intolerable situations and the understanding that misunderstandings are the founding variable of lasting growth. We are a miracle. We are the result of a painful combination of riotous situations slated to break us yet we have overcome! We have endured past messes that we caused ourselves in situations where we thought the poor decisions we made were in our best interest. Life is a miracle because someone saw fit to give us chance after chance after chance to get it right.

We have finally made it!
We are finally doing it right!

Say Aloud: My Life is a Miracle!

February

"

I Will ENJOY Life!

"

"What's [MOST] important is that you dance."
—RAMONA JONES

This should be the quote of our lives! With no desire to appear "perfect" or to seem like we have it all under control, we should always seek to DANCE through life instead of allowing lows to keep us down.

Life is NOTHING without joy as its reward!

What is there to life if we can't celebrate the joy that we experience along the way? What do we have if not for memories that we cherish and the joy that laughter and happiness bring? We cannot simply exist with no perception of all the happiness existing within our worlds! Life is FULL of joy if we seek to find it! Life is full of lessons if we seek to learn. Life is full of secrets If we seek them out!

Say Aloud: **I Will Enjoy Life! I Will Dance Through It!!!**

*The most important thing
is to enjoy your life—to be happy—it's all that matters.*

AUDREY HEPBURN

February 15

"
GOD is AWESOME!
"

In case you hadn't completed your personal reminder already today *or* if you haven't reminded yourself at all recently:

GOD is AWESOME!

God is simply AMAZING!!! Life is SO much better when you realize this! Learn to accept your experiences and the outcomes as the AWESOMENESS of God aiding in your purposed growth.

There is PURPOSE in your path. Stay prayerful, stay positive and PURSUE! Stop discounting God's omniscience by complaining about what coulda, shoulda, woulda—accept what IS! GOD is! Each time you think to complain and let others into your world, verbally acknowledge God's awesomeness and let HIM into your world! Praise God at ALL times claiming your victory against fear and defeat.

Wind chimes are beautiful and they make a beautiful noise, but *only* when the wind is blowing. The wind *will* blow—as it does, make your joyful noise unto God!

Today's To-Do's...
- ★ **Write out how awesome God has been in your life.**
- ★ **Write down your praises to Him for being awesome.**
- ★ **Read these aloud each time you think to complain.**

Say Aloud: **God IS Awesome! God is Simply Amazing!**

February

GOD is EXCELLENT!

God is the excellence within our lives! He is our operation within our BEST selves. God is the essential component that allows us to operate *outside* of ourselves to accomplish daunting tasks when we have nothing left to give. The power of God enables us to operate in that which is greater than ourselves. Through faith in God's excellence we're able to dig deeper, go further and perform better than we could without that power. The excellence of God causes us to be pleasing to ourselves once we accept and utilize the many gifts that we've been blessed with! God is simply EXCELLENT!

Our lives are the marvel of God's excellence in creation. We find security in knowing that we are God's children. We are loved with all of God's being. Purity and selflessness define His treatment of us—His children. God is excellence in all of His ways. Through goodness, by grace, God is excellent perfection. We are God's blessed children.

Say Aloud: God is Excellent! I Am God's Marvelous Creation!

Joy is the infallible sign of the presence of God.

PIERRE TEILHARD DE CHARDIN

February 17

"

GOD is GREAT!

"

God is GREAT! He is SO awesome to us! God is everything that we are not and all that we can never be. He is for us what we cannot be for ourselves. God is the GREATNESS that resides within us. *He* is our *best* selves. He is the solace that keeps us grounded and the calm that keeps us at peace. God helps us to maintain. He makes it possible for us to *grow* the extra mile. He gives us something to believe in—a power greater than ourselves. We are the BEST we can be because of all that God *is*.

For all that you can't do for yourself, put your trust in God to do what is only *His* to do. Allow God to be the GREATNESS that exists within your life! Be FULLY PERSUADED that God has the POWER to do EVERYTHING He has promised to perform. Call Him out on His promises and GET OUT OF THE WAY!!!

We limit the GREATNESS of God when we place too much on our own shoulders. Do what is within your control and leave the rest to life to figure it out. Don't create burdens that wouldn't otherwise exist if you were wise enough to be *mortal* at times.

Say Aloud: **God is Great! God is the BEST of Me! God's Got It!**

February

GOD is MERCIFUL!

There isn't a soul who can imagine the chaos going on within your walls. There isn't a soul, but you, who understands the composition of your mind. Truthfully, these things don't require expression. There is One who already knows what it is that you're *growing* through. He knows what it is that you're in need of. He knows the desires of your heart.

Say Aloud: **God is Merciful! I Rest in God! He's My Peace!**

During the times in life when your heart is just tired from nonsense—times when you don't know how you've gotten where you are—realize that you are exactly where you need to be. You are SAFE in the arms of our merciful God.

Say Aloud: **God is Merciful! I Rest in God! He's My Peace!**

Affirmation Journal
- ★ **Where within my life has God shown His mercy?**
- ★ **Where within my life can I stand to accept more mercy?**
- ★ **How is the mercy of God valuable to my future?**

*Because God has made us for Himself,
our hearts are restless until they rest in Him.*

AUGUSTINE OF HIPPO

February 19

"

GOD LOVES ME!

"

Say Aloud:

The love of God is a precious gift given to me. By His grace and His love, God blesses me with talents to be used for His glory. Before the day that I was born, God loved and accepted me! Using a thought process and methodology that greatly differs from my own, God has positioned me for the BEST life possible. HE LOVES ME! Even when I didn't know how to love myself, God Loved Me from the start—since the creation of the world!

No human alive loves me like God Loves Me! God Loves Me, and I LOVE God! THAT is true love. God Loves Me without recompense and without remorse! There is NO reason that I should ever ignore Him!

My impatience with a loving God finds me at the mercy of my own frail humanity. The tug of war that I play with God is not acceptable because of the deep assurance that His love promises me.

I accept that I don't know it all. I don't even know everything about myself. In order to learn new things about myself—to multiply my capacity for growth and learning—I must place my FULL hope in The One who knows ALL!

God Loves Me! I Am Thankful for God's Love!

February

"

I Am THANKFUL!!!

"

Always be thankful for your receipt of the promises of God and the joy that they bring. Reminding yourself of God's promises on a regular basis helps you appreciate the process. You then understand that better is yet to come.

Be thankful for being provided with opportunities to excel and serve in ways that you would have never imagined understanding also that you have been gifted with the skills to see the opportunities through to talented completion. In gratefulness, you will be overjoyed thinking of the personal and spiritual growth that you have witnessed about yourself. Pray that progress is steadily made so you can continue to make *yourself* proud.

Be thankful for friendship and family—for the love and concern that is directed toward you on a regular basis whether you welcome it or not.

Thank God for the eventful life you have that brings as much joy as you allow! Open your heart to more gratefulness and you will see that blessings abound in your life!

Say Aloud: **I Am Thankful! I Live a Life of Abundance!**

One of the BEST things we can do in life is come to accept that ALL of the BAD works together for our GOOD. Life goes on PRET-TY smoothly after that!

D NICOLE

February 21

"
I Am
a Wonderful Reflection
of GOD's Love!
"

In all that we do, we have the opportunity to humbly share and express the goodness of God's love. Our lives should be a reflection of all that we are and all that we have been blessed with. Why not express this goodness with others every single day?

God's love abounds in each of our lives. We are vessels of The Master's greatness. Our gift to God and to those around us is to share the message of His grace and favor by mirroring what we acknowledge through acceptance of His love. Exemplification of God's love can be demonstrated in numerous ways. We can do silent deeds or give to those in need. We can be faithful members within our social groups and concerned members of our communities.

The easiest way to express the love of God is within our lifestyles. Our smiles and laughter tell of His love toward us. When we smile, laugh and outpour the happiness that we have within, there is no denying the power of love because we show that our joy is exactly what gets us from Point-A to Point-B in life. If it is not us loving ourselves that helps us to progress, it is someone else's reflection of God's love that does that trick. These exhibitions of love are examples of God working within and through us.

Always strive to be a wonderful reflection of God's love.

Say Aloud: **I Am a Wonderful Reflection of God's Love!**

February

"
I Am in GOD's Favor!
"

Favor places us in positions that we couldn't earn within environments that we shouldn't be worthy of. Faith gives us opportunities that we don't deserve. God's favor affords us the ability to match our faith with our works, the combination of which grants us lifestyles that we could only dream of. By putting faith into action, we witness the favor of God. His many works begin to move in our lives as we see manifestations of God's promises to us.

Thank GOD for favor, talent and experience—let's not forget LOVE!!! You're entrusted with being a vessel of thanks to make God's love visible to the world!!! Appreciate God for trusting you to get the job done!!! No amount of money can buy that type of trust.

Thank God for His Love and for His Favor!

Affirmation Journal
- ★ **What does it mean to be in the favor in God?**
- ★ **Where can I see evidence of God's favor in my life?**
- ★ **How can I best take advantage of the favor of God?**

Say Aloud: **I Am in God's Favor! I Am Thankful for His Love!**

> *It doesn't matter if a million people tell you what you can't do, or if ten million tell you no. If you get one yes from God, that's all you need.*

TYLER PERRY

February 23

" I Am PROUD of My PAST! "

The problems of our past are nothing to be ashamed of! We ALL have overcome much that we would like to forget, but in all of your forgetting, don't forget what was gained in the process of maturation. The bad events combine with the good events to form useful experiences that shape our individual characters. We become who we are because of everything we've been blessed to confront in the past.

Be proud of the learning opportunities that your past life has afforded you. Without the building blocks of the past, there could be no current you and there would be nothing upon which to build your bright future! Take pride in the progression of your life understanding that each plight could have broken you, shattered you or defeated you, yet these trials were exactly what you needed to develop into the prosperous leader you now are!

Don't be so quick to leave the past in the past. Let the pride of your past bolster your motivation for the future! Be all that you can be while taking lessons of the past with you on your journey. Your BEST stories and BIGGEST successes are found within your troubled past!

Say Aloud: I Am Proud of My Past and All That I Have Learned!

February

F E B

"

I Am PROUD of My PROGRESS!

"

Progression in life takes time. Nothing happens overnight and longstanding positive progress doesn't typically happen amidst unplanned, hurried change. As tumultuous as change may be, appreciate the strides achieved in *any* progress that you have made. Even if the main goal you were seeking isn't obtained in the end, there is priceless value to be celebrated within lessons gained along the way.

Affirmation Journal
- ★ **What obstacle has been hardest to overcome in my life?**
- ★ **How was the situation in the beginning?**
- ★ **How is the situation now?**
- ★ **What progress have I made?**
- ★ **How do I feel about that progress?**

There is no failure in patience and waiting. There is no failure in defeat. There is only failure in quitting.

Don't let lack of progress cause you to quit. Be proud of the progress you make. Learn from it! Take enlightened steps that pave the way toward your BEST future.

Like success, failure is many things to many people.
With Positive Mental Attitude, failure is
a learning experience, a rung on the ladder, a plateau at
which to get your thoughts in order and prepare to try again.

W. CLEMENT STONE

February 25

I Am PROUD of My SALVATION!

Life is perfectly orchestrated for our timely acknowledgment and reverence of the POWER and precision of GOD! God WILL take care of YOU! God is your salvation! God will even save you from your own self-inflicted blissful misery!

Your saving relationship with God helps you to commit to yourself because you put your faith in that which is greater than you: The AWESOME Power of God! Human frailty causes you to waiver in many decisions, but acceptance of God places divine power within your own very capable hands. No need to continue failing in your personal capacities when you are endowed with the blessed power of God within you! Weakness within your own abilities causes you to hold on to people, places and habits that impede your progress and other things that do NOTHING for your sense of self-worth. God is your saving grace!

Be proud of the relationship you develop with Him trusting that, in God, you have ALL you will ever need!

Affirmation Journal
- ★ **What does it mean to be proud of my salvation?**
- ★ **What makes me personally proud of my salvation?**
- ★ **What is God's direct role within my salvation?**
- ★ **What is my individual role within my salvation?**

Say Aloud: **I Am Proud of My Salvation!**

February

"
I Am PROUD of My EXPERIENCES!
"

Are you proud of your experiences? Are you proud of the life you have created? Are you proud of the route you have taken? Have you welcomed each experience you've had?

If we are to live the best lives EVER, we must accept our experiences for EVERYTHING that they're worth whether they be good, bad, GREAT or ugly! Taking clear pride in experience means that our stories become more worthwhile since we see the value within each hidden gem of experience. We then speak from a position of wholeness in clarity versus speaking from a tainted, bitter position of just barely overcoming defeat.

Our lives are an example of beatitude if we believe them to be such. Welcoming pleasant *and* unpleasant experiences aides us in understanding that the changes we encounter in life are essential to our joy. There is no true appreciation of happiness until we have been blessed to experience pain. There is no true win until we have experienced defeat. There is no true love until we have seen everything but that.

Say Aloud: I Am Proud of My Experiences!

The joy of life comes from our encounters with new experiences, and hence there is no greater joy than to have an endlessly changing horizon, for each day to have a new and different sun.

CHRISTOPHER MCCANDLESS

February 27

With Each New Day Comes New Fulfillment of PROMISE!

Say: **With Each New Day Comes New Fulfillment of Promise!**

Aren't you grateful that you wake up each day with a new opportunity to try again? With each waking moment, you are blessed with yet another chance to get things right! You have all of the needed resources at your disposal to do life EXACTLY how you choose to. No need to be hung up on the past or to hold onto anything negative. The past creates your stories yet the future gets the glory!

Today is one more day that you have on earth to create the BEST life that you can! All of the promises of your life are waiting on your ACTION to fulfill them. Today, and every day, that opportunity is lying within your grasp. TAKE IT! Take today and extract from it exactly what you will! Accept no less than what you are worth and work as hard as your goals deserve!

The fact that you are alive means that you still have *much* to offer. In all of your giving, be willing to receive the offerings that life provides to you in return. These gifts are part of your promise to continually be fulfilled.

Say Aloud: **I Will Give! I Will Receive! I Will Fulfill Promise!**

February

"

I Will LAUGH!

"

Laughter involves so much more than just a smile and sounds of joy. Laughter entails a good feeling on the inside. Laughter is contagious and each time we experience it, all is right with the world in that moment. For that reason, practice laughing as much as possible! Listen to the laughter of others. Listen to your own laughter and relish in the moments where you have the good fortune to laugh. Create moments of laughter for yourself.

Life is not much if not for the joy that we share within it.

Say Aloud: **I Will Laugh! I Will Create a Joyful Life!**

Affirmation Journal
- ★ **Where is there an abundance of joy in my life?**
- ★ **Where is the joy lacking in my life?**
- ★ **How can I create fullness of joy throughout my life?**

The only way to get through life is
to laugh your way through it.
You either have to laugh or cry. I prefer to laugh.
Crying gives me a headache.

MARJORIE PAY HINCKLEY

February 29

> ❝ **I Am VERY Comfortable with Myself and My Experience!
> I LOVE ME!!!
> I FULLY Embrace Who I Am! I TRUST ME!** ❞

We live in a world where we are overly concerned with social acceptance. Many of us are absorbed in the idea that others require our appraisal and that we also require theirs. Our lives shouldn't be wrapped up in the pretense that we *could*—or should ever endeavor to—be people-pleasers. We shouldn't seek to find our assurance in the judgments—spoken or unspoken—of our fellowman. All that we are, and all that we could ever hope to be, can never be bound by the admiration of the human race.

The standards of any other human being are too obscure to finitely judge you with, in all of your splendid individuality. Quit lending your time to the claims of these unauthorized approval agents! Be your own judge!

Affirmation Journal
- ★ Am I comfortable with myself? How do I show it?
- ★ How can I become even more comfortable with myself?
- ★ How can I fully embrace who I am?
- ★ How can I show more love and trust for myself?

If YOU are not comfortable with yourself and your decisions, how can you expect others to be comfortable with you and your decisions?
GET COMFORTABLE!

D NICOLE

Peace

March 1

> ## I Will Work on WHOLENESS!

Peace is unconditional resolve in our hearts to maintain a spirit of acceptance, calm and joy. Through peace, we maintain solid character despite life's troubles knowing that our help resides in a power that is greater than ourselves. Joy is found in peace. We acknowledge the fullness of life because of our faith, and by faith we have fullness of joy.

Peace Affirmation *(Repeat this aloud)*
My substantive relationship with God puts me in a peaceful place of inner stability that is undaunted by outside stress. Peace keeps me at rest and poised for a blessing. My inner wholeness creates lasting peace.

Peace affords us the blessing of wholeness. We are whole, not based on a perfect life in reality, but based on a perfect life in spirit. Through wholeness, we accept life as it comes and live it as we go, one day at a time, not ever getting outside of ourselves by attempting to make sense of it all. We are whole based on our inner sanctity and spiritual resolve.

Say Aloud: **I Will Alter My Spirit! I Will Work on Wholeness!**

March teaches us about creation of internal peace within ourselves and also throughout various aspects of our lives. We learn to center ourselves by way of The Creator and through conscious practice.

March

" I Will MOVE On! "

It is *your* heart—you take *much* pride in it. It is a BIG heart!!! There is a lot to go around too, which means there's a lot to be broken! Each day, you live through the beating of your heart—not the pulse part—the tick! You have had MANY bouts, some of which you are *still* fighting yet you LIVE! Perhaps you boast a heart that has rarely faced any of its bullies, so you're still afraid of them. You're still hurting because of them. You're still beating yourself up because of them.

Release the negativity. Let go of the bad times. It is time to move on. Are you ready? Aren't you tired? You need your heart and *all* of its pieces, to give first to yourself and then to give to others.

Affirmation Journal
★ What have I been holding onto that I need to release?
★ How can I best move on past these situations in my life?
★ How can I ensure that I no longer hold onto negativity?

Say Aloud: **I Will Move On! I Will Let Go of Negativity!**

*Even if things don't unfold the way you expected,
don't be disheartened or give up.
One who continues to advance will win in the end.*

DAISAKU IKEDA

March

I Am in GOD's Will!

In all that we do and within every decision that we make, God gives us the will to carry out tasks in line with our calling. We make decisions to and fro. We traverse a great many paths haphazardly searching to obtain the objects of our desire yet we find a sweet resting place once we find ourselves in the will of God.

Say Aloud: **I Am in God's Will! I Find Peace in God's Will!**

Within the will of God is where our perfect peace resides. Within His will is where we should also reside. Life becomes much easier when we find ourselves walking along the path that has already been set before us.

Affirmation Journal
- ★ **What is the will of God for my life?**
- ★ **What paths have I taken to lead me into God's rest?**
- ★ **How is life different for me within God's resting place versus when I am not in His will?**

Say Aloud: **I Am in God's Will! I Find Peace in God's Will!**

March

GOD Will PROVIDE!

We spend entirely too much time attempting to solve problems that are not of our concern. We dwell on things that we have no power to change. We worry ourselves restless trying to fix what is outside of our control.

For all that God has already done in our lives, we should learn to trust Him more and more. There shouldn't be a single moment where our faith becomes shaky when considering all that God has already blessed us with.

We are too strong in our own free will sometimes. We don't know *when* to let go or *what* to let go. We don't trust that we can leave the impossible to God while we focus on what *is* possible. God has always provided. God always will.

Affirmation Journal
- ★ **What has God already provided for me?**
- ★ **What major things have I trusted God with in the past?**
- ★ **What was the outcome?**
- ★ **What am I trusting God to provide right now?**
- ★ **What am I trusting God to provide in the future?**

Let go! Leave your problems to God! God will provide!

Never be afraid to trust an unknown future to a known God.

CORRIE TEN BOOM

March

GOD Will REPLENISH!

When in a time of need or lack, first understand that you *already* have **ALL** you need: Breath is flowing through your lungs and blood pumps through your veins. Praise God for that ALONE! Outside of that, have faith that God will give you the desires of your heart. What is it that you want? Pray earnestly, trusting God to fulfill your needs and also to replenish what you lack! Believe that God has the power to do it. Know that He will! Be faithful to God even in your loss. Continue your relationship with God through it all.

Pray, meditate and keep a sound, clear mind while you grow through travail. Let God be your comfort. Accept the promise of His peace and build up your faith through true belief, not through panic or desperation. When you pray, pray with POWER, believing that you can and WILL receive all that you ask for in faithfulness.

Affirmation Journal
- ★ **What am I lacking in life?**
- ★ **How am I remaining peaceful during this time?**
- ★ **How do my prayers show my faith?**
- ★ **How can I infuse my prayers with more power?**
- ★ **How can I keep being faithful once my needs are met?**

Say Aloud: **God Will Replenish! I Will Be Faithful in Peace!**

March

I Am PROSPEROUS!

Many of us don't go far in life because we aren't willing to invest in ourselves. Just as we invest in clothes, cars or other tangibles, we should also invest in our betterment, our education and our legacies from a financial perspective.

To be prosperous, create a flourishing lifestyle—a lifestyle that compels you to thrive! Put yourself first! Direct yourself to make all sacrifices required to feed YOUR vision. Remove yourself from the company of those with limiting mindsets and align yourself with visionaries! Don't allow your fruitful vision to be tainted by the limits of negative minds—which includes your own!

Change Your Posture! Change Your LIFE!

Affirmation Journal
- ★ How am I flourishing in life?
- ★ What am I doing NOW to create a life of prosperity?
- ★ How can I continually compose a life that compels me to thrive?

Say Aloud: **I Am Prosperous! My Life Compels Me to Thrive!**

Find out what poor people read and...
DON'T READ IT!

JIM ROHN

March 7

"

I Am Right ON SCHEDULE!

"

There are those of us on a trip with a repeat course. We are going in circles—starting to become all too familiar with the scenery. We are *quickly* getting bored because nothing is changing. Then, there are those of us who find ourselves in a CRASH course with STAGNATION—*longing* for a destination—with little to no path, no plans, and no preparation. We are wanting to be somewhere, on a time schedule, yet we have NO clue how to get there!

Regardless of our personal plans for our lives, we have to accept that *everything* happens exactly as it should. There is purpose in our engagements. There is purpose in our interactions. There is purpose in our timing. Anything that seems to be on hold or progress that seems to be thwarted is predestined to lead us exactly where we need to be.

When finding ourselves in situations that leave us stuck, we must look *within* for answers while always understanding that there is something to be gained from any stagnation within our lives.

Affirmation Journal
- ★ What are the stagnant areas of my life?
- ★ What lessons am I being taught amidst the stagnation?
- ★ How are the lessons gained *now* crucial to my progress?

Say Aloud: **I Am Right On Schedule! I Find Value in Timing!**

March

I Am SUCCESSFUL!

It's tough to professionally network and socially interact with others when you consider EVERYBODY your competition! Everyone is NOT your competition! YOU are your only competition! YOU are successful ALREADY, so there is NO need to compete with anyone else. Instead, cherish and encourage others. Learn from them. Take all that you can by learning from their experiences and support them as much as possible! Be successful TOGETHER with them!

For the individuals who *could* be considered your competition, try your hand at networking with these the MOST! Your success can only be further increased by rubbing shoulders with the best in your field. Don't compete with them—glean from them! Learn everything you can from others within your targeted areas so that YOU can be even MORE successful than you already are!

Say Aloud: I Am Successful! I Am Happy with My Progress!

Success is getting what you want,
happiness is wanting what you get.

W.P. KINSELLA

March

I Am ENOUGH!

Never walk through life creating comparisons of yourself based on the accomplishments of other individuals. You don't know their lives or what has been involved in the makeup of who they currently are. The only thing that you *do* know for *sure* is yourself, and YOU are ENOUGH! Point blank. PERIOD.

YOU! ARE! ENOUGH!

No amount of money in this world, no kind of GREAT fortune and no miraculous stroke of luck can compare to how awesome **YOU** already are, all by yourself! The benefits that come along with your individual awesomeness include friends, family, accomplishments and other accolades that may tickle your fancy, but you—you with your very unique self—**YOU** *are* enough!

Say Aloud: **I Am Enough!**

Constantly remind yourself at every juncture, at every fork in the road and amidst every obstacle that YOU are enough! In every single God-given moment, you are enough! You are the best you can be in *that* given moment in time and whatever you're being then—so long as it's your best—is ENOUGH! Give your everything whenever you have your everything to give. Your best is ALWAYS good enough.

Say Aloud: **I Am Enough! My BEST is Always Good Enough!**

March

" I Am SURE! "

Our faith waivers when we don't trust God! Our faith waivers when we aren't secure in the promises of God. When our connection to God lacks earnestly and commitment, we don't operate using the power of God that lies within us—we operate instead out of our own power. Without God, we are nothing. Without God's peace we become unstable, emotional, flighty individuals who are sure of nothing, especially not ourselves.

Rest in the peace of God—in the wisdom that God is a sure thing! By God's power, you can also be sure of yourself! Don't doubt the power that you have within you. You are here for a reason, and by God, you will fulfill the purpose given to you. Trust yourself and be MISSION FOCUSED! Be ever-ready to fulfill that which you are destined for. Be SURE of who you are never doubting your power to perform.

Affirmation Journal
- ★ How can I be sure of myself?
- ★ What about myself am I sure of?
- ★ Why is surety essential to my goals?

> *You've got to be sure of yourself before you can ever win a prize.*
>
> NAPOLEON HILL

March 11

I Will Not Fear OTHERS!

There is no person in your world more powerful than YOU! You have the power to be as great as YOU choose, so why let another human being intimidate you? Why let the success of another impede your own progress? You are SO much better than you believe yourself to be! You are far better than you could ever imagine, so **WHY FEAR?**

Be PROUD of who YOU are and what YOU have to give! Let *that* be motivation enough for you! Be blinded by your own goals enough not to let any other human being stand in the way of where YOU yearn to be!

Don't question the skills that you've been given, and don't compare yourself to anyone other than yourself! No one can be you and you can measure up to no one else! There is NO measurement adequate enough to compare two men! In this respect, we were *not* created equal!

Everyone has the potential for GREATNESS!
What will you do with yours?

Affirmation Journal
- ★ **What am I afraid of?**
- ★ **What is my potential?**
- ★ **What will I do with it?**

Say Aloud: **I Will Not Fear Others! I Have No Reason to Fear!**

March

I Will Value PEACE!

Enjoy the quiet times. Welcome the moments of peace that grace your life. Appreciate these moments—the times when it's just you and yourself within the world. Value the inner peace that only you can create.

Be a vessel of peaceful practice in all that you do. Engage with others only on a level that is favorable to your continued solace. Don't participate in emotionally destructive activities, relationships or habits. Break the chains of emotional bondage and prioritize your happiness at all costs. Control what you can control within your environment and accept the grace of God regarding the rest.

Understanding that storms will come, be the calm in the midst of each storm that you face. Silence yourself, meditate and apply hard mental work toward fully developing your peaceful resolve.

Affirmation Journal
- ★ How do I demonstrate that I value peace?
- ★ How can I practice being the calm amidst storms?
- ★ How can I practice prioritizing my happiness?

Learn to value yourself, which means:
fight for your happiness.

AYN RAND

March 13

"GOD Will RESTORE!"

Restoration is all about getting back what was lost or taken from you. Changing your posture and changing your life is a means toward this end.

In faith, continually believe in the promise of restoration. Use your own power to compel goodness into your life. Allow God to provide everything else. Declare that you WILL live a life of goodness and abundance because you are blessed with the grace and favor of God.

When waiting on restoration, wait in peaceful anticipation of all that is coming to you. Don't allow your heart to be troubled. In centering yourself on your promising future, let go of what was lost in the past. There is nothing outside of your reach if you maintain your connection with God never doubting that He will restore to you all that you have lost.

Affirmation Journal
- ★ What am I looking for God to restore in my life?
- ★ How have I let go of what I lost?
- ★ How is my heart managing during this time?
- ★ How can I ensure that my heart remains pure and that I remain peaceful while I wait?
- ★ How has my connection with God been while waiting?
- ★ How am I placing myself in the best position to receive?

Say Aloud: **God Will Restore That Which Belongs to ME!**

March

> ## I Will LET GO!

Periodically, we find ourselves in atmospheres where the views of those around us are quite contradictory to our own. We look around, and our frequented environments and social settings have become wholly foreign to us—the people we share our free time with no longer seem to be the best accompaniment for our refined track of life. These scenarios SCREAM at our desire to find ourselves in situations where we don't just *feel* comfortable, but we yearn to partake in situations that challenge us to *be* our BEST selves! Being the BEST is hard to do when obligations and familiarity keep us hanging on when letting go is most advantageous.

Find yourself in the seasons of life that *compel* you to be GREATER! When your personal growth has surpassed that of those around you, don't make that *your* problem! Regularly rid yourself of *any*thing and *every*thing that isn't profitable to your future development. Find yourself in company that doesn't stifle you— everyone isn't going where you are going in life! Everyone can't travel the path that YOU will take. Be OK with that! People, places and things that need to be left behind WILL be left behind! LET THEM GO!

Letting go gives us freedom, and freedom is the only condition for happiness. If, in our heart, we still cling to anything—anger, anxiety, or possessions—we cannot be free.

Thích Nhất Hạnh

March

I Will LET GO of Bad Habits!

When will you move on? When will you stop allowing pain to define you? When will it be time to let go? Value yourself enough to let go of bad habits. Let go of bad thoughts. Let go of bad relationships. Just **LET GO**! Hands down. **LET GO**! No questions asked. Drop the baggage and let go.

Exhale. Breathe in deeply, *very* deeply and let go of the weight of yesterday's problems. Let's repeat: Exhale. Breathe in deeply. Breathe in *very* deeply and let go of ALL problems.

Don't hang onto painful situations. There is no value in having a pity party for yourself or being the pity party for anyone else. Piss poor habits only add to the weight of pain. Repetition of bad habits further connects you to the pain and makes disconnection all the more difficult. Exercise emotional resolve solid enough to cause you to yearn for change. Do what it takes to let go NOW!

Today's To-Do's...
- ★ **List out at least 5 poor habits that you need to stop.**
- ★ **Create deadlines for removal of these habits.**
- ★ **Find a friend or coach to hold you accountable.**

Affirmation Journal
- ★ **Why do I need to break my bad habits?**
- ★ **What does my life look like after I break bad habits?**
- ★ **How can I ensure that new bad habits don't develop?**

March

I Will LET GO of Painful Memories!

Don't hang onto too much garbage. Don't live in the shadows of yesterday's problems reminiscing on too many bad memories of lost love and love lost. Leave it ALL behind! Do. NOT. **DWELL**! Wipe your hands of painful recollections. Literally! Be done with the pain!

Bring to mind the most pressing issues that have consumed your time this week. Recall the pain, the questions, the answers, the guesses and the messes. Got it? Now, **LEAVE IT**!

Today's To-Do's...

- ★ **List out at least 10 problems that have been plaguing you. Yes... 10!!!** (Don't be ashamed if you can reach this number quickly. You are not alone!)
- ★ **Go through your list acknowledging and accepting the current status of each problem, and... Let! Them! Go!**
- ★ **As you review each of them, cry, write, do whatever you need to, but release the negativity within your mind.**
- ★ **Once you are done trash your paper, along with the burdens, and literally wash your hands as a physical reminder that you have let go!**

The trouble with having an open mind, of course, is that people will insist on coming along and trying to put things in it.

TERRY PRATCHETT

March 17

I Am Walking in My DESTINY!

I have come across many people who are afraid of their purpose. For various reasons, they openly avoid the recognized path for their lives. I raise my hands, both hands, and attest to the fact that I have been one of those people! I was not at all afraid of pursuing my purpose—I was opposed to the methods! I didn't want to do what "everyone" was doing. I didn't want to find myself in the same occupations as "everyone" I knew!

Calculations may be off a bit, but 90% of my paternal family preaches or teaches OR we marry preachers or teachers! I didn't want to be a preacher or teacher and I definitely didn't want to marry a preacher or teacher! *(Don't get me wrong! I LOVE preachers and teachers—and bosses! I LOVE BOSSES! haha)* I simply wanted to be different.

In trying hard not to do it the way it was inevitably going to be done, I have managed to receive certification as a Christian Coach and Trainer. I have become BOTH a preacher *and* a teacher. Most of my clients are pastors and their leadership teams. My first speaking engagement as a Life Coach found me in a church pulpit!!! Go Figure!

I am walking in My Destiny!

No matter how much you try to avoid it, your destiny WILL find you. Walk in it!

Say Aloud: I Am Walking in My Destiny! I Embrace It!

March

MAR

" I Will Value My PURPOSE! "

Everyone has a calling in life—a purpose—a destiny to fulfill. Some people are aware of what that purpose is while others are yet unaware.

If you are reading this book, you are one of those who either knows your purpose OR you are currently on a journey to find it.

Affirmation Journal
- ★ **What is my purpose?**
- ★ **What am I doing NOW to develop my purpose?**
- ★ **How will I demonstrate the value of my purpose?**

Don't be afraid to try new things in order to find your purpose. Many times, it takes that exquisitely unique—sometimes chaotic—combination of trial and error for us to finally get to the place where we say, "YES! This is IT!!!"

When you know what your calling is, honor it and honor God through passionate pursuit of your purpose!!!

Value Your Purpose!

Say Aloud: **I Will Value My Purpose!**

Your destiny is to fulfill those things upon which you focus most intently. So choose to keep your focus on that which is truly magnificent, beautiful, uplifting and joyful.
Your life is always moving toward something.

RALPH MARSTON

March 19

" I Will Fear No Evil! "

We fear too many things in life: aids, cancer—and while this book is being written—EBOLA! Seems we're afraid of nearly EVERYTHING—seen and unseen, heard and unheard of. And why? *For no reason at all!* Many of the things that we fear are of no immediate personal concern of ours, yet we're afraid anyway, and for what? What gain is had in such an overload of fear? Why do we buy into it? *(These are personal questions to ask yourself. Evaluate your attachment to fear and REMOVE IT! QUICKLY!)*

STOP BEING AFRAID OF **EVERYTHING**! There is NO justifiable reason to be afraid of nearly everything under the sun *AND everything* beyond *the sun too*! CUT IT OUT! YOU are much more powerful than your fear!

Today's To-Do's...

- ★ Focus ALL of your energy on being peaceful, positive and prayerful.
- ★ Every time you feel fear or negativity, get to the bottom of the issue and DEAL WITH IT! Find out *why*!
- ★ As a result of your findings, change what's most important about the situation: YOU!
- ★ Regularly practice measures that help remove fear: Pray, Meditate, Walk, Be Silent, *Woosah*, and... STOP WATCHING THE NEWS!!!

March

"

I PRAY!!!

"

No matter what we are facing, we must learn to honor the fact that prayer is *so* much deeper than what we can ask for or what we *think* we need. Prayer is our humble acknowledgment of the POWER of GOD and our bold acceptance of that same POWER within OURSELVES! We must learn to stop *begging* for what we *think* we need and instead get a better handle on the things we already have!

Through prayer, we learn honor, submission and patience. Prayer is our recognition that we need help. Prayer is how we share with The Master our yearning for things greater than ourselves. We cannot traverse life's roads alone. Prayer supports our will to take God on the journey with us!

Affirmation Journal
- ★ **What is my prayer life like?**
- ★ **Why do I practice prayer?**
- ★ **What am I hoping to receive through my prayer life?**

Say Aloud: **I Pray! I Yearn to Take God Along On My Journey!**

Prayer is not asking. It is a longing of the soul.
It is daily admission of one's weakness. It is better in prayer
to have a heart without words than words without a heart.

Mahatma Gandhi

March 21

> ## I Will Not Operate in FEAR!

While death can be a truly daunting prospect, LIFE scares many of us much more than *anything* else including death. We're fearful of living! We're fearful of shining! We're fearful of being successful! We are afraid to *actually* get it RIGHT! And sometimes, just sometimes, we're afraid to fail.

Fear of failure is more prominent than failure itself! Many fail because they don't even try! If you try, you win EVERY single time simply because you have put forth the effort needed to WIN! Fear can keep you from doing that. Fear can keep you from the bare minimum of even trying, so what then do you do?

Feel the fear and DO IT ANYWAY!!!!

If you have to be fearful at all, make fear work in your favor! Work *past* the fear—don't operate *in* it. If anything, let fear be a motivator for you to do your BEST! Let fear inspire you to higher heights so that you can prove fear WRONG! For all the times that fear caused you to think you would fail, create a *new* accomplishment to show yourself that there is no need to fear success! There is no need to fear life, so don't be afraid to live!

Affirmation Journal
- ★ **What causes me to operate in fear?**
- ★ **How will I work past my fear?**
- ★ **How can fear work in my favor?**

March

I Will Not Allow Outside Factors to Take Away from My HAPPINESS!

Circumstances control you only if you let them. Leave the past in the past and live primarily in the present. Embrace each opportunity for what it is and release the past for what it wasn't. Take the time needed to empty yourself of all pain, all woes, all headaches, heartbreaks and toothaches! Create a carefree life worth living—one where you will not be burdened by the cares and concerns of others. Focus on what matters, and that is YOU! Remove outside factors that impede forward progression in the direction of happiness. Never allow *outside* factors to take away from your *inner* happiness! Change your circumstance!

Change Your Posture! Change Your LIFE!

Affirmation Journal
- ★ What would make me happier?
- ★ What am I doing *daily* to ensure my happiness?
- ★ What outside factors am I allowing to take away from my happiness?
- ★ What will I do to adjust the impact of those things?

Do not let circumstances control you.
You change your circumstances.

JACKIE CHAN

March 23

> ## I Will Not Fear!

Fear is damaging. Fear is limiting—and still worse—fear is crippling. Limits are often self-inflicted and they can always be overcome with time. When allowed, fear will slow you down. Progressively, fear causes complete, longstanding immobilization. Fear paralyzes you—it takes all that you have been given and makes those gifts useless.

The constructs of fear that you develop can cause you to feel that you *have* nothing, that you *are* nothing and that you will amount to nothing. Do not let fear cause you any further damage than it already has.

Get in FRONT of Fear!
Don't be left behind!

Affirmation Journal
- ★ **What am I afraid of?**
- ★ **How do my fears impact my future?**
- ★ **What *could* I do if I were not afraid?**
- ★ **What *would* I do if I were not afraid?**
- ★ **What *will* I do without the limit of fear?**

Remove your self-imposed limits by taking fear COMPLETELY out of the equation! When it comes to your success, fear will always be much more damaging than it is helpful! Act out of FAITH, not fear!

Say Aloud: **I Will Not Fear!!! I Will Not Let Fear Limit Me!**

March

"

I Will Be FEARLESS!

"

Fearless people take over the WORLD! Fearless people are the leaders, the winners, the conquerers, the learners, the teachers and the trailblazers! Fearless individuals are those who succeed despite obstacles—not because of the absence of fear—but because of their ability to continually work *through* fear! If you're not afraid, you're not doing it right!

Fear can be used to our benefit when we work *with* it:

Dynamic People exact fortuitous change within *all* while creating a more vibrant landscape that pulses with creativity.

Introspective People evaluate truths to find progress suited to wholeness for continuous peace within and without.

Resourceful People examine opportunity from various angles and find viable solutions that evoke lifelong learning.

Which are you?

Are you fearless?

Affirmation Journal
- ★ **Of the fearless examples provided, how do I relate?**
- ★ **How do I show fearlessness?**
- ★ **How does my fearlessness impact my future?**

Do one thing every day that scares you.

ELEANOR ROOSEVELT

March 25

"To Whom Much is Given, Much is Required!"

For all that you dream and ALL of the plentiful blessings that God has in store for you, there will be MUCH effort needed on your part to see those through to fruition! Glory cannot be had without there being an equivalent story telling the pathway that led to the ultimate successes you see in life. Be PROUD of your story and ALL of the glory that your individual path will bring. Don't be afraid to work HARD for all that you strive for understanding that there WILL be sacrifices to be made and difficult challenges to overcome. In the end, you will arrive at the end result that you have created based on your efforts, your disposition and your giving. All that is for you is for YOU! No one can take that away, so be sure that you get out of your own way in order to obtain exactly what is YOURS! You will have ALL that you desire through work, ethics and discipline!

Say Aloud: **To Whom Much is Given, Much is Required!!!**

Affirmation Journal
- ★ **What am I willing to sacrifice for the sake of my dreams?**
- ★ **How much effort am I willing to put into my goals?**
- ★ **What has been given to me? What was required?**

March

I Am GOD's Child!

God sees ALL that we *grow* through. He sees every challenge, every bit of courage and all the faith that we put into our efforts. With this knowledge, we trust that our work is never in vain. Our effort doesn't go without benefit. We are cared for and we are taken care of. We have everything we need in life and we are blessed INDEED because we *have* life!

We Are Children of GOD!

God is our savior! God is our Provider! God cares for us! By all that God is and by all that *we* are, we know without a doubt that we are children of The Most High!

Believe in the POWER of GOD and the power of the blood flowing through your veins! You were created in the image and likeness of God! Use the power that you possess to call forth ALL that God has set aside just for YOU! *Reign* in life through God's divine favor! You are God's child! Be BOLD with the power you possess and yearn after God more and more each day to awaken the blessings you have in store!

Say Aloud: **I Am God's Child! God Takes GREAT Care of Me!**

God is waiting eagerly to respond with new strength to each little act of self-control, small disciplines of prayer, feeble searching after him. And his children shall be filled if they will only hunger and thirst after what he offers.

RICHARD HOLLOWAY

March 27

I Am Under GOD's Protection!

When our connection with God lacks sustainable certainty, we flip flop back and forth between blind faith and emotional desperation. Our faith in God cannot be that shady—we have to understand who He is and who *we* are in Him! **We Are God's Children!** We are under God's protection! There is NOTHING in this world that can change God's love for us, so we rest assured in His promises knowing that He is ALWAYS on our side and He is ALWAYS right on time!

We need reassurance that God is an ever-present, ever-ready vessel should we find ourselves in trouble. God never leaves our side. He protects us at ALL times. These things we know by faith! We know them because of the many times He has protected us in the past—even from ourselves!

Trust in God's everlasting love and His everlasting protection. God is on your side—forever and always!

Say Aloud: **I Am Under God's Protection! God is On My Side!**

Affirmation Journal
- **What does it mean to be under God's protection?**
- **When has God protected me in the past?**
- **How does my assurance in God's protection aide me?**

March

I Am at PEACE!

Grace & Peace. Grace & Peace. Grace & Peace.

If you pray to God for *anything*, peace should be it! If you are ever at a loss for what exactly to pray for, pray for peace and accept God's grace.

We don't always wholly accept the grace that God affords us, so we end up praying for what we already have. We ask God for an abundance of peace when peace is something we have the power to create in our lives.

If you want to be at peace, DO IT! *Decide* that you want peace and do what it takes to create a life FULL of total calm and peace within. Troubles will come and storms will rise but a mind at peace will never lose its calm.

Affirmation Journal
- ★ **Am I at peace?**
- ★ **What do I do to create and maintain peace in my life?**
- ★ **What does it mean to accept the grace of God in my life?**

Say Aloud: **I Am at Peace! I Accept God's Grace and Peace!**

Peace comes from within.
Do not seek it without.

GAUTAMA BUDDHA

March 29

" I Am BLESSED! "

Regarding free will, be careful not to walk away from the Angels that God has strategically placed in your life to protect, guide and prosper you. Sometimes, the Angels watching over you may be those you war most with. ☺ Be enlightened, even in closed-mindedness. Whether the closed-mind be yours or another's, seek rest in the fact that ALL things happens for a reason—your steps are ordained by God. Find the blessing in each interaction you have knowing that you are blessed beyond measure!

You are as blessed as you allow yourself to be. Get out of the way of your blessings and let life show you true favor. Find peace in your blessings. Find solace in honoring God with your blessings through giving, service and honor for all that you have received.

Affirmation Journal
- ★ How blessed am I?
- ★ Which blessings of mine am I most grateful for?
- ★ Which blessings of mine have brought me the most peace?
- ★ How can I continually be a blessing to others?
- ★ What does it mean to find peace in my blessings?

Say Aloud: **I Am Blessed! My Blessings Are Beyond Measure!**

March

"

I Am WHOLE!

"

Wholeness is such a grand treasure to possess. By obtaining the blessing of wholeness, we find that negative traits within our human nature are removed. This paves the way for peaceful practice and joyful appreciation of ALL experiences, good or bad. An individual who finds wholeness finds respect, value, reverence, honor and undying love for self. Once these are obtained, they project themselves outwardly in love, admiration and appreciation for ALL mankind.

Wholeness is the perfect breeding ground for joy, peace, kindness, gentleness, and self-control. When we arrive at wholeness, problems bother us less. We are then patient with ourselves and the rest of the world. We deal gracefully with all things and quickly bounce back from defeat. Internal battles are less frequent and are easily quelled when they *do* occur because of self-love and self-respect. We are lacking little when we are whole. In wholeness, we feel complete even when things are missing.

Affirmation Journal
★ **How can I find and sustain completion in wholeness?**

*Happiness is when what you think,
what you say, and what you do
are in harmony.*

MAHATMA GANDHI

March 31

My Life is PEACEFUL!

Peaceful lives are created through peaceful practices. Any number of peaceful procedures, activities and behaviors can be incorporated within our daily lives to create peace. Peaceful lives are simple lives. Simplicity in life isn't found through removal of complex agendas. Simplicity exists in practices such as learning to enjoy the small things, learning to be at rest as much as possible and learning to create positivity all around.

Peace starts in the mind. Through the practice of mental discipline, we learn to silence that which doesn't allow us peace. We learn to listen to our souls and seek the answers to our prayers in calm surroundings.

Peaceful lives can be obtained through these practices and through exhibitions of faith. Faith grants the peace we need and teaches us to live lives of harmony.

Is your life peaceful?

Say Aloud: My Life is Peaceful! My Life is in Harmony!

The Simple Path
Silence is Prayer
Prayer is Faith
Faith is Love
Love is Service
The Fruit of Service is Peace

MOTHER TERESA

Wisdom

April 1

> ## I Will Use WISDOM!

Above all of the character virtues, wisdom reigns supreme. Wisdom guides attainment of all other virtues because it necessitates incorporation of them all based on the overall goal of sound judgment.

Wisdom Affirmation *(Repeat this aloud)*
Wisdom is the spiritual trait of emotional intelligence in action. Through wisdom, I elevate my desires to focus on things that are spiritual in nature. By focusing on the spiritual, my physical environment becomes all the more pleasing to my natural eye. Wisdom is the admiration, facilitation and validation of truth.

April visits the concept of wisdom. This month, we find that wisdom isn't just a mental or intellectual concept. Wisdom is very spiritual in nature. We learn to use wisdom in our daily activities by adhering to spiritual guidelines and wholesome principals.

Say Aloud: **I Will Use Wisdom! I Will Use Sound Judgment!**

April

I Will Be THANKFUL!

Thankfulness to God comes as a result of your appreciation for the abundance found in your life. Clarity shows you that God's presence is everywhere and in all things within you and around you. In thankfulness, find blessings in *everything*.

Affirmation Journal
- ★ Where is there abundance in my life?
- ★ Where do I find lack in my life?
- ★ How can thankfulness contribute to further abundance?

Today's To-Do's...
- ★ Reflect on the things that you are thankful for.
- ★ Reflect on the things that you take for granted.
- ★ Compose a prayer of thankfulness that you can reference during times of doubt.
- ★ Post the prayer where you can easily access it.
- ★ Remind yourself of all that you are thankful for daily.

Say Aloud: I Will Be Thankful!

It's the simple things in life that are the most extraordinary; only wise men are able to understand them.

PAULO COELHO

April

> ## I Will Use My TIME Wisely!

Time is precious. It is a gift that we have been given. Time is a gift that we give to others as they give their time to us in return. Time shouldn't be taken lightly since all that we do is based on time. For this reason, we use our time wisely.

We give of our time understanding that everything doesn't warrant our attention, let alone the time we have to give. This knowledge means that everything isn't worthy of our time or attention. We prioritize those things that *deserve* our time always remembering to keep ourselves first when it comes to time considerations.

Regarding others, we give our time to those who deserve it. We teach others to be deserving of our time—we give our time to those who respect it, cherish it and appreciate it. We give time to those who don't waste it.

Time isn't freely given nor is it freely received, so be sure that those who have your time also have your attention in those moments. Commit to each moment you spend in the presence of others or you will find your time to be wasted.

Affirmation Journal
- ★ How can I make better use of my time?
- ★ How can I direct others to do the same?
- ★ How does effective time management positively impact my future?

April

I Will Use My TALENTS Wisely!

The favor of God is a precious gift given unto us. God's favor finds us in command of talents, opportunities and awareness that we wouldn't otherwise have.

Cherish all that God has favored you with. Use your talents to widely express your appreciation for the blessings of God.

In gifting you with talents, God shows that He trusts your ability to get the job done! Thank Him by using ALL that He has made available to you. Don't squander what you've been blessed with.

Use your talents to make God's love visible and appealing to the world! No amount of money can buy God's trust. No amount of money can express gratitude for God's favor so thank Him for favor, talent and experience through your wise use of them.

Say Aloud: **I Will Use My Talents Wisely!**

Talent without discipline is like an octopus on roller skates.
There's plenty of movement, but you never know
if it's going to be forward, backwards, or side-ways.

H. JACKSON BROWN, JR.

April

" I Will Be CONFIDENT in My VOICE! "

Through all you encounter in life, never show yourself to be lacking in confidence. Based on the challenge of your goals, raise your self-confidence to a comparable level. If your goals don't challenge you in that manner, GET SOME NEW ONES! People should be able to see your FUTURE based on who you show yourself to be TODAY! YOU should be able to see your future based on your confidence *today*!

Be confident without compromise! KNOW your worth! As faithful as you are to God who provides ALL, place your FULL trust in God's powers when you lack confidence in yourself!

Match faith in God with confidence in your VOICE—develop a voice WORTH believing in! Speak LIFE into yourself! Repeat daily affirmations ALOUD to hear positive self-talk in your own voice! There isn't a single person in this world who should be encouraging you more than you encourage yourself. USE YOUR VOICE! Eventually, your confidence will begin to speak for itself! TRUST in it! Trust in the power of YOU!

Say Aloud: **I Will Be Confident in My Voice! I Trust MYSELF!**

April

I Will Use My WORDS Wisely!

Words define us. The things which we utter out of our mouths define that lives that we live and the lives that we aspire to. Be sure that everything coming out of your mouth is something you can be proud of.

Think before you speak.

If you can't say anything good, don't say anything at all.

The words that come from your lips are as important as the clothes that you wear and the decisions that you make. In fact, words are *more* important since they explain the decisions you've made.

Create definition using words. Define yourself and define your life. Through words, shape whatever perception you choose—perception determines identity. Ensure that the words you speak energize your life and the lives of others. Make your words appeal to your audience. Gain their attention whether they are being attentive or not.

Say Aloud: **I Will Use My Words Wisely! Words Energize Me!**

*He that can compose himself
is wiser than he that composes books.*

BENJAMIN FRANKLIN

April

" I Will Value CLARITY! "

When looking at life through broken lenses, you see a poor picture of reality—you view the entire world without removing the damage caused to your personal viewpoints. Instead of taking the time needed to fix what has been impaired, you assess life through your own distorted view. Minor disfiguration causes major disdain over extended periods of time and you forget that your lens was ever damaged in the first place—better yet, you begin to look at the rest of the world as if ALL of IT is broken, not just your lens.

Clarity is essential to viewing the world on an even playing field. Clarity won't be found within an outlook that hasn't healed from past brokenness. To obtain fair viewpoints, free yourself of hatred, anger, bitterness, resentment, unforgiveness and all negativity that leaves you feeling damaged and depleted. Devote much time finding the clarity in your life. Expose all demons that you've swept under the rug including the truths that you're hiding from yourself and others. Do what it takes to release the headache of chaos. Happiness is found at the opposite end of confusion.

Don't spend another day broken and unclear! Face yourself and clean up your troubled reality. Find clarity, and find it NOW!

Say Aloud: **I Will Change My Perspective! I Value Clarity!**

April

> ## I Am FULL of CLARITY!

Each of us sees things only as clearly as we allow ourselves to see them. Some matters of clarity are beyond our control, but as it relates to spiritual, emotional and mental awareness, we are all given the clearest clarity that we open ourselves up to.

Clarity is the ability to see far-reaching implications of a situation—it is a facet of wisdom. Clarity becomes the tool of those willing to exercise knowledge that goes beyond the typical. Considerations include personal awareness, external awareness and the ability to project and theorize based on one's own learning. We see things not just because *they* are clear, but because *we* are clear.

How clear are you?

However clear you find yourself to be, ensure that your brain doesn't turn to muck once you find the missing links. Clarity presents the ability to make clear, *clean* decisions with your new level of vision. With newness in clarity, pray for increased productivity so that you best operate with the clarity that you've found.

Be Clear. Be Direct. Be GREAT!

The art of being wise is the art of knowing what to overlook.

WILLIAM JAMES

April

I Will Value My INTELLIGENCE!

Don't let people affix their (negative) judgments to you in a manner that causes you to change into who THEY want YOU to be. Make your own assessments of who you are and who you want to be. Even if you agree with the inferences of others, come to terms with the information yourself, *for* yourself and *within* yourself. Make changes from the inside.

You have enough intelligence to guide your own life and to deal with the outcome of each decision that you make. You are powerful enough to change as much as you desire to within yourself and also within your environments. As you see the need to change, trust that you will make decided adjustments in the manner that's most profitable to you. This isn't saying that you don't need the input of others or that you disregard the value found in feedback that you receive. With all that you receive from others, be sure to involve yourself in the decisions you make because the accountability for YOU is YOURS and yours only.

For any and all changes that ever need to be made within your life, be sure to inquire within—within yourself.

Say Aloud: **I Am Intelligent! I Will Value My Intelligence!**

April

I Am Full of INTELLIGENCE!

When others around you are hurting, be the powerful shoulder they can lean on for support. Pay attention to the people around you. Listen to the things they will never say. Without asking for permission, do what you can to ease their unspoken pain! Use your intelligence! Your personal awareness and deep connection with *yourself* best postures you to bespeak the internal engagements of others. Tap into your emotional intelligence! Use it to heal what ails others. You don't need anyone's permission to make them better. Do it anyway! Do it by your fine example, by your sound judgment and by your thoughtful wisdom. In wisdom, let your intelligence go further than only what you can do for yourself. Intelligence will teach you that whatever you do for others is *always* in the best interest of yourself.

Affirmation Journal
- ★ **Where have I found opportunities to use emotional intelligence to help others?**
- ★ **What have I done with this awareness?**
- ★ **How will I use my emotional intelligence in the future?**

The wise man will make more opportunities than he finds.

FRANCIS BACON

April 11

> ## I Am MASTERFUL!

"Coaching is the process of awakening an individual's internal awareness in a way that acknowledges who and where they currently are while also developing purposed actions that propel them toward who and where they yearn to be."
—D Nicole

You are Masterful!

Say Aloud: **I Am Masterful!**

As masterful as you are, don't limit your efforts to only that which *seems* possible! Show yourself that you are composed of more GUT than you could ever imagine! Awaken your internal awareness in a way that taps into your *vision* of life! Through PASSIONATE visualization, develop purposed actions that PROPEL you toward the lifestyle that makes you MOST happy! Don't allow weakening within your soul or any output within your environment to take away from your trust in your own masterfulness. You *can* overcome EVERYTHING! You can be ANYTHING! You *have* it ALL!

You are Masterful! PROVE IT TO YOURSELF!

Say Aloud: **I Am Masterful! I Will Propel Myself to Greatness!**

April

"

I Am LEARNING!

"

New learning abounds within each new day that we are given. Each new relationship presents us with newfound acceptance of who we are and acceptance of new individuals. Each chance meeting allows for more understanding of the meaning of life. We are given endless opportunities to learn!

With every new day, every new opportunity and every new relationship, we're constantly reminded that we are evolving—always learning, always growing. There isn't a single occurrence within our lives that excludes a moment to learn! It's up to us to maximize each moment that we're given and to take full advantage of our potential to increase our knowledge.

Say Aloud: **I Am Learning! I Am Sharing! I Am Growing!**

Through learning we grow and through sharing we grow together.

> *By three methods we may learn wisdom:*
> *First, by reflection, which is noblest;*
> *second, by imitation, which is easiest;*
> *and third by experience, which is the bitterest.*
>
> CONFUCIUS

April

I Will PRAY!

As the overly dogmatic visionaries we often are, we limit the power of prayer and the power of God when we subject them to the limitations of personal religion. Just as God comes in various forms, so too does prayer. Prayer is accomplished through verbal and nonverbal practices of meditation, quietude, dreaming, vision building, etc. Through these practices, we make our desires known and we communicate with the universe on exactly how we might acquire them. With proper silence and reverence of our own power—in conjunction with God and the universe—we find answers to our prayers and thusly attain the desires of our hearts.

Find newness in your prayer life. Study new means for connecting with The Creator—your best self. Silence yourself long enough to heighten communication with yourself. Lift yourself up from within. Drive your *literal* life by reigniting your *prayer* life. Start NOW!

Today's To-Do's...
- ★ Compose a prayer that incorporates acceptance of your past, present and future.
- ★ Post the prayer where you can see it daily. Pray it daily.
- ★ Open yourself to new prayer methodologies for connecting with your higher self. Use them often.

Say Aloud: **I Will Pray! I Stay Connected Through Prayer!**

April

What GOD Has for ME is for ME!

There is great wisdom in making a conscious acknowledgment that God exists. The acceptance of God's existence empowers our lives as it endows us with capacities beyond human understanding. Outside of the general gifts available to all human beings, each of us is endowed with a unique set of skills designed for us to effectively execute that which we are purposed to complete. Arming ourselves with the whole amour of God, we leave fear, doubt, judgment, insecurity and mixed emotion behind.

Relish in the favor of God. He has given you EVERYTHING you have need of. Rely on faith and begin to FULLY embrace all that you've been given knowing that what is for you is YOURS only!

Say Aloud: **What God has for Me is for Me! I Believe in God!**

Affirmation Journal
- ★ **What is the role of God in my life?**
- ★ **Why is it wise to acknowledge God's existence?**
- ★ **How does my acceptance of God impact my purpose?**

Don't Gain The World & Lose Your Soul,
Wisdom Is Better Than Silver Or Gold.

Bob Marley

April 15

"I Will Stand FIRM Behind My Truths!"

Obedience isn't as optional as we would like to make it, yet our timely acknowledgment of God's grace *is* optional. The fact of the matter is that God *still* grants grace to ALL people regardless of our personal acceptance of His grace. THANKFULLY, our lack of recognition—or lack of obedience—does nothing to limit God's desire bless us. These are truths we can believe in!

While standing *firm* in the knowledge that God seeks to bless us, we should be more intentional in our prayer life! For all that we desire, we need to STOP praying prayers of basic "restoration" and instead KNOW that God has the power to do exceeding, abundantly above ALL we could EVER ask for or think of! Don't discount the unlimited power of God! Don't discount the weight of your blessings! Be a GREAT steward over what you have NOW and command more goodness in your life by accepting God's grace while reverencing His power!

Affirmation Journal
- ★ What does it mean to accept God's grace?
- ★ How can acceptance of God's grace change my life?
- ★ Within God, what truths can I stand firm in?

Say Aloud: I Will Stand Firm Behind My Truths!

April

"

My THOUGHTS Are POWERFUL!

"

Limiting thoughts limit personal capacity. BIG thoughts accomplish BIG things! Throughout history, we've seen proof of this in genius, medicine, science, technology and other areas. Imagine how mighty initial thoughts were *before* coupled with the capacity of the humans behind them! Revolutionary thinkers accomplished what they *desired* to!!! They accomplished what they *thought* to!

What are you thinking? What types of thoughts consume your daily life? Are they typically negative or positive?

Monitor your thoughts for the next 24 hours. Each time it crosses your mind, stop and jot down what you're thinking and whether the thought and associated feelings are negative or positive. Where is your *power* being directed? What are you creating within your mind? Practice shifting your thoughts to be constantly positive. No matter what happens, find GREATNESS in everything! Control your thoughts enough to alter them at a moment's notice. Your mind is too powerful not to control it!

Say Aloud: **My Thoughts Are Powerful! I Am What I Think!**

A man is literally what he thinks,
his character being the complete sum of all his thoughts.

JAMES ALLEN

April

> ## I Will Be HONEST with MYSELF!

With good intent, many of us encourage others to *be* and to *do* better. We rarely realize when we lack some of the selfsame healing principles that we seek to inspire within others. This happens when we are out of sync with ourselves. Life passes by quickly. If we aren't careful, we can pay so much attention to everything and everyone else that we lose the primary focus on self. Change starts with self—therein lies the root of ALL wisdom!

Being honest with ourselves requires wisdom in taking the time needed to evaluate our lives using effective measures. We follow evaluation by enacting adjustments that change us for the better. Instead of applauding speedy changes, we prioritize those which take considerable effort. In turn, we see enduring change that we can be proud of.

Say Aloud: **I Will Be Honest with Myself!!!**

Affirmation Journal
- ★ **What does it mean to be honest with myself?**
- ★ **How can I be more honest with myself?**
- ★ **Why is it wise for me to be honest with myself?**
- ★ **How does being honest with myself help my purpose?**

April

My MIND is POWERFUL!

Don't spend too much time *do*ing. You waste time when you are *do*ing too much. Spend more of your time *thinking*. Concocting. Planning. Create a progressive combination of thinking *and* doing so that you can be aggressively productive in your exploits.

The mind is a powerful tool. Use it appropriately. If you spend more time thinking, your actions will be more relevant and less wasteful. Questions can be reviewed and worthwhile answers can be discovered within the framework of the mind. Many answers in life are more intuitive, so instead of always looking on the outside, start to find yourself within.

The mind is a powerhouse of near effortless creation. Use it wisely—always for good, never for evil.

Say Aloud: **My Mind is Powerful!!! I Will Use It Wisely!**

Affirmation Journal
- ★ **What am I *do*ing too much of?**
- ★ **Within my life, where can I stand to do more thinking?**
- ★ **Why should I start within when solving life's problems?**

Rule your mind or it will rule you.

HORACE

April

"

My Life is PURPOSED!

"

Say Aloud: My Life is Purposed!

Your life is PURPOSED!

Once YOU know exactly what your purpose is, DO SOMETHING ABOUT IT! Be FIRM in our resolve to passionately pursue your purpose! Pursue your purpose with a clear, well-defined vision and learn to dream!!!

It's true that dreams will set you free! Dreams free your mind of limits, fear and human frailty because dreams aren't solely based on mere mortal potential. Dreams tap the surface of MIRACLES!!! They place within your grasp accolades that cannot be achieved by anything less than divine intervention, so gird your mind and press toward the HIGHEST mark of YOUR calling!

In knowing your purpose, NEVER compromise. Don't let others interfere with your vision! Your stark determination should find your character well built for the tests of will that you are guaranteed to face. As down and out as you will be at times, STAY FOCUSED! You never know when YOUR time will come, so be EVER ready—even in turmoil! Remember: Your purpose is larger than life! So, too, are YOU!

Say Aloud: My Life is Purposed! I Am Here to Fulfill Purpose!

April

I Will LIVE!

In childhood, our parents should prioritize teaching us how to dream! Parents should give children EXPERIENCES! One of the BEST things we can do for any young person is to bestow within them the JOY of EXPERIENCE!

Say: **I Will LIVE! I Will Encourage the JOY of EXPERIENCE!**

There is wisdom in experience—GREAT wisdom resides in getting all you *can* and canning all you *get*! If you find yourself around people who aren't open to experience, teach them, inspire them OR get rid of them! NOW! People who don't dream limit the potential of others based off their own limited exposure.

Say: **I Will LIVE! I Will Teach Others to Do the Same!**

This path that you have been on leads right to your destiny. Take charge of it and LIVE! Cherish every experience, every emotion and every opportunity! Make the best of your life! Create the life you've always dreamed of and LIVE!

May you live every day of your life.

Jonathan Swift

April 21

"I Will TRUST My INSTINCTS!"

When you believe in others more than they believe in themselves, think:

**God believes in us more than we believe in ourselves!
God is patient with us—He doesn't give up on us.**

Be patient with others! Don't give up on them. Allow your instincts and your faith in God to guide your stewardship. Don't push *your* vision upon others. Be instinctive in your interactions and trust what you've been given. Your God-given intuition isn't to be taken lightly. Give of yourself in discernment. Give others HOPE. Give others LOVE. Give them the example of YOU using the valuable instinct that you possess.

Affirmation Journal
- ★ What does it mean to have instinct?
- ★ Why is it essential for me to trust my instinct?
- ★ How can I use my instinct for the benefit of myself?
- ★ How can I use my instinct for the benefit of others?
- ★ How can I ensure that I am always in full use of my instinct?

Say Aloud: **I Will Trust My Instincts! I Will Trust My Vision!**

April

I Will LISTEN to My INSTINCTS!

Instinct provides us with the ability to *see* things more clearly. We have increased clarity based on this *feeling* in spiritual awareness. Instinct is very closely linked to vision. With vision, we are able to positively map our future because of our abilities to vividly dream, to create and to trailblaze. Intuition guides these skill by allowing us to operate on an emotional level of the more perceptually driven concept of vision. With both intuition and vision, our decisions operate outside of simple logic. We begin to tap into the realm of spirit by being guided by feeling as well.

Don't be afraid to maximize this wavelength wherein you align yourself more closely with The Creator. In doing so, you elevate your faith while expanding your personal power and prowess.

Don't be afraid to tap into the miracle of vision. Let your wise instincts guide you. Be wise and listen.

Say Aloud: **I Will Listen to My Instincts. I Will Use Wisdom.**

Knowledge speaks, but wisdom listens.

JIMI HENDRIX

April 23

I THINK!!!

The only effective way to change how we *see* things in life is to change how we *think*. To change our thoughts, we practice *behaviors* that create new thoughts. One example of this is the practice of affirming ourselves. Another way to change our thoughts is to take *actions* that create new thoughts. This is demonstrated in the practice of dressing for the job that you want. The act of dressing a certain way causes us to see ourselves differently—literally and otherwise. Because of our attire, we feel differently, we behave differently, we *think* differently and we have thusly gotten ourselves onto a path where we *see* differently based on actions and behaviors.

Thought is a remarkably powerful aspect of life. The outcomes of our encounters are directly related to how we think. Even our current circumstances correlate directly to our thoughts. The future will take us to a destination consistent with the present thoughts contained in our minds.

Understanding that we have such control, it goes without question that we must put much effort into directing our thoughts in the EXACT direction that we would have them go. Changing our circumstances, our responses and our encounters is a matter of redirecting our thought. We use the power that we've been given to create the life of our choosing. We must *think* and *be* GREAT!

Say Aloud: **I Think! I Will *Think* and *Be* GREAT!**

April

I Will Value My THOUGHTS!

With the goal of valuing that thoughts that bless your mind, meditate on good things. Don't conflict your mind with evil when you can always direct your mind to dwell on the good. Put MUCH thought into your future and use positive memories of your past to drown out negative thoughts in the present. Wisdom resides in directing your thoughts to pleasurable things while clearing it of things which tarnish your otherwise positive outlook.

Say Aloud: **I Will Value My Thoughts! I Dwell In Happiness!**

Life is too short to lose the value in controlling the mind by allowing any ole thought to dwell there. Value your thoughts by always dwelling on that which is good. Your enduring happiness depends on it.

Affirmation Journal
- ★ **Why is it important to place value in my thoughts?**
- ★ **How do I show that I value my thoughts?**
- ★ **How can I practice controlling my thoughts?**

Everybody in the world is seeking happiness—and there is one sure way to find it. That is by controlling your thoughts. Happiness doesn't depend on outward conditions. It depends on inner conditions.

DALE CARNEGIE

April

" I Make SOUND Decisions! "

Along this road of life, you are blessed with the power of free will. You're given the opportunity to make your own decisions on a daily basis regarding your past, your present and your future. Based on your thought processes, goals and experiences, you wield power that is in tune with your individualistic desires.

Your outcomes may not always make you proud, but you can always ensure that the decisions you make are your own. Don't be led by others to make decisions that you can't be proud of. Whatever the route taken to arrive at the choice, YOU bear the outcome of every single decision you make—good or bad—so be sure that each decision you make from this point forward always brings results you can be proud of.

Say Aloud: **I Make Sound Decisions!**

Affirmation Journal
 ★ Why is it important to make sound decisions?
 ★ What is the importance is making my own decisions?
 ★ How do my sound decisions contribute to my desires?

April

I Am RICH in Right-Thinking!

Be fluid in the progression of your thoughtful decisions. Whenever you encounter a shift or experience temporal delays, PERSIST knowing that setbacks aren't the same as failure! Take in new information and circumstances being mindful to grow with fresh learning opportunities made available to you versus choosing to grow against change. You *will* come across inopportune events that definitely need to be discarded. In other cases, adjustments and shifting perspectives are a beneficial—a welcome option—if you allow yourself to "flex" more, so LIGHTEN UP!

Trust your thought processes and trust yourself to make sound decisions. Every decision that you make won't always *look* or *feel* like it's the correct one, but there is benefit in apparent missteps whenever you seek to gain *all* that you can at *every* juncture. With this mindset, you will *always* know that you are RICH in right-thinking!

Say Aloud: **I Am Rich in Right-Thinking!**

It isn't what you have or who you are or where you are or what you are doing that makes you happy or unhappy. It is what you think about it.

DALE CARNEGIE

April

I Am a LEARNER!

Every experience of yours isn't solely for your personal gain. Some of what you grow through is specifically designed for the benefit of others. By the same token, understand that your immediate environment presents you with limitless opportunities to learn based on the experiences of those around you. There are persons within your life who have experienced situations simply so that they could help YOU—*or* so that you could help them. To get the most out of these learning opportunities, be less critical of yourself and others. Don't judge others. You never know who you will need and you never know who will need you.

In wisdom, be clever enough to take advantage of each opportunity to give to others. Don't miss any moment to learn, and don't miss any opportunity to help. In doing so, your growth proves itself to be limitless.

Say Aloud: **I Am a Learner! I Learn from Others, and I Give!**

Affirmation Journal
- ★ **What have the people around me been able to gain from my experiences?**
- ★ **What have I learned from those around me?**
- ★ **Why is it beneficial for me to learn from the experiences of others?**

April

I Will STUDY to Show Myself APPROVED!

Do you remember your educational experiences? Do you remember having to go to school and not really wanting to? Do you ever recall thinking, "What am I going to do with this information?" OR "I can't use this!"? Well, as a adult you have the ability to learn exactly what you *want* to learn, so what are you teaching yourself? What personal educational activities are you investing your time and efforts into? Are you bettering yourself through bettering your mind?

Say Aloud: **I Will Study to Show Myself Approved!**

Take advantage of the many learning opportunities readily available to you. If you're going to invest your resources into anything, invest them into *yourself*! Don't waste your time in activities that don't increase the value of your mind or your worth. STUDY to show yourself approved! Put your money where your MIND is! Learn all that you can while you have the opportunity to do so. Immediately apply your learning to your lifestyle and begin to prosper in life!

Say Aloud: **I Will Study to Show Myself Approved!**

Formal education will make you a living;
self-education will make you a fortune.

JIM ROHN

April

I Am FULL of PURPOSE!

Before we are born into this world, we're purposed with a destiny to fulfill. There's a path that is already laid before each of us, and our environments are contrived so ALL that we are predestined to do can be effectually carried out. In line with the goal of FULLY embracing and passionately pursuing our God-given purpose, there will be a great many pointed shifts in our personal and professional endeavors over the course of time. As we fine tune our skills and increase our awareness of God's will for our lives, shifts become more widely appreciated and accepted because obedience is more advisable than sacrifice.

Eventually, shifts that you have operated within combine into the sole force that will impact not only your life, but also the lives of those around you. Through these processes of revolution, you find purpose, so be OK when current business models and pursuits give way to consolidation of the whole.

Affirmation Journal
- ★ What notable shifts have I experienced in life?
- ★ How have these shifts directed me to my current point?
- ★ How have these shifts impacted my overall purpose?
- ★ What are the noticeable building blocks seen in the path I have taken?

April

"

I Am WISE!

"

Discernment is an interesting concept. While clear insight is great to have, we mustn't fall short of the subsequent decisions required as a result of *thorough* understanding of a situation. Increased clarity could cloud better judgment or open us up to unanticipated results. The goal must go further than the simple ability to view concepts more clearly, so with discernment, pray also for increased wisdom.

With wisdom comes the goal of proper utilization. Wisdom must be groomed from within. The true essence of having wisdom is also knowing how best to *use* it by being wise in facilitation of the skill. Wisdom is mistaken as arrogant intelligence if not managed effectively. Introspection is required to optimize wisdom at full potential—you have to first know yourself. If you don't know yourself, your handle on wisdom will be especially lacking.

Find out who you are! Use what you know about yourself to more closely understand the happenings within your surroundings. Master yourself and you master your environment! Such is the nature of wisdom.

Knowing yourself is the beginning of all wisdom.

ARISTOTLE

Diligence

May 1

I Will WORK on DILIGENCE!

Every effort presents us with the opportunity to perform to the best of our abilities. In all we do, we are tasked with putting forth our best by giving our all. How often do we actually do it? Sincere commitment to ourselves within each task means working diligently, in earnest. Diligence represents our integrity, character, skill and our interest level. It is always in our best interest to put forth worthy effort to complete the projects placed within our hands.

Diligence Affirmation *(Repeat this aloud)*
Diligence is zeal and my personal integrity to be persistent! It is decisive effort and work ethic that protects me against laziness. Diligence is maintaining my personal convictions at all times.

Diligence is our topic for May. This month, we learn about practices that keep us on track toward our goals. Through diligence, we commit not only to our goals, but we also commit to ourselves!

Say Aloud: **I Will Work on Diligence! I Will Commit!**

May

> ## I Will Work CONSISTENTLY!

There are a great many things that we encounter over the course of our lifetimes that could impede our progress and stand in the way of success. While embarking on our personal journeys, we find numerous instances of self comparison along the way. We take our lives and place them within the realms of lives that are not our own. We compare ourselves to others and are often discouraged when their lives seem less difficult. We look at their external progress and think their routes to be effortless and without travail. Such comparisons stand in the way of GREATNESS!

Without EVER comparing yourself to others using negative methods, *always* do what it takes to see YOUR needs met! Be consistent in your efforts. Work diligently no matter what others are doing and despite obstacles that you're sure to encounter! Live your life CONSTANTLY in pursuit of your dreams. Live earnestly, in great discipline and without any regret!

MAKE the BEST life by being consistent in ALL you do!

Say Aloud: **I Will Work Consistently! I Will Use Discipline!**

Everyone must choose one of two pains:
The pain of discipline or the pain of regret.

JIM ROHN

May

"

I MUST!!!

"

Say Aloud: I Must! I Must!! I MUST!!!

Each accomplishment of ours is always achieved based on personal commitment. There is no one else to complete the activities that we are designed to complete. There is no one else to fulfill our roles. The job is ours and we MUST commit! Personal motivation to get our jobs done isn't optional. It is REQUIRED! We MUST have the perseverance that it takes to complete our tasks. We MUST be driven enough to see assignments through to the end, and we MUST be connected with ourselves enough to be the personal encouragement we need when no one else is around.

Affirmation Journal
- ★ **What motivates me?**
- ★ **What do I feel that I MUST do?**
- ★ **What am I doing NOW to get it done?**

Find out where your passion resides and start there to find the depths of your motivation. Motivation comes easy once you find out where your heart is! Match your passion with a plan, consistency and the discipline needed to see it all through to the end. Once you complete smaller tasks, bigger ones seem much more attainable.

Say Aloud: I Can! I Will! I Must! I Am Motivated to Succeed!

May

> ## I Will CREATE a Great Life!

Say Aloud:
> *Life is what I make it. It is exactly what I choose.*
> *I create my problems. I decide: Win or Lose?*
>
> *Life is what I make it. When I decide to start my day,*
> *I should opt to make it a good one.*
> *I control that in my own way.*
>
> **D NICOLE WILLIAMS**

Life is EXACTLY what we make it! This will ALWAYS ring true. Understanding that we have the full power and capacity to *make* our lives exactly what we choose, why choose anything less than the best?

Affirmation Journal
- ★ **What great moments have I had in my life?**
- ★ **What great moments have I *created* in my life?**
- ★ **What great moments have I planned for the future?**

> *Never miss the moments!*
> *Don't miss anything. Don't miss the game.*
> *Don't miss the performance, don't miss the movie,*
> *don't miss the show, don't miss the dance.*
> *Go see everything and experience all you possibly can.*
>
> **JIM ROHN**

May

> ## I Will PURSUE My Dreams!

What is your dream life? What is your *dream*—not your goal? What type of life would you like to create that supersedes your general goals? What type of life would you like to create that could only come about as a result of life's *miracles*? What are you doing RIGHT NOW to create a life in line with your dreams?

Without pursuit, there is no dream. Without plans, there is no attainment. Take steps RIGHT NOW to build the life you've always wanted! Don't wait on life to be perfect before you create a path of GREATNESS! Don't wait on your lucky stars to line up in order for you to get the job done. Act now! Do what it takes NOW to follow your dreams! When you do, don't act lackadaisically about it either! Pursue your dreams with PASSION! Back up ALL of your lofty goals with matching ENERGY to see them through! Your dreams deserve it! Your life deserves it! YOU deserve it!

Say Aloud: **I Will Pursue My Dreams! I Will Pursue in Passion!**

Affirmation Journal
- ★ **What is my dream life?**
- ★ **What am I doing right now to create a life in line with my dreams?**
- ★ **How important is planning in conjunction with my dreams?**

May

I Am DETERMINED!

As our lives progress, we sometimes get stuck. We find ourselves residing within junctures that either make us or break us. We get left at crossroads where we must determine the measures needed to embrace the change opportunity at hand. These passes test our determination. They test the weight of our goals and the diligence in our *why*.

Why are you doing "it"? Is your reason worthwhile enough for you to press past hurdles over and over again? Is your reason worthwhile enough for you to defy even *yourself* at times to be sure that projects are completed? Does your reason inspire UNSTOPPABLE determination? Are YOU determined?

Affirmation Journal
- ★ **What is my overall goal in life?**
- ★ **Why is this my goal?**
- ★ **Why is *that* my reason?**
- ★ **How worthwhile is this reason?**
- ★ **What am I willing to do to show my determination?**

You've done it before and you can do it now.
See the positive possibilities. Redirect the substantial energy
of your frustration and turn it into
positive, effective, unstoppable determination.

RALPH MARSTON

May

" I Will PURSUE My PASSION! "

Have you figured out your passion in life? Have you felt what it like is for an activity to completely ENERGIZE you? What is *that* activity? What are you doing to incorporate that activity into your life's dreams and goals?

Change Your Posture! Change Your Life!

Take steps NOW to mesh your passion into your lifestyle. Do things that bring joy to your immediate environment. Do things that add positive vibes to your world. Do what makes YOU feel good! Add to the longevity of your life by working within your passion. Give yourself LIFE by partaking in your passions on a daily basis.

LIVE yourself HAPPY! Pursue your Passion!

Change Your Posture! Change Your Life!

Affirmation Journal
★ **What is my passion?**
★ **What is it about my passion that energize me?**
★ **How have I incorporated my passion into my life?**

Say Aloud: **I Will Pursue My Passion!**

May

I Will Take the FIRST Step!

Diligence develops a process, but there is no progress without plans and goals. There are no plans and goals without steps. Take the first one! Contrary to popular belief, the first step is the EASIEST! The first step is always the one with least complication, least risk and MOST reward! You hardly even know what you're doing with that first step, which means there is less chance to mess anything up! All other steps result from the step which was most inspirational: The first one!

You're sure to be a little skeptical at first, but stop worrying about who's looking, who's judging you or who's going to steal this or that idea. What is for YOU is for YOU! You'll get it no matter WHO tries to mimic or stop you! Don't worry so much about others stepping on your toes. Just be PROUD that YOU are taking steps in the first place!

Say Aloud: **I Will Take the First Step! I Am Ready to Begin!**

Take one step toward your purpose, and your purpose will take MANY steps toward you. What are you waiting for?!

*A journey of a thousand miles
begins with a single step.*

LAO TZU

May

> ## I Will PURSUE My PURPOSE!

The value of purpose is limitless. Purpose is the value of our lives! Without purpose, we are NOTHING, so what is *your* purpose? What are you doing to fulfill that purpose in life?

The purpose of life is a life of purpose! It is up to us to take the reins and passionately pursue the value for which we were created. The trick lies in first figuring out exactly what our purpose is in life.

If you're having trouble finding your purpose in life, recall those things that excite you the most—the things that give you LIFE! What activity do you do that makes you feel GREAT?

If you are having trouble finding your purpose, speak with a coach who can help you find clarity in that area. Once you're able to pinpoint the value that you bring to life, bring it to pass! Embark on a journey to FULLY embrace the gift you've been given!

Affirmation Journal
- ★ What is my purpose?
- ★ What am I doing to fulfill my purpose?
- ★ What are my gifts?
- ★ How am I using my gifts?

Say Aloud: I Will Pursue My Purpose!

May

" I Will PURSUE My VISION! "

Once your purpose has been defined, it must be matched with an equally weighted plan. You can't have a HUGE, world-altering purpose and create plans that alter only the local community! Create a vision worthy of your purpose AND PURSUE IT!

It's pointless to plan and not also plan your pursuit! Take ALL actions necessary to obtain the reward worthy of your purpose. This requires imagination! Learn to dream again! Create a vision bigger than your britches! Have FUN while you carry out that vision.

As a child, imagination was always about the FUN you could have and the adventures that you could create with the people who journey through life with you. Don't forget to take the same guidelines with you as a adult!

Say Aloud: **I Will Pursue My Vision! I Will Dream HUGE!**

Affirmation Journal
- ★ **What is my vision?**
- ★ **What am I doing to fulfill my vision?**
- ★ **Why is visualization essential?**

In order to carry a positive action
we must develop here a positive vision.

DALAI LAMA

May 11

> ## I Will PURSUE My GOALS!

Only you know what your goals are. You have them in your mind. You have listed them on paper, but have you started to PURSUE them? Have you added deadlines to your goals?

Goals need formal plans. They need actions to progress. If you don't match effort with goals, you get nowhere! If you don't match deadlines with goals, you go through life more slowly than you should.

Take the steps RIGHT NOW to place your *life* within reach of your *goals*. Take sure steps that will get you on the path toward pursuit!

Today's To-Do's...
- ★ List your top 5 goals for the next year.
- ★ List your top 5 goals for the next 5 years.
- ★ List your top 5 goals for the next 10 years.
- ★ Add deadlines to each of these goals.
- ★ Add steps needed to complete each of these goals.
- ★ Add deadlines to each step.
- ★ Create a calendaring system where you list these goals, the needed steps, deadlines AND REMINDERS!
- ★ Don't wait until the last minute to remind yourself something needs to be done.
- ★ Give yourself enough lead time to actually complete it!

Say Aloud: I Will Pursue My Goals!

May

"

I Will GIVE My ALL!

"

Giving ALL of yourself demands that you embrace ALL of your skills and ALL of your talents. Giving your all means that you have to first get in tune with the parts of yourself that you sometimes leave out! It means embracing ALL of YOU!

Love who you are and accept all that you will be so you can firmly place yourself within every single moment and always execute to the BEST of your abilities! Get to know yourself, and let the world get to know who you *really* are. This is the only way you can tackle each project with the diligence that is worth your efforts. Don't commit to something without endeavoring to put your BEST foot forward. Commit to yourself FIRST! *Then*, in EVERYTHING you do, give your ALL!

Affirmation Journal
- ★ **What does my BEST consist of? Is that what I give?**
- ★ **Have I embraced ALL of my skills, talents and feelings?**
- ★ **How can I better embrace ALL of who I am?**

Say Aloud: I Will Give My ALL!

You only get out of life what you put into it.
Put your LIFE into it!

D NICOLE

May 13

"

I Will WORK!

"

You are able! You can! You will! You must! You must WORK!

Say Aloud: **I Will Work! I Can! I Will! I Must!**

Ever see diligent individuals work? You wonder how they get so much done. They progress much more quickly than others simply because they take ACTION! While others are waiting for perfection, funding and strategically aligned stars, diligent individuals are getting the job DONE!

Stop spending so much time thinking and start DOING! Don't *think* yourself out of ACTION! Create plans that inspire action. Take on tasks, projects and roles that inspire further action. Find yourself within circles that increase your work efforts and drive you toward inspirational diligence.

Affirmation Journal
★ **What is impeding the progression of my work?**
★ **How can I work *around* the hindrances?**
★ **How can I work *through* hindrances?**
★ **How can I remove them?**
★ **What will I accomplish once I begin to work?**

Say Aloud: **I WILL WORK! I CAN! I WILL! I MUST!**

May

I Will Work HARD!

In each and every endeavor you commit to, always do your best. Work HARD! It isn't enough to merely get the job done. Complete tasks to the BEST of your abilities. Such diligence and effort in simple concerns carries over into character and tenacity within bigger projects. These combinations create a life that's sure to find its way to GREATNESS!

Dedicate yourself to your tasks no matter the size, the notoriety or the resources available to you. Pave the way for your own greatness by being dependable by every definition of the word. Let others know that if *ever* there is a job to be completed, YOU are always the ideal resource. In this way, you show *yourself* how task driven you are which then encourages you to continually press toward your mark!

Say Aloud: **I Will Work Hard! I Will Press On!**

Affirmation Journal
- ★ **Why is commitment to work essential?**
- ★ **How does I show my personal level of commitment?**
- ★ **How does my own commitment further encourage me?**

No matter what you're going through, there's a light at the end of the tunnel and it may seem hard to get to it but you can do it and just keep working towards it and you'll find the positive side of things.

DEMI LOVATO

May 15

> ## I Will Work CONFIDENTLY!

Don't work toward anything that you don't believe in. Don't commit to personal tasks that you don't truly support. For yourself, only work on those things that add happiness to the value of your life. In this way, you will be confidently committed to ALL that you do.

Confidence in your work efforts causes you to work better and more effortlessly. Work no longer feels tedious because it's much more pleasing and fulfilling for you. The increased pleasure causes you to perform better because you're happy to do the job. You serve better because you believe in what you're doing and you stand behind it. The combinations of these newfound capacities leads to increased longevity since your personal well-being is enhanced by finding joy in your own diligence.

Say Aloud: **I Will Work Confidently! I Will Pursue in Passion!**

Affirmation Journal
- ★ How can I become more confident within my work?
- ★ Why is confidence in my work essential?
- ★ How can my confidence increase my longevity?

May

" I Will Work DILIGENTLY! "

Every task that you take on should be considered a labor of love—**NO HALF-STEPPIN'**!!! If you can't put your FULL effort into each project you work on, why are you participating?

We understand that we aren't always proud about everything that we *have* to do, and we understand that all jobs aren't pretty. Sometimes, we're even selected to do things against our will!

Regardless of the process that found you within a particular role, have pride enough to stand out in ALL of your efforts! Commit yourself to the task at hand and work diligently to see the job through to the end! Be willing to overcome hurdles, obstacles, set-backs, challenges and defeat in order to see projects through to completion!

Say Aloud: **I Will Work Diligently! I Am Worth It!**

Be diligent in your efforts! Don't let ANYTHING discourage you! Through blood, sweat and tears, put your best efforts into getting the job done no matter what!

Say Aloud: **I Will Work Diligently! I Am Worth It!**

Being forced to work, and forced to do your best, will breed in you temperance and self-control, diligence and strength of will, cheerfulness and content, and a hundred virtues which the idle will never know.

CHARLES KINGSLEY

May 17

I Will Speak with CONFIDENCE!

When speaking, always present yourself with confidence. Know who you are! Trust who you are never doubting what you have to offer. Be sure of yourself. Understand your potential acknowledging that you can ALWAYS learn and grow more.

You don't have to vocally *demand* that others acknowledge you within any setting. In 99% of cases, confidence speaks for itself! When needed, *command* the attention of others using your confident presentation of YOU. Be confident without compromise! Know your worth and operate within your optimal value.

As hard as you've worked to get where you are, confidence is warranted, expected *and* appreciated. No situation is intimidating when you are in full command of self-confidence. You know yourself better than anyone, so in speaking of yourself, speak in resolute boldness without any sign of fear!

Say Aloud: **I Will Speak with Confidence! I Am Not Afraid!**

Affirmation Journal
- ★ How can I build my confidence?
- ★ How does confidence remove fear?
- ★ How can self-awareness contribute to confidence?

May

"

I Will STOP Wishing and START Working!

"

Think on all the great many things that you want in life: things for yourself. Things for your children. Things for your entire family. You want one of those emergency funds you keep hearing about, and you want to travel internationally—not just for the first time, but during the first of spring EVERY year!!! GREAT!

Now that you have your mind sufficiently distracted with *things*, go ahead and list them out! Why not?! This listing of your Heart's Desires is an excellent reminder of what you're working toward! During the moments of weakness that are sure to come, use this list to remind yourself why you're doing it all in the first place.

Fittingly, we could also go ahead and couple this with your List of Why—why are you doing it? Dig a little deeper on this particular list and include more important things like education for you and your family. Include extracurricular activities and any notable purchases you'll be required to make in the future. Once you're done, it's time to get to work!

Say Aloud: **I Will Stop Wishing! I Will Start Working!**

*Discipline weighs ounces,
regret weighs tons.*

AUTHOR UNKNOWN

May 19

"I Will Be PERSISTENT!"

To everyone doing hard work that you think no one notices, work that you get no credit for OR if you're doing work that seems purposeless at times:

KEEP IT UP!

Don't be discouraged by slow progress—patience builds character. Continued progress toward your goals will find you better able to handle the resulting success once you finally arrive at your destination. Be persistent in your efforts no matter what life looks like. Don't give up! Don't give in! Show yourself how determined you are by passionately committing yourself to the task at hand. Take breaks as you need to, but get back to your projects revitalized and further inspired to see them through to completion.

When times get hard, visualize the future that you dream of. Think of the great many things that you've already accomplished and all of the future accomplishments that you will have. Use these as motivation to persist!

Say Aloud: **I Will Be Persistent! My Time is Soon to Come!**

Kudos to you for your fortitude, dedication and humility. Your time is soon to come!
CHEERS!

Say Aloud: **I Will Be Persistent! My Time is Soon to Come!**

May

> **I Will KEEP ON Keeping On!**

Initially, when beginning new endeavors, we do so without thoroughly embracing our full potential. We take the steps of newbies—movements that are timid, unlearned and routinely unpredictable. Amidst our progress, missteps and all, we face a number of growth opportunities including those that seem to challenge us *beyond* our means and abilities. It is within these difficult situations where we must develop tenacity to keep on keeping on! We must not face life with our eyes to the ground, so chin up! Shoulders back! Look life STRAIGHT in the eyes! **Keep Your Head UP!!!**

New challenges are new territories. They are new dimensions that are unfamiliar. Embrace the freshness with clear outlook and clever boldness. You can't top the charts with fear or complacency. With each new obstacle, understand that you are one step closer to completion— you have one new learning opportunity added to your list of unique experiences. Embrace the world around you and dig in!

Say Aloud: **I Will Keep On Keeping On! I Have Just Begun!**

Success is stumbling from failure to failure with no loss of enthusiasm.

WINSTON CHURCHILL

May 21

"

I Will GROW!!!

"

Say Aloud: **I Will Grow!**

When you start developing yourself—once you begin changing your posture and changing your LIFE—you'll grow out of the people and the problems that previously bothered you. You'll find new people and new problems to match your new competencies. Look forward to the growth! Life doesn't change—YOU do—only if you *want* to though. Always strive for growth in EVERY way. ALWAYS!

Think back on some of your past problems and relationships. Just LAUGH—reflecting on how you USED to be. **chuckle, chuckle**

Say Aloud: **I HAVE Grown!**

As you continually progress, remember that as you grow, so too should your circles of influence. Don't be left with social and professional circles that don't match your vision or position. Proactively target interactions with individuals who inspire you to be your BEST self. Make no quibbles about leaving others behind, and NEVER endeavor to *drag* anyone along with you!

Say Aloud: **I Will Grow! I Have Grown Considerably!**

May

" I Will CHANGE My Approach! "

To get out of your comfort zone and get the BEST out of life, you must change your approach! This change in approach requires you to change your mind! Approaching life differently entails getting *outside* of your mind at times to undergo some very uncomfortable things. You will be chart unfamiliar territory, and you can't exist within your current mindset to make needed adjustments, so GO AHEAD! Get out of your mind a little! Get out of the limits and the baggage *and* the headaches that you cause yourself! Be CRAZED with the goal of betterment!

Change your approach!

Affirmation Journal
- ★ How comfortable am I with my life right now?
- ★ How uncomfortable must I get to reach my goals?
- ★ What changes are needed within my approach to life?

Say Aloud: **I Will Change My Approach! I Will Be Better!**

You cannot change your destination overnight. You can change your direction.

JIM ROHN

May 23

" I Will WORK with PURPOSE! "

Less accomplished people sometimes wonder how successful people seem to get so much done. If inspired by the success and curious enough about the efforts, less successful people question how they can do the same. The response:

JUST DO IT!

Seriously, that's what works! *DOING* it. Planning is essential, yet sometimes—many times—it gets in the way for over-thinkers! Think about it! *(Don't think* too *much though.)*

Whatever you do, do it with purposed intent. It's not good enough to participate in an activity and not be present in the moment. Let your presence warrant your resolve to be actively involved in the occasion. Have a PURPOSE for your participation. Have a PURPOSE for your commitment. Have a reason to show up!!! Even if you can't find a reason other than for yourself, show up ANYWAY and present yourself with purpose! Be driven by forces that supersede logic. Your purpose is larger than life. Act like it!

Affirmation Journal
- ★ Why is it important for me to work with purpose?
- ★ Why is it important for me to commit to my activities?
- ★ How does a person who works with purpose behave differently than one who doesn't?

Say Aloud: I Will Work with Purpose!

May

" I Will Be DISCIPLINED in My Efforts! "

The journey you take through life will always be a labor of love. It will be ripe with reminders that EVERYTHING that you do starts with your. *You* are the focus of your life! *You* are the person responsible for every bit of progress you make and *you* will be held accountable to every bit of discipline that you employ.

Be TOUGH on yourself—tough enough to get the job done efficiently, but not too tough that you can't enjoy the fruits of your labor. Discipline yourself enough to see the light at the end of the tunnel in ALL situations. Once you reach your targets, bask in the sunshine!

The many sacrifices that you've already made aren't nearly as worthwhile as the sacrifices you should be looking forward to making in the future! Sacrifice for your future and be disciplined in your efforts! Each night you don't sleep; every misstep you take; every set back you have; every hurdle you overcome and every tear you shed should remind you that life is your *own* salvation. The obstacles are well worth it. Your enduring happiness is worth enduring discipline.

*Without discipline,
there's no life at all.*

KATHARINE HEPBURN

May 25

> ## I CAN!!!

Whatever route you decide to take in life—whatever winnings are yours for the taking—GREATNESS can only be achieved by you if you *believe* that greatness is yours for the asking!

> **I Think? I Can?**
> **I Think = I Can**
> **I Think! I CAN!**

Using the above rewrite of the childhood mantra, understand that you CAN *achieve* whatever it is that you *perceive*. Place in your mind magnificent thoughts, visions and plans! Piece together the most lavish goals that you can, and PURSUE!

Place yourself within the realm of excellence by committing to your desires. Dreams are nothing without worthy actions backing them! Back up your dreams with ACTION! YOU CAN DO IT!

> **I Think! I Can!**
> **I Think! I Can!**
> **I Think! I Can!**

Say Aloud: **I Can! I Will! I MUST! I Can Do It!!!**

May

> ## I Am READY!

Finding your purpose, your passion and the motivation to fervently pursue the life of your dreams follows a line of fortuitous events that place you on a path of GREATNESS! Readiness to follow that path means making a committed decision to undergo changes necessary to fulfill your goals. ACTION results from readiness. Readiness shows your commitment to yourself, your commitment to your project and your commitment to the people your endeavors will serve.

There is never a single, simplistic source of motivation. Motivation to pursue your dreams is everywhere you look! Find those motivations and write them down! Record them and post them where you can reference them during quick moments of discouragement.

Your purpose is much bigger than you. Remember that and GET READY! Be Great! The world is waiting to fulfill your dreams!

Say Aloud: I Am Ready! I Will Fulfill My Dreams!

> *The secret of discipline is motivation.*
> *When a man is sufficiently motivated,*
> *discipline will take care of itself.*
>
> Sir Alexander Paterson

May 27

> ## I Am FULL of CAN-DO-IT-Ness!!!

Each of us has encountered troubles that have been mentally, physically, emotionally and spiritually draining—troubles we thought we couldn't possibly overcome, yet we overcame anyway!

We made it! We did it! We're still here!

CAN-DO-IT-ness gives us the gumption to succeed! Life teaches us by providing a great many opportunities for us to learn. Past experiences remind us that we've done it before, so we can do it again! We CAN make it! We WILL make it!

Say Aloud: **I Am Full of CAN-DO-IT-ness!**

When life consistently presses you, you'll find that each struggle includes a clever opportunity to impress yourself. Encourage yourself through each trial that you face. Be reminded of past successes while working through troublesome situations. You CAN make it! You WILL make it!

Say Aloud: **I Am Full of Can-Do-It-ness! I CAN and I WILL!**

May

"

I Will Do My BEST!

"

Each day, if you aim to be better than you were on the day before, you effectively control the only thing that you definitely control for sure: yourself. By exercising such power, you are always able to do your best! Through this, you free yourself of hangups based on another's progress, and you maximize your potential because of the GREAT effort you personally put forward on a regular basis.

Your best will never be the same as another's and theirs will never be the same as yours. Make up in your mind that the only person you're competing with is yourself, and strive to be the BEST *you* that you can be!

Affirmation Journal
★ **What does it mean to do better today than I did in the past?**
★ **What will life look like if I always strive for the best?**

Say Aloud: I Will Do My Best! I Compete Only with Myself!

Always Do Your Best. Your best is going to change from moment to moment; it will be different when you are healthy as opposed to sick. Under any circumstance, simply do your best, and you will avoid self-judgment, self-abuse and regret.

MIGUEL ANGEL RUIZ

May 29

> **I WILL!!!**

Within each of us, there exists the passion to complete a number of things. That passion often prioritizes a single overall goal including the minor tasks that are involved along the way.

Affirmation Journal
- ★ **What job would I do if no one else was watching?**
- ★ **What job would I do if no one gave me credit?**
- ★ **What job would I do if I never earned a dime?**

Your answers to these questions will help you to define your passions in life. They will get you closer to the things that you will *happily* commit to. The tasks that involve your passion are those where you already understand: *I WILL!* You already know: *I WILL commit!* You already trust: *I WILL succeed!* Maintain this level of certainly by reviewing your reasons for doing it in the first place! Make your List of Why readily accessible, especially when embarking on a new journey. If ever you become discouraged, regularly review your reasons for getting started! Take your passion to the next level by continually motivating yourself to achieve bigger and greater!

Say Aloud: I Will! I Will Commit! I Will Succeed! I WILL!!!

May

" I Will Work on ME! "

Self-respect is the most crucial aspect of one's life. If you don't understand how to appreciate yourself and your own worth, how do you expect others to? Life is too short to maintain toxic behaviors. In order for you to flourish, you need to work on yourself. Don't expect others to love or respect you if you don't fully love and respect yourself first.

Say Aloud: **I Will Work on Me! I Will Better Myself!**

People accept poor jobs, poor relationships and poor futures because they don't respect themselves enough to realize they deserve better. Too many people become complacent in these aspects and stop striving for greater things.

Work on yourself! Do what you can to take your awareness to new levels. Place yourself within the mindset to *be* and to *do* better than you ever have before. Create and maintain a continual, evolutionary path of betterment for yourself and watch yourself achieve great things in life!

Say Aloud: **I Will Work on Me! I Will Better Myself!**

*For a man to conquer himself
is the first and noblest of all victories.*

PLATO

May 31

" I Believe in ME!!! "

One of the more difficult concepts that I convey to my mentees is learning to depend on themselves. The difficulty lies in the sensitive balance between being self-sufficient without being stubborn while also being bold enough to ask for help and humble enough to *receive* it.

The first of these young women reminded me of myself so much that I was plagued by the idea of having her conceptualize being even tougher than she already. It wasn't something I desired to do, but for the right reasons, I did. I had to! I had to get my sister, as she calls me, to understand that she could ALWAYS lean on and trust in herself if there were ever a time that even I couldn't be there for her. I promised her that those times would come while simultaneously assuring her that in our weakness we find our strength—in our weakness God is made strong! YES!!!

It's much easier to have faith in ourselves when we put our faith in something BIGGER than ourselves! Faith gives us POWER beyond anything we could accomplish by our own skill or will.

Faith can move mountains,
but don't be surprised if God hands you a shovel.

AUTHOR UNKNOWN

Self Control

June

> ## I Will Work on SELF-CONTROL!

Self-control guards our being. It keeps us in line with our personal values, morals and future desires. Through self-control, we exhibit restraint, poise and dutifulness. Truth be told, self-control keeps us out of MUCH trouble! We practice being our BEST selves by exhibiting self-control.

Self-Control Affirmation *(Repeat this aloud)*
Self-control means having possession of myself and command over my own behavior. Self-control means that behaviors come *from* oneself, not *by* oneself.

We focus on self-control this month. We learn to understand the extent of our rule over self and practice behaviors consistent with having utmost regard for ourselves and others. Our study on self-control will visit exertions of internal and external control so that we are BEST armed to move forward with command of our *full* being.

Say Aloud: **I Will Work on Self-Control!**

June

"

I Am ABLE!

"

Matters of self-control require hard mental diligence, commitment and boldness in courage. There is no formal preparation required in self-control, only a motivating pressing goal is needed for one to make enduring resolutions toward self-stewardship. Command of self-control includes awareness of what one can, will and *must* do when committing to imperative matters.

With the goal of self-control, figure out your motivating desires and KNOW that you're able to achieve them! There is no blueprint for the journey you're on. Everyone's path is different. Don't think that others have been prepped with key pointers that you're missing out on. The only key that most people really have is the key called LIFE! You have the power to decide if you want to open doors at the bottom OR if you aspire to bust doors WIDE open at the top! So CHOOSE! Whatever your final playing field, know that you are *more* than able to see it through to the end.

Say Aloud: My Ability is a Matter of Self-Control! I Am Able!

Self-control is one mark of a mature person;
it applies to control of language, physical treatment of others,
and the appetites of the body.

JOSEPH B. WIRTHLIN

June

" I Will LET GO of LIMITING BELIEFS! "

No matter how many times you hear it, or how cliché it may be, it will forever remain true that you can achieve WHATEVER you *believe*, yet this FACT is only true if you believe it. If you are to create actions that will boost your self-esteem and encourage you to persevere in life, you *must* change your way of thinking—let go of ALL limiting beliefs!

Create belief systems that leave NO room for worry and take ACTIONS that leave no room for failure! Shaky faith and timid actions aren't representative of FIRM belief in yourself and your outcomes, so believe—without a shadow of doubt—that you *can* and *will* have ALL that you strive for.

Make decisions that show your faith. Take actions that *test* your faith! Leave no option for yourself other than to move FORWARD! Move forward with no awareness of fear, defeat or limitations. Bury the limitations of your mind!

Say Aloud: **I Will Let Go of Limiting Beliefs!!!**

Affirmation Journal
- ★ **What are limiting beliefs?**
- ★ **What limiting beliefs do I maintain?**
- ★ **Why must I rid myself of these beliefs?**
- ★ **How does letting go of limiting beliefs open up a better and brighter future for me?**
- ★ **How can I help others let go of limiting beliefs?**

June

> ## I Will STOP Fighting and START Winning!

We battle too much. We battle with ourselves. We battle with our lives. We battle with dreams, fears, the past, the present and the future. We battle with friends, our families, our mates, and we even battle with strangers. Why are we doing so much fighting?

We are doing entirely too much fighting and not nearly enough WINNING! And for what?! Too often we fight about things irrelevant to our own cause. WHY?! Stop and think about that. WHY?!

Affirmation Journal
- **Who am I fighting with?**
- **What am I fighting for?**
- ***Why* am I fighting?**
- **Am I winning?**

Whatever it is that you are fighting for, with OR against, just STOP! Why fight when you can WIN!?! Change the *conception* of your hangup. Life is not a battle! Life is your playing field! Be inspired by your struggles and do what you can to CHANGE them! Do what you can to WIN!

You have to have inspirational dissatisfaction!
You have to be dissatisfied with your present condition and ask yourself, 'What more can I do with what I have?'

SENI HAZZAN

June

I Will List Concrete ACTIONS to Overcome My Fears!

We ALL have fears! It's true. REALLY!

The most successful people in life practice working *with* their fears instead of working *against* them. For example, fears that keep you from making progress are fears that are working *against* you, while fears that cause you to prepare yourself for the next challenge are those that are working in your favor.

What are *your* fears doing to you? Are they working *for* you OR are they working *against* you?

Affirmation Journal
- **What am I afraid of?**
- **What is the *worst* that could happen if I try?**
- **What is the *best* that could happen if I try?**
- **What happens if I don't try?**
- **What concrete actions will I take to overcome my fears?**

Today's To-Do's...
- **List the concrete actions you will take to overcome fear**
- **List actions you will take to pursue your goals.**

Whatever your fears are, never allow them to impede your progress. Use caution, use wisdom, but do not STOP!!! GO in the direction of your dreams, and just as you list out concrete actions to overcome your fears, list equivalent actions to pursue your goals!

June

> **I Will Turn My DREAMS into PLANS!**

Never be afraid to dream, and when you do, dream BIG! DREAM HUGE! Take the dreams that continuously replay themselves in your head and put organized plans behind them! By their very nature, dreams supersede goals since they are comprised of desires that can't be directly achieved by human ability. As magnificent as dreams are, they *still* require plans followed by humanly possible ACTION. HUGE dreams require BEAST effort, yes, BEAST: That which is greater than BEST! ☺ If you aren't mentally (AND SPIRITUALLY) prepared for your dreams, you WILL run into problems! The better your planning and preparation, the better your own mental support for yourself and the better your chances of success!

Start planning out your dreams. Take the first few steps and see how it works for you. At the very least, give yourself time to dwell on your plans long enough to consider various scenarios. Don't go into it blindsided! You'll be more successful if you take time to wrap your head around it all first!

Good Luck!

You do not need permission to be great!
Just dream and do the things you dream about!!!

SENI HAZZAN

June

" I Will Use My WORDS! "

Too much in our lives goes without being said. Too much goes misunderstood. We allow too much invalid, improper, unsolicited and miscommunicated communication. More effortless success in life is found through using ALL tools available to us. Such tools include using the foundational variables of communication: words.

Words are the expression of our thoughts, our feelings, our innermost selves. Words display our verbal perception of a mental, hidden reality. Every justified occasion should find us readily eliciting our thoughts by way of our words. We shouldn't miss any worthy moment to share our thoughts, feelings and decisions through communication.

Open yourself up through self-expression. Fill the voids in your life by uttering your desires through language. Find personal identity through the definitions created by your words. Define yourself and allow that picture to be the reality seen by others.

Don't allow life to pass you by without commanding each moment through use of words. Even unspoken words carry great weight. Use them!

Say Aloud: **I Will Use My Words! I Will SPEAK LIFE!**

June

" I Will Use My VOICE! "

We miss too many moments to share. We share too many quiet times when words would better express our desires and find us more closely aligned with the lives we dream of. We let too many moments pass where prioritization of silence causes us to miss priceless opportunities.

Don't let your thoughts be limited only to your mind. Empty yourself of unspoken dreams, visions and feelings by speaking them audibly into the environment. Express yourself to remove the voids from your life.

Affirmation Journal
- ★ Which thoughts of mine need to be expressed?
- ★ What have I gone too long without expressing?
- ★ How can I best express that which has gone unsaid?
- ★ What is the value of using my words and my voice to express myself?
- ★ What method of self-expression works best for me?
- ★ In the future, how will I better commit to self-expression?
- ★ How has my affirmation journal helped me this year?

Words mean more than what is set down on paper.
It takes the human voice
to infuse them with shades of deeper meaning.

MAYA ANGELOU

June

I Will Use My RESOURCES!

We ask for so many things in life. We require so many things from others, yet we don't position ourselves to best *receive* what we pray for. Life is less about the *asking* and more about the *receiving*.

Learn to receive well! Put yourself in the best place to receive all that you yearn for—this is cause for *drastic* mental alteration. All of the pride, self-sufficiency and independence that you have built up to this point will have to be *let go* in order for you to embrace ALL that is being gifted to you. **Let it go!**

Release the NEED you have to do EVERYTHING by yourself! You'll get absolutely NOWHERE like that! Any progress that you *do* happen upon will be short-lived as you QUICKLY realize that you simply cannot sustain yourself *by* yourself, so get over it! Be HAPPY to let others help you! Be happy to move forward with ample support systems at your beck and call! Move forward with tenacity in grace knowing you don't have to *grow* this road alone—you NEVER had to!

Say Aloud: **I Will Use My Resources! I Will Receive Well!**

Affirmation Journal
- ★ *Who, What* and *Where* are my resources?
- ★ How am I using my resources?
- ★ How can I better use my resources?

June

" I Am MASTER of My DESTINY! "

Too many people *want* things, but they don't want to *do* things. They aspire to take over the world, yet they have no gumption to get up and DO something about it. They dream with no plan. These people don't realize they have the power to create and obtain EVERYTHING they desire in the world! They don't realize that dreams require ACTION to see them through.

Magnificent levels of power rest right in your own hands! What are YOU doing with the power you possess? Are you taking CONTROL of your life, dreams and vision using YOUR power to do what you can?! Take the INITIATIVE and DO something! Don't sit and wait on things to happen—MAKE things happen! You are master of your destiny! Behave like a master would and take control! Take the steps needed to pursue your dreams TODAY using ALL that is within you and everything that is around you!

Life is too short to leave your destiny in the hands of another. Take control! Find a coach and start NOW!

Say Aloud: **I Am Master of My Destiny! I Am in Control!**

*If you conquer yourself,
then you conquer the world*

PAULO COELHO

June 11

> **The More I Do,
> the More EMPOWERED I Feel
> to KEEP GOING!**

Think back on all you've accomplished in life. Take the time to compose your listing of Accolades and Accomplishments. You will LOVE this list during times when you get discouraged or when you need that extra PUSH anytime you think to quit. You need to be reminded of all that you *have* done and all that you *can* do! These little trinkets of success will be enough to keep you reminded that there is NOTHING too hard for you to do!

Today's To-Do's...
★ Update your list of Accolades and Accomplishments.

Affirmation Journal
★ How do I feel about the things I have accomplished?
★ What are my future plans?
★ How will my list of Accolades and Accomplishments help me with my future plans?

KUDOS to the many amazing victories that you've had! Keep up the great work! Take actions that keep you on a path toward greatness and continue empowering yourself to *be* and to *do* better in life!

Say Aloud: The More I DO, the More Empowered I FEEL!!!

June

> # I AM!!!

By this point in the book, you've arrived at a place where you acknowledge, accept and agree with the statement:

I AM!!!

You ARE!

Today's To-Do's...
- ★ **Create a detailed definition of YOU!** *(500 words PLUS!)*
- ★ **Preface your** Defining Statements **with *I AM!***
- ★ **Update your list as often as needed noting growth!**

You are WHOEVER you *desire* to be! You have MASTERED this understanding by now. You have arrived at a point where you are FINALLY pursuing your dreams! You have created your definition of YOU, so what is it? Who do YOU say you are? Are you being *that* NOW?

Say Aloud: **I Am Dancing, Singing, Smiling and Living! I Am Dreaming, Hoping, Planning and PRAYING! I Am Giving, Receiving, Laughing and Learning! I Am Loving! I Am SUCCEEDING! I Am!**

I always wanted to be somebody,
but now I realize I should have been more specific.

LILY TOMLIN

June 13

> ## I Am a CREATOR!

I Am A Creator!

The power of creation lies within our hands. Creation lies within our thoughts and is birthed through our voices! The exact lives that we desire rest in the power of our fingertips, our minds and our affirmations.

What are you creating with the voice you've been given, with the thoughts that you share and with the affirmations that you declare? Create goodness! Create GREATNESS! Be ALL that you desire to be using your power to create the that life you deserve!

Develop your thoughts into those that are limitless and declare with your voice EXACTLY what you *will* have! Do all within your human ability to claim what you desire and watch life meet you with plentious blessings matched to your efforts.

Affirmation Journal
- ★ What am I creating within my thoughts?
- ★ What am I creating through my actions?
- ★ What type of life do I desire to have?
- ★ How am I going about creating exactly that?

Say Aloud: I Am a Creator! I Will Create a Life That I LOVE!

June

"

I Will DEFINE My Life's DESIRES!

"

Define your life's desires by putting into plain sight the things that you long for; Align yourself mentally, physically, emotionally and spiritually with the desires of your heart; Take actions in tune with the picture of life that you've created; Alter your thought process so that it fits your goals; Find a peaceful center that will sustain all external battles by starting from within; Become more in tune with your spirit and the power of God that resides within you. Through these practices, your planned lifestyle design comes within reach.

Knowing that you have the ability to create the exact life that you want, do EVERYTHING within your power to create the BEST life. Define a life that you DESERVE—a life that is worthy of YOU!

Affirmation Journal
- ★ What do I want out of life?
- ★ What am I doing to get it?
- ★ What mental changes have I made to get what I desire?
- ★ What physical changes have I made to get what I desire?
- ★ What emotional changes have I made to get what I desire?
- ★ What spiritual changes have I made to get what I desire?

Say Aloud: I Will Define My Life's Desires! I Deserve the Best!

June 14

" I Will Use My TALENTS! "

Use EVERYTHING you've got!

Take FULL advantage of every single last one of the talents that you've been graced with. Buried talents are of NO use to anyone, so don't complain, don't be disobedient and don't be lazy about utilization of what you've been personally given. Without use, your talents are GUARANTEED to leave you! Use what you have while you have it! Don't allow distractions to bury your talents! *NOTE: Society, media, NEWS, fears, worries, concerns, lack, ignorance and slothfulness ALL limit your focus!*

Don't discount your talents! It is by no mistake that you've been endowed with the unique tools you have at your disposal—USE THEM! By putting your talents to use, you will become as POWERFUL—literally, intellectually and spiritually—as you want!

WHAT ARE YOU WAITING FOR?

Say Aloud: **I Will Use My Talents! I Will Not Bury Them!**

When I stand before God at the end of my life, I would hope that I would not have a single bit of talent left, and could say, 'I used everything you gave me.'

ERMA BOMBECK

June

> ## I Will Hold My Head High!

Ever stop and think, **"What in the WORLD is going on?!!!"** If so, that is a GREAT place to find yourself in! It's a place where you are *wholly* tired, frustrated and fed-up with whatever IT is. You are therefore in a good place to proceed in a NEW way!

No matter the battles you've overcome or the heartfelt lessons you've learned, accept the struggle for ALL that it was and carry on with your head held HIGH! Be PROUD of ALL you've accomplished and ALL that you've grown through to arrive safely at your currently PROGRESSIVE state of mind! You've grown through a great deal—WE ALL HAVE!

Don't be ashamed of your story! For all that it's worth, your story—however trying it might've been—was *exactly* the perfect combination of events required to grow you to the essential point of maturation where you now find yourself. Be grateful! Live in HIGH ANTICIPATION of *new* lessons that you will gain on your path toward GREATNESS!

You can't change the past, so accept it! Be proud of it! Be proud of now! Be proud of YOU! Hold your head HIGH!

*Not being able to govern events,
I govern myself*

MICHEL DE MONTAIGNE

June

"
I Am BEING!
"

Choose what to *Be*.

Choose EXACTLY what to be! *Be* GREAT! *Be* LOVING! *Be* POSITIVE! *Be* RESPECTED! Whatever you choose to *Be*, *Be* sure that YOU are to *Be* APPRECIATED! When you learn to *Be* loving, respectful and appreciative of yourself, it becomes increasingly easy to *Be* loving, respectful, appreciative AND FORGIVING of others. Stop letting bitterness, ignorance and selfishness cause you to *Be* disrespectful to others. People don't deserve that from you!

Say Aloud: **I Am *Be*ing!**

Dear friends, when you tire of complaining, being sad, lonely, heart broken, bitter, petty, needy, depressed, difficult, etc., just STOP! Most things in life are actually that simple! Most things in life are as simple as *Be*ing, so when you choose to *Be* anything, choose to *Be* GREAT!

Say Aloud: **I Am *Be*ing!**

I Am *Be*ing GREAT! I Am *Be*ing Loving! I Am *Be*ing Respectful! I Am *Be*ing Appreciative! I Am *Be*ing Forgiving! I Am *Be*ing Selfless! I Am *Be*ing HAPPY! I Am *Be*ing FREE!

I Am *Be*ing ME!

I Am *Be*ing AWESOME Sauce! I Lead Others to *Be* the Same!

June

" I REFUSE to Be Ordinary! "

Refuse to be ordinary! Take a stand RIGHT NOW to be the BEST that you can be! Don't settle for mediocrity or average gains. In ALL that you do, strive for GREATNESS—it's what you're destined for! Greatness is what you WILL achieve if you put forth the required effort, time and PASSION, so...

REFUSE TO BE ORDINARY!

Be encouraged despite your falls and be challenged through your toughest times. Your life isn't meant to be typical. For all that you'll achieve, you WILL endure hard times. Your atypical future presents you with many opportunities to build your atypical TENACITY. Strive to *be* and to *do* the BEST in EVERY project that you take on.

Say Aloud: **I Refuse to be Ordinary! I Will *Be* and *Do* My Best!**

Let others lead small lives, but not you..
Let others argue over small things, but not you..
Let others cry over small hurts, but not you..
Let others leave their future in someone else's hands,
but not you.

JIM ROHN

June

> ## I Will CHANGE for the BEST!

When it comes to change, we aren't always excited about adjusting the *current* state of life in order to find ourselves in a better position for the future. Change often comes with much angst and anxiety because we're often at the mercy of our immediate environment *or* we're being forced to change in ways that go against the person we currently know ourselves to be. Whatever the cause or scenario, accept change as a positive. Change leads to progress. Change is for the BEST!

If ever you're stuck in life, look for opportunities to change YOURSELF! When you find yourself at odds with your environment, look for opportunities to change YOURSELF! The battles you face in life are NEVER about another person—they are ALWAYS about YOU! The challenges you face in life involve SELF and GOD—you are *always* tasked with making adjustments that lead to the greater good of YOU! You are tasked with decisions that lead you toward the life you desire. Always be HAPPY about changing for the BEST!

Change takes patience, respect and humility, so be gentle with yourself and with those around you as you sort through alterations. Respect the transformation that is occurring. Prepare yourself for changes that will position you for a bright future and a new LIFE!

June

"

I Will Be ACCOUNTABLE!

"

You *are* what you attract! You must constantly remind yourself of this. Many times, you may find yourself disgusted by the challenges you face, by the environmental settings you find yourself in or by the nature of your personal and professional interactions. Take a step back and analyze these situations. *You* are the common denominator within them all! Figure out where the problem lies and solve it! This is the time for you to be wholly honest with yourself. It requires alone time, vulnerability and CHANGE!

While you can't wear your identity on your forehead, you *can* expect your life to resemble your mind. A fruitful mind equals a fruitful life! A chaotic mind produces a chaotic life. Be accountable for *who* you are and *how* you present yourself. Your outer life is the product of your inner thoughts.

You are only as good as what you attract. If you want change, YOU must change!

Change Your Posture! Change Your LIFE!

The next time you're tempted to make an excuse... DON'T! Accountability is tough, so start within. If you won't commit to yourself, what WILL you commit to??? No Excuses! If you have an excuse, don't utter it. Start there.

D NICOLE

June

"

I Will CHANGE My LIFE!

"

Success isn't measured by what you have now. It *is*, however, directly impacted by what you're *doing* now and even more importantly, success is measured by what you're *thinking* now. Instead of being discouraged by where you currently are in life, use that same energy to propel yourself into a better future! There is no need to be continuously disturbed by what you see within your immediate environment—simply change it! The lack that you feel may not be apparent to anyone else, and that isn't a bad thing. You have simply outgrown your current settings—so change them!

Affirmation Journal
- ★ **What situations in my life have caused me discomfort?**
- ★ **What actions am I taking to change these situations?**
- ★ **How will my actions change my life?**

Do not limit yourself! Don't remain within settings that have become negatively uncomfortable for you.

Today's actions drive tomorrow's future. Do what it takes to change for the BEST!

Say Aloud: **I Will Change My LIFE!!!**

June

"

I Will CHANGE My OUTCOME!

"

Frustration is the perfect catalyst for progressive change. Too much time in frustration will put you in a mindset to change and to change IMMEDIATELY!

If you're currently going in circles, you're too comfortable—you haven't yet become frustrated by your steps in the *same* direction which lead to the *same* known outcome—you're TOO comfortable with going NOWHERE!

When you're too stagnate for too long, you *must* be too comfortable! You haven't yet become frustrated by your lack of steps. You have NO direction!

When life comes at you from ALL sides, you FINALLY get to a place where stagnation, repetition or both, have caused a cataclysmic CRASH COURSE where you NEED direction!

In these moments, pinpoint the outcome you want and work diligently toward that desired end! Step into unknown realms to create new pathways for yourself. Surround yourself with people who inspire you and those who will motivate you to try new things. Get uncomfortable!

Say Aloud: I Will Change My Outcome!!!

Yesterday is not ours to recover,
but tomorrow is ours to win or lose.

LYNDON B. JOHNSON

June

"
I Will Make Myself a PRIORITY!
"

Do you ever question why YOU are the *center* to *everyone's* existence?! Do you ever wonder why YOU are the *glue* that holds *everything* together?! The answer is quite simple! It's because you ALLOW yourself to be!

You find yourself as the focus of everyone else's life because:
1. You have a need to please.
2. You have a need to be needed.
3. You're too unimportant in your own life to give yourself the time, attention and REST that you NEED.
4. OR You're **ALL OF THE ABOVE!**

If you can relate to *any* of the above statements—and *especially* if you can create extensive journal entries about them—THERE IS A PROBLEM and you need to solve it!

Making yourself a priority doesn't mean that you'll always be #1, but it *does* mean that you WILL be counted. Don't create a life for yourself where you don't matter because you *choose* not to matter. The person you should matter to the *most* is yourself, so start there!

Make yourself a priority NOW! In this very MOMENT, do something that will please YOU and make it a continual practice throughout your day and within your life. Learn to do what it takes to please YOU! Make yourself a PRIORITY!

Say Aloud: **I Will Make Myself a Priority! I Am Number One!**

June

" I Will CHANGE My OUTLOOK! "

When undergoing alterations in any present state of affairs, the changes can feel SO drastic that we are seemingly at the mercy of life, with no boat and no oars to row. Like a ship without a sail. Like a map without a destination. Like a trip with no bags, and EVERYTHING is ALL over the place. This, my friends, is a GREAT place to find ourselves in! How so? This is the MOST opportune time for us to CHANGE! Change what?

CHANGE YOURSELF!!!

Life often presents itself in a way that causes us to feel that there is nothing we can do personally to change the hell going on around us. What, then, shall we do?! We can alter the hell going on *within* us!!! Life appears exactly the way we imagine it to be. If we imagine goodness, we see goodness. If we imagine chaos, we see chaos. Imagine a clear outlook and a blissful life! Change yourself from within!

Say Aloud: **I Will Change My Outlook! I Will Change My Life!**

When you wake up every day, you have two choices.
You can either be positive or negative;
an optimist or a pessimist.
I choose to be an optimist. It's all a matter of perspective.

HARVEY MACKAY

June

" I Will CHANGE My POSTURE! "

Say Aloud: **I Will Change My Posture!**

Changing posture means doing what it takes to acquire what you want in life *especially* when you can't readily see it! Changing posture means to change your mind, your outlook and your approach in order to alter your outcome.

Change Your Posture! Change Your LIFE!

Imagine test driving a car right before purchase. You want the car, so you do what it takes to get it—a test drive! Before pulling off, you adjust your mirrors. Consider this the equivalent of taking **actions** to change thoughts. You adjust your seat, which changes your **posture**—you need to be able to see where you currently *are* even if you don't yet know where you're *going*. While traveling along the journey, you drive carefully—changed **behavior**. You put on a GREAT safe-driver show for the salesperson! You stop, look *and* listen! You start to feel yourself a little because you *are* behind the wheel of a brand new car!!!

The same happens when you change your posture in life. You feel like a brand new car!!! haha ☺ When changing your posture in life, you incorporate actions and behaviors that lead to a desired outcome.

Say Aloud: **I Will Change My Posture! I Will Change My Life!**

June

" I Will CHANGE for ME!!! "

Problems are life's way of showing us that we need to change things up a bit! Problems often show us that our mindsets aren't yet BIG enough for the reality we seek, so we require CHANGE! We then get a crash course with life—and I *do* mean **CRASH** course—that causes us to step back and ask:

What in THE WORLD is going on?!!!

Substantive growth and maturation causes us to be more outwardly observant and inwardly introspective. We become more accountable and less accusing. Instead of blaming others, we take an actionable approach and ask:

What in MY MIND is going on?!!!

Figure THAT out—and please, take considerable time to figure it out—*then*, do what it takes to change for *you*! If nothing else motivates you to make proper adjustment, *be* the motivation you need to change. Self-motivation will take you far in life. When you're at your wits' end, muster the courage to be strong for yourself. *Get out of your own way!*

> *If you could kick the person in the pants*
> *responsible for most of your trouble,*
> *you wouldn't sit for a month.*
>
> THEODORE ROOSEVELT

June

" I Will Make MYSELF Proud! "

Are your goals BIG enough that you will deny YOURSELF?!

Whenever you consider quitting, be reminded that your goals are BIGGER than emotional discomfort or temporal defeat! Your goals are BIGGER than YOU!!! If that means facing yourself each time YOU don't cut the mustard, be prepared to do what is possible NOW and watch God *move* in your FUTURE!

Take one step in the direction of your dreams TODAY! Make yourself proud. Get out of your own way! Don't let thoughts of quitting be so pervasive that you actually give in. Combat fear with positive self-talk!

Say Aloud: **I Will Make Myself Proud! I Will Deny Myself!**

Today's To-Do's...
- ★ **List out 5 things that cause you to consider quitting.**
- ★ **For each of these, list methods of combating them.**
- ★ **Create deadlines for overcoming each obstacle.**
- ★ **Make Yourself Proud!**

June

> ## I Will Find a Way!
> ## I Will Not Find Excuses!

YOU have charge over EVERY single day that you're alive! EVERY single one of them! Stop letting yourself be at the mercy of life, and let LIFE be at the mercy of YOU! Exercise POWER even when you're not in control! Find a way to get things done!

What are your goals? List them out. Create deadlines. Find support. Use resources and GET THINGS DONE!

The more excuses you use, the more excuses you will find.

Excuses are NOTHING, so stop using them! Completely remove excuses from your communication! Don't even accept them from others! By limiting your acceptance of excuses, you automatically propel yourself and others into greater performance. Knowledge that you can't *use* excuses comes also with the knowledge that you no longer *need* them—you no longer respect them, listen to them or acknowledge them. Perform better for yourself, and make others perform better for you. Find a way. Don't find excuses!

Say Aloud: **I Will Find a Way! I Will Not Find Excuses!**

If you really want to do something, you'll find a way.
If you don't, you'll find an excuse.

JIM ROHN

June 29

> ## I Will Attain What is MINE!

Within you resides the ability obtain EVERYTHING that you desire! It is within YOUR very own power to have EVERYTHING you can dream of! All you have to do is put in effort that matches the weight of your dreams! Attainment is your choice, so what do you choose?! What is your goal in life? What are you doing NOW to attain it?

Don't EVER be fearful of others *taking* your ideas or *stealing* what is yours. You MUST trust and BELIEVE with ALL of your heart that—outside of you—there isn't a SINGLE person in this world who can attain what is YOURS to have! Rest assured in the fact that NO ONE can do what is YOURS to do, so DO IT!

Quit being fearful of every little thing! Quit being discouraged by every little hurdle that comes. You are better than that! You are STRONGER than that!

What is meant for YOU is for YOU!

Be Encouraged!

Say Aloud: I Will Attain What is Mine!

June

" I Will Take Steps TODAY to Change My Life FOREVER! "

Change in life demands ACTION! You have to take planned steps to get to the next level. Put considerable thought into the specific tasks that should be completed so you can change your life TODAY! Don't wait around for perfection or for adequate timing. Preparedness is a facet of the imagination in most cases. Prepped or not—ready or not—do exactly what is needed to position yourself for the BEST life you can have.

Always be willing to give up your current behaviors for those that earn you the greatest gain in life. Even when you can't see the outcome, trust that your shift toward success will ALWAYS find you winning!

Change Your Posture! Change Your LIFE!

Commit yourself to the time, dedication and effort required to be your BEST! As slowly as your progression may sometimes appear, never lose your ability to take the next step toward a changed life.

Say Aloud: **I Will Take Steps Today to Change My Life Forever!**

I have learned that I really do have discipline, self-control, and patience. But they were given to me as a seed, and it's up to me to choose to develop them.

JOYCE MEYER

Goodness

July

" I Will Work on GOODNESS!

"

Good people *feel* good! Good people are proud of who they are based on the GREAT qualities they possess. They are strong and upstanding in character, not shaken or easily moved by external forces. The good within GREAT people is evident in how they approach life. The internal goodness of great people resonates with others simply by how they carry themselves at all times.

Goodness Affirmation *(Repeat this aloud)*
Goodness is the state of being good, morally excellent and virtuous. My good character is recognized through my conduct. Through goodness, I am strong in kindness and I am pleased by being good.

During July, we remind ourselves to be good!

Say Aloud: **I Will Work on Goodness! I LOVE Being Good!**

Life is always pleasing to good people because they make the BEST out of *any* situation. Their internal qualities positively reaffirm their optimism during trying times, so good people seem to effortlessly maneuver through trial after trial—never once altering their GREAT character. Goodness is shown through strength, resilience and stability of mind, body and soul. The aim of great people is to continue in goodness throughout the course of a lifetime.

July

"

I Am a GREAT Person!

"

Do you *know* who you are? Do you *trust* who you are? Do you *love* who you are?

Are you a GREAT person?

We are only as powerful as our beliefs allow us to be! We are only as sure as our thoughts guide us to be! We are only as successful as our dreams drive us to be!

If you're GREAT, let the WORLD know through your actions, your deeds and your successes! Don't be afraid to be exactly who you are! Be EXACTLY who you were created to be! Be unapologetically YOU—the *great* you, of course!

Affirmation Journal
- ★ **Do I know who I am? Who am I?**
- ★ **Do I trust who I am? Do I love who I am?**
- ★ **What is so GREAT about me?**

SO! *Are* you a GREAT person? If you are, **SAY SO!** Let your greatness be exampled in how well you treat the world around you! Be great yourself and be great to others!

Too often we underestimate the power of a touch, a smile, a kind word, a listening ear, an honest compliment, or the smallest act of caring, all of which have the potential to turn a life around.

LEO BUSCAGLIA

July

"I Will Walk with CONFIDENCE!"

Be proud of who you are. Let your confidence speak for itself! Don't feel the need to prove yourself to *anyone* about *anything* (unless it's job or school related)! ☺

All too often, people walk around flamboyantly *stating* that they're to be admired when *true* worthiness is exhibited by inaudible behaviors, actions and accomplishments. *Show* more than you tell. In your silence, let your confidence speak for itself. You require the approval of no one, so be a quiet representation of appealing essence. Create a silent standard of brilliance that causes others to proudly communicate their admiration of your goodness. Be the framework that shapes the character of others who will model themselves after you, and then go on to break the mold! Confidently *be* what others aspire to.

If you can be *any* one thing in this world, be confident. Confidence is intimidating to weaker vessels and valuable to worthy counterparts. Life will immediately separate you from those unworthy of your presence and place you in the graces of noble acquaintances. Undeserving characters will rarely approach you when they see your pride. They know they can't compete with you—the individual who knows the value of self-worth. Wallow in your confidence. Make the world honor you and step in line.

Say Aloud: I Will Walk with Confidence! I Am Proud of ME!

July

" I Will Stand STRONG! "

Strength is found in weakness. Strength is found when we persist during the times when we have nothing left to give. It's found in our determination amidst insurmountable pain, and it is found during those times when quitting is not an option. Strength presents itself during the times when we are most weak. It is the untapped energy that we find buried deep within our darkest moments where we stand—not just because we *want* to, but we stand most steadfast because we *have* to. Life often gives us no other choice or we would've already given up the fight! Strength is our awakening, our renewal, our fortified resolve.

Affirmation Journal
- ★ What situations within my life require steadfast strength?
- ★ What are my thoughts regarding these situations?
- ★ What are my goal in these situations?
- ★ How can I encourage myself in these situations if I become weak?

Say Aloud: I Will Stand Strong! I Boast Fortified Resolve!

Be strong.
Live honorably and with dignity.
When you don't think you can, hold on.

JAMES FREY

July

> ## I Will Be TRUE to My WORD!

Create structure within your life! Create a balance that you can *challenge* yourself to adhere to. If it doesn't challenge you, it's too comfortable a structure, CHANGE IT!

Change Your Posture! Change Your LIFE!

The structure that you create for your life should be adhered to by ALL parties involved! Don't compromise on your self-prescribed personal standards and don't allow others to. Be true to your word and be true YOURSELF!

Today's To-Do's...
- ★ **Make a schedule and keep it!**
- ★ **Commit *yourself* to YOUR schedule.**
- ★ **Require others to do the same.**

People won't respect your time if you don't. When setting appointments, set time blocks for your days and honor them! Don't allow your FULL day to be full of OTHERS! Structure increases efficiency and encourages discipline. Set this professional expectation for yourself, your clients, your peers, family and friends! Focus on PLANNING and PUNCTUALITY to further your personal and professional progress. Be true to your word!

Say Aloud: **I Will Be True to My Word! I Will Be Structured!**

July

" I Will Be HONEST! "

What is honesty to you? What is the value of honesty? How does your personal brand of honesty help you maneuver through life? How does the honesty of others help you? As you read on, ponder these questions.

Honesty goes far beyond the surface of telling the truth. Honesty is about being bold, conscious and vocal about your awareness. The value in honesty resides in the communication of your truths. An honest person endeavors to correct wrongs by being introspective and resolute about clearly communicating in truth.

Affirmation Journal
- ★ What does it mean to be honest?
- ★ What is the value of honesty?
- ★ How does my personal honesty help me maneuver through life?
- ★ How does the honesty of others help me?

Say Aloud: **I Will Be Honest! I Will Communicate in Truth!**

Honesty is more than not lying.
It is truth telling, truth speaking, truth living,
and truth loving.

JAMES E. FAUST

July

"
I Will Value the TRUTH!
"

Truth is found in awareness. It is found in openness, honesty, vulnerability and introspection.

Say: **I Will Be Open, Honest, Vulnerable and Introspective.**

You must be ever-ready to risk your own credibility by being honest with yourself *first* and then all others. In this manner, you increase your personal integrity and further build your sound character.

Be truthful at all times. Accept truth from others without discouraging their expressions of openness. Don't use truth for negativity. Further positive interaction by being truthful and you will further enlighten the character of others.

Affirmation Journal
- ★ How do I already show that I value the truth?
- ★ How can I demonstrate my increased value for truth?
- ★ How can I encourage others to do the same?
- ★ How can I be better at exemplifying value in truth?

Say Aloud: **I Will Value the Truth! I Am Open and Honest!**

July

"

I Will Value the TRUTH About ME!

"

Each of us is born with qualities specific only to us. We each boast a combination of innate tendencies that no other human being on this planet shares with us. The fullness of our character is as unique as a snowflake—we cannot be duplicated.

As special as we are, we sometimes faultily decide to hide our wholeness for the sake of others or even for ourselves. We occasionally think to leave portions of our identity under the radar—undetectable—as if *hidden* is the best way to live.

There is no truth in hiding who you are. There is no pride in being ashamed of your uniqueness. Be exactly who you are in *all* of your wholeness and be OVERJOYED with the fact that you just cannot be duplicated! Appreciate your individuality. Accept your truths—VALUE them! Shine your light in ALL of its splendor. Don't give the world an incomplete view of yourself. The world deserves to know who you are, YOU deserve to know who you are! If you can't be honest about YOU, you can't be honest about a thing!

Say Aloud: **I Will Value the Truth About Me! I Value Myself!**

If you do not tell the truth about yourself
you cannot tell it about other people.

VIRGINIA WOOLF

July

"

I Am EXCELLENT!

"

What would you do if you *could*? What masterful goal would you check off your lofty list if you could? Do you have a list? Have you drafted up your List of Goals and Dreams? If not, start it NOW!

To-Do's...
- ★ **Create your** List of Goals and Dreams.
- ★ **Update your list as often as needed noting changes!**

Affirmation Journal
- ★ **What would I do if I could?**
- ★ **What *masterful* goal would I check off my list if I could?**

For EVERYTHING humanly possible that was included on your list, TRUST that you have the POWER to achieve them! Even some of those non-humanly possible things can be considered! ☺ Put forth the EXCELLENCE required to meet your goals and employ GREAT faith to help you see your dreams come true! Validate EVERY sacrifice that you have made in the past worthwhile by busting your BUTT to execute! Don't let your suffering have been in vain!

PURSUE with PASSION matched by EXCELLENCE!

Say Aloud: **I Am Excellent! I Match My Pursuit with Passion!**

July

> ## I Am FULL of AWARENESS!

Life sometimes finds us in situations where our emotional reactions to an experience or toward particular people catches us wholly unaware. In these situations, we either don't care *enough* OR we care all *too much*. Whatever the response, the problem is that we're not always conscious that our feelings have been compromised without our acknowledgment of the change.

Awareness requires us to be present in *every* moment as much as we possibly can. Surprises prevent us from adequately responding to life in an effective manner! Feelings never come as a surprise for those who are in touch with themselves. We enjoy experiences thoroughly and gain much more from them by being *proactive* about our participation in anything involving feeling. Awareness of feelings keeps us accountable to ourselves and also to others.

Don't miss *any* opportunities to be aware!

Say Aloud: **I Am Full of Awareness!**

A life without regret can be attained by full awareness of one's actions in their present moment.

MICHELLE CRUZ-ROSADO

July 11

> ## I Am FULL of POTENTIAL!

Say Aloud:

My full potential is found in my awareness of it. I have the power to be, to create, to do or not to do *anything* that I desire. I have FULL control of my mind, my soul and my being. I will direct this power toward the passionate pursuit of purpose! I will see my goals reached! I will see my dreams fulfilled! I am writing my vision. I will make it plain.

This is MY life! I have FULL control of it! I will do with it what I desire to. I will live life to the fullest in wholeness, prosperity and understanding. I will create the BEST life for myself and my family. I will be the BEST for myself and for those around me. I declare that I will have great things. I will have great riches! I will have great success, great value and great legacies based on my fulfillment of my divinely guided purpose.

This world is mine! The world is at my beck and call.

I have command over my past! I have closure within my past, and I am FULLY vested in the present. I am emotionally aware. I am intuitive. I am socially present. I am community involved. As I make myself better, I challenge others to the same. I am my BEST self at ALL times! NOTHING comes in the way of that.

I am not afraid of ME! I am POWERFUL beyond measure. I no longer speak in terms of my potential.

I already AM the person I desire to be!

July

"

I Am FULL of POWER!

"

Each day that you wake, life affords you with the LOVELY opportunity to live your dreams and also with the opportunity to help others live theirs! The closer you get to fulfilling your overall visions and goals in life, the more INVIGORATING they become! Use the magnificent power you possess during that time to amaze yourself even further! Capitalize on the exhilarating energy you find and work during inspired hours. If those times are outside of your normal sleeping patterns, SO WHAT?! Tap into the energy when it's PULSATING within your veins or you'll miss the most opportune moments to MAXIMIZE your personal greatness!

Allow your passion to EXCITE you! Ignite your life using the energy you feel during passionate times. Allow your vision, your present and your future to fascinate you as you position yourself to take advantage of every talent made available.

Change Your Posture! Change Your LIFE!

Say Aloud: **I Am Full of Power! I Have Power Over Myself!**

He who controls others may be powerful,
but he who has mastered himself is mightier still.

Lao Tzu

July

" I Am PROUD! "

Be Proud of *Who You Are*!

Recall the things that make you proud and write them within your Listing of Accolades and Accomplishments. Remind yourself of all you've achieved in life and don't be afraid to share these successes as you journey. Find the things that make you proud. Explore them! Relive them! Learn them and LOVE them! Therein lies your identity! Be PROUD of who you have *become*!

If life offered nothing more than what you already have, be sure that all you've accomplished up until now has been worth the journey. Be PROUD of what you've *done*!

SMILE! Your life is your own and no one else can live it like you! Share it as you must, but keep it as your treasure! You have created a standard of existence that will go unmatched. Be PROUD of what you have to *offer*!

Affirmation Journal
- ★ **What is it about my identity that makes me proud?**
- ★ **What have I accomplished that makes me proud?**
- ★ **What experiences of mine make me proud?**

Say Aloud: **I Am Proud!**

July

" I Am IMPORTANT! "

Make yourself of utmost importance in your life. Compare yourself only to *yourself*!!! If you aren't all that great, up the ante! Step it up a notch! Challenge yourself to *be* better, to *do* better and to *think* differently. To achieve what you never could, you must *be* what you have never been and *do* what you have never done. Start from within!

Affirmation Journal
★ **What is it about me that makes me feel important?**
★ **What makes me feel unimportant?**
★ **What can I do to "up the ante" of my importance?**

Think of the American Dream and assess what its really all about. The dream is to lead a life of importance! The dream is to lead a life of past value, present value and future value. Importance is the name of the game!

Do what you can while living to be as important as you want to be. Make a practice of *feeling* important daily.

You may not always have a comfortable life and you will not always be able to solve all of the world's problems at once but don't ever underestimate the importance you can have because history has shown us that courage can be contagious and hope can take on a life of its own.

MICHELLE OBAMA

July 15

> **I Am PLEASED!**

Don't spend your entire life complaining it all away! Find something to be satisfied with. Design a life that you can be HAPPY with! Be pleased with *some*thing! In a personal evaluation of your life, if you find something—*anything*—that displeases you, CHANGE IT! Don't let troubling things ruin your better posture. Don't be afraid to grab life by the jugular and LIVE! Create a pleasing life for yourself, and don't be afraid to live!

When adding pleasure to your life, start with your disposition. Change your outlook! Be more pleasing to yourself and you will be more pleasing to others. People will be more pleasing to you in return! Smile more! Your journey has been filled with enough pain, gloom, stress, heartache and sorrow—don't personally add more negativity to that list!

Don't sweat the small things. In all that you do, focus on the overall goal of increasing your personal happiness. Through this, you will be constantly pleased.

Affirmation Journal
- ★ **What about my life has always been pleasing to me?**
- ★ **What about my life is most pleasing to me now?**
- ★ **What pleasures can I add to my life for the future?**

Say Aloud: **I Am Pleased! I Focus on My Personal Happiness!**

July

" I Am LAUGHING! "

The best way to encounter life is to laugh your way through it! Laugh your way through the tough times, the unbearable moments and the tragic situations that you face. Laughter cures all that ails the soul. Whenever you find yourself amidst trouble and defeat, arms yourself with the shield of passionate laughter to relieve yourself of pain.

Infuse your life with MUCH jovial laughter and welcome the healing that you are sure to find in carefree merriment. With sincerity and time, you will find the impact of laughter to be enduring and well worth the concerted effort you put into creating joy as much as possible. Physically, spiritually and mentally, you will reap benefits of the wisdom found through laughing. Without avoiding healthy emotion, counteract pain and dread with goodness and laughter to minimize negative impact. You will certainly be glad that you did!

Say Aloud: **I Am Laughing! Goodness is Found in Laughter!**

*There's nothing like deep breaths after laughing that hard.
Nothing in the world like
a sore stomach for the right reasons.*

STEPHEN CHBOSKY

July

"

I Am POWERFUL!

"

Some of us hold onto our pain as if it has some sort of sentimental value.

Let it go!

Stop defining yourself based on pain. You are more powerful than that. You are MUCH more powerful than ALL of your hurts, hang-ups, headaches, mess ups and missteps. Stop living in the guilty shadows of your past. By the power vested within YOU, free yourself of the burdens in your past! Heal yourself so you can change your outlook on life.

Even though parts of your past were VERY trying, you are STILL alive! In the midst of trials, it's often hard to keep the faith and stay encouraged, but DO IT ANYWAY! The *bad* doesn't come to hurt you, it comes to HELP you. Empower yourself with this reminder as often as you need to!

Say: **I Am Powerful!**

Today's To-Do's...
- ★ **Choose happiness over pain.**
- ★ **Deal with pain QUICKLY so you can move on.**
- ★ **Don't embrace pain.**
- ★ **Embrace the lessons learned and move on.**

July

I Am BOLD!

Be willing to broach difficult situations with others. Be willing to broach matters that no one else dares to mention. Tough conversations involve both positive and negative progression. Make sure that the boldness you exemplify has the power to inspire positive progress for ALL!

In negative situations, putting bold effort in clearing up misunderstandings is the best way to move forward. Leaving on a positive note is the BEST way to maintain open communication if feasible agreements can't be reached at the time. Be bold in a manner that warrants respect. Mutual respect goes a long way toward continued profits AND prospects! Deal with others frankly and make no quibbles about feelings if they interfere with what is RIGHT!

Boldness sets you FREE! Boldness will place you immediately within the realms of greatness. Since you're not timid about your steps, you won't be fearful of yourself and you won't be afraid of others!

Say Aloud: **I Am Bold! I Boldly Interact Respectfully!**

Freedom lies in being bold.

ROBERT FROST

July

" I Am STRONG! "

Some of us, especially powerful people, have a problem being vulnerable. We have a problem admitting that there are sensitive issues that we need to deal with. In an effort to hide brokenness within and around us, we put entirely too much energy in covering those things up through work. Where is the strength in that? That's not strength! That's insanity!

Strength is found in weakness. Strength is found in the very traits where you think it's not. Strength isn't found in being so tough that you can't be weak. It isn't found in being so big that you can't be little. Strength isn't found in being so successful that you can't be humble.

Be strong enough to know when you need help. Be bold enough to *ask* for it! Be courageous enough to accept help and be powerful enough to *give* it! THAT is power. That is strength!

It takes a strong person to be weak. Weakness is a vulnerability and vulnerability is where our greatest truths reside. Find your weaknesses and fix them. There you will find your strength.

Say Aloud: **I Am Strong! I Find Strength Even in Weakness!**

July

"

I Am COURAGEOUS!

"

If your goals don't scare you, you're not even tapping the surface of your potential—you're just *barely* LIVING! Your goals should STRETCH you. They should CHALLENGE you! Your goals should get you OUTSIDE of your comfort zone and find you in a place where you're *constantly* abuzz with inspiration and fresh ideas!

Be courageous! Challenge yourself to get into a new zone. Take your life to optimal levels by creating challenging dreams that test your courage. Don't be complacent or mediocre with your goals. Mediocre goals inspire mediocre thoughts. Go beyond thinking big—think HUGE! Train you mind to construct GREAT thoughts on a GRAND scale and watch your life flourish! Basic thoughts result in a basic life. Courageous thoughts turn into an adventurous lifestyle that will always persevere through the burden of fear. Think, "COURAGE," and conquer ALL fear and doubt!

Say Aloud: **I Am Courageous! I Conquer Fear and Doubt!**

I learned that courage was not the absence of fear, but the triumph over it. The brave man is not he who does not feel afraid, but he who conquers that fear.

NELSON MANDELA

July 21

" I Am Proud of My SKILLS! "

Appreciate the abilities, capacities and talents that life saw fit to give YOU! Using what you have, help others fulfill their dreams, their personal endeavors and their professional goals. Before doing *any* of that, help *yourself*!

Be PROUD of your skills!!! You've got TALENT! USE IT!!! It's what you're here for! Be grateful that life saw fit to endow you with such unique, powerful and RELEVANT skills! Continually use your gifts to help and support yourself and others in order to show how grateful you are!

Develop your skills further by always seeking constructive feedback from people you trust and respect. Sometimes, you'll have to go outside of your immediate circle for this feedback, and that's absolutely fine! In fact, it's recommended! The people around you tend to be "nice" about the feedback they provide. Seek input that will solidify the positive feedback that you already expect. Seek input that challenges you to steadily IMPROVE! Within your circle of friends, ask very pointed, direct questions that keeps the input guided in a way that's most effective for your specific needs. Don't be offended by any feedback that you receive. To be better, use what you can and rid yourself of the rest.

Say Aloud: I Am Proud of My Skills! I Am Proud to Be Better!

July

"

I Am SMART!

"

To be smart is to be effective, sharp and on top of things. To be smart is to use what you have in a way that works for you never allowing weakness in yourself or others to overcome your intelligent resolve. Smartness involves mental aptness and aptitude slated so that you shine within any area. Smartness is less related to literal mental intelligence and more related to how you utilize the level of intelligence that you possess.

What level of smartness do you possess?
What are you doing with it?

Affirmation Journal
- ★ Within my life, where can I readily see my smarts?
- ★ How do I apply smartness within my interactions?
- ★ How does being smart position me for greatness?

Say Aloud: I Am Smart! I Do My Best with What I've Got!

Smart people always choose comfort over luxury.

CELSO CUKIERKORN

July 23

I Am COMPETENT!

Put your best foot forward in all that you do! No matter what the competition *looks* like, understand that YOU are the only person who is competing against you on a daily basis. Trust your own competence knowing that YOU can get the job done! Your steps will be different from everyone else's—that's to be expected since your capacities are different from theirs. You have a different walk from theirs and different shoes to fill.

As you trek, allow for falling short at times while never ceasing to progress along the journey—stay the course. We ALL fall short at times. Throughout it all, affirm yourself by constantly building on the positives that already exist within you. Be boldly introspective enough to address the negatives and be honest enough to effectively change all that needs adjustment.

Say Aloud: **I Am Competent! I Am My Own Competition!**

Affirmation Journal
- ★ How can I better accept and trust my own competence?
- ★ How can I accept that I am my only competition?
- ★ How does that awareness alter my outlook?
- ★ How does that awareness propel me toward success?

July

" I Am CREATIVE! "

Why do people spend so much time attempting to change others? People spend ENTIRELY too much time attempting to *tell* others how to live their lives. We want to create duplicates of ourselves without first being our best selves!

The BEST brand of creation that you can EVER aspire to is creation of YOURSELF! Build your own MASTERPIECE! Either DIY or DUY: Do YOU *yourself*!

Be CREATIVE! CREATE the YOU that you WANT to be! Be ALL that you've ever dreamed, imagined, thought or saw at a board meeting or on a TV commercial. Just BE! CREATE! Don't worry about what others think of you or how you can mold, shape, define or make *them*! Mold, shape, define and make *you* instead! Create, create,, CREATE!!!

Say Aloud: **I Am Creative! I Will Define the Best ME!!!**

Affirmation Journal
- ★ **Why is it important that I define myself and create my own identity?**
- ★ **Why is creativity essential overall?**
- ★ **How does this awareness impact my future?**

The most creative act you will ever undertake is the act of creating yourself.

DEEPAK CHOPRA

July 25

" I Am PROUD of My INDEPENDENCE! "

When life has placed you in the season to passionately pursue your purpose, be prayerful and vigilant about who you allow to accompany you on that journey. Your success is too sacred to have just any ole body on your team! Don't be under the faulty impression that someone *has* to accompany you on your journey. There isn't a single person *required* on your pathway but you. Take advantage of that realization as often as needed! Allow others to help you as you navigate, but trust and know that even by yourself, you can *still* move mountains!!!

The most important support that you require is your own! All other support is a bonus, but you can't even appreciate *that* if you can't appreciate and support *yourself*!

Independence has negative connotations when used for evil and not good. Be proud of your ability to depend on yourself, but don't be so prideful that you can't benefit from others. Take lessons from others and readily apply them. Take help from others and readily reciprocate it. Take pride in your independence and you will grow far!

Affirmation Journal
- ★ **How has my pride in my independence harmed me?**
- ★ **How has my pride in my independence helped me?**
- ★ **How can I adequately balance prideful independence in a way that is most beneficial?**

July

I Am POWERFUL Beyond Measure!

Very rarely does life give us time to respond. It doesn't pause for complaining, pouting or even PLANNING in many cases. Life makes us STEP UP to the occasion... NOW! The sooner we adjust in a positive manner, the sooner we move on.

Life doesn't stop. Neither should we.

> *"March on. Do not tarry. To go forward is to move toward perfection. March on, and fear not the thorns, or the sharp stones on life's path."*
>
> —KAHLIL GIBRAN

Say Aloud: **I Am Powerful Beyond Measure!**

Affirmation Journal
- ★ **What does it mean to be powerful beyond measure?**
- ★ How can I test my personal power?
- ★ How can I tap into the potential of my power?

When your desires are strong enough,
you will appear to possess superhuman powers to achieve.

NAPOLEON HILL

July

"

I Am BEAUTIFUL!

"

In reference to goodness, beauty describes the quality traits that characterize an individual. You are beautiful based on the good virtues that you exhibit. Beauty in this case has absolutely nothing to do with literal aesthetics yet the same defining characteristics that make you intrinsically beautiful are the selfsame traits that make you ostensibly beautiful as well.

How beautiful are you?

Do you possess traits that make you good, both internally and externally? Do you possess traits that make you *feel* good? How proud are you of the goodness that you possess?

Affirmation Journal
- ★ **What beautiful traits do I possess?**
- ★ **What is beautiful about me in the eyes of others?**
- ★ **Why is it important to be a beautiful person?**
- ★ **How does such goodness impact my future?**

Shower the world with your beauty. Shower the world with your praise. In modesty, accept the power of your beauty and share your goodness with the world.

Through awareness of your own goodness, you create beauty within the world. LOVE the beauty that you possess, and be sure to love the beauty that you find in all others.

Say Aloud: **I Am Beautiful! I Am Goodness in Human Form!**

July

"

I Am AWESOME!

"

When you wake up each day—before you begin the day's tasks—be PROUD of what you are made of! Be proud of who YOU are!!! Don't let ANYONE or ANYTHING take away your pride in who YOU are as a person! YOU are AWESOME! NEVER forget that!

Accept who you are. Love yourself in wholeness and BOLDNESS! There isn't a single thing in this world worth losing your self-love for. For all negative situations that you encounter, use them to further love and love *on* yourself! Take every opportunity to show yourself love and require others to do the same.

Make your awesomeness non-negotiable! Live up to that standard. Only YOU truly know whether you are awesome or not in spirit, deed and truth. Don't just *think* you're awesome. BE awesome and awesome you will be!

Affirmation Journal
- ★ **What is AWESOME about me?**
- ★ **What can I do to ensure my long-term awesomeness?**

*Positive feelings come from being honest about yourself
and accepting your personality,
and physical characteristics, warts and all; and,
from belonging to a family that accepts you without question.*

WILLARD SCOTT

July

"

I Am GREAT!

"

You are GREAT!

Say Aloud: I Am GREAT!!!

YOU are your BEST thing! Be inspired by your own efforts, and be exactly what YOU need! If you need a friend, a love, or a teacher, start by teaching, loving and being friendly to yourself! The world can't want more for you than you want for yourself, and you can't gain ANYTHING from others without first understanding that YOU can have whatever it is that you desire. Anything is possible! Put yourself in the best position to receive by first understanding:

YOU ARE GREAT!

Let the greatness that resides within teach you how to better live, laugh and love! Learn how to ENJOY life! In raw form, appreciate ALL that you offer. Show the world your transparency and resilience! Live without regret, making no apologies for your pathway through life! Learn from all that you encounter, and have an encounter with all that you learn! ☺ Be your BEST self!

Say Aloud: I Am Great! I Am My BEST Thing!

July

" I WILL SET a GREAT Standard! "

Standards are the guiding models we use when individually engaging with the world. We acquire them based on upbringing, socioeconomic status, culture, educational environments and also based on personal goals. Standards are easily displayed within our reactions to adverse situations, and they can equally be acknowledged when comparing our past selves to our present and future selves.

As we grow and evolve, so should our standards. Each time our bar of accomplishments is raised, it should be met with a heightened level of relevant standards. Each time we face adversity, we can witness our newly productive responses which demonstrate our worthwhile growth. Over time, problems don't impact us like they once did. Developing standards should find us as models of grace and peace. If ever life presents us with hurricanes, high standards allow us to be calm in the midst of the storm—at the center of it all.

Say Aloud: **I Will Set a Great Standard!**

By constant self-discipline and self-control you can develop greatness of character.

GRENVILLE KLEISER

July 31

"

I Will SHINE!

"

Today is for YOU! Today is for loving YOU! Today is for accepting yourself, knowing yourself, understanding yourself—and if you don't yet do *any* of those things, start by learning to love yourself UNCONDITIONALLY!

This is how you shine! You shine from within! Your internal light of goodness empowers your shine to expand outward to others and throughout the world. Continue striving to be a better YOU constantly!

Be happy for your own successes and your failures, your past, your present and your future, your love, your life, your loss and your laughter! SHINE!

Be happy with yourself and be COMFORTABLE in your own skin! Shine by way of your maturity, your focus, your dreams and your passionate pursuit of purpose!

Love being YOU and take life no other way!

Always SHINE!

Say Aloud: **I Will Shine! I Will Take Life No Other Way!**

You can turn off the sun,
but I'm still ganna shine!

JASON MRAZ

Patience

August 1

> ## I Will WORK on PATIENCE!

Patience can sometimes be a daunting task, especially when the concept is new to us. Furthermore, patience is a skill often acquired only through laborious suffrage which means we aren't always in the best of moods when being pupils of this task. The best preparation for trials of patience is hard mental focus, personal awareness and gentleness. Although detachment is the less favorable option, we almost feel the need to emotionally detach ourselves from situations that test our patience so that we can safely maneuver within them. The same result can be had by simply learning to control passion while simultaneously increasing patience.

Patience Affirmation *(Repeat this aloud)*
Through patience, I exhibit restraint while enduring pain and persecution. Patience is a demonstration of leniency. It is the opposite of gutlessness and gloom. In patience, I am hopeful in courage actively resisting frustration or failure.

August's affirmations walk us through reminders of patience. We learn how to position ourselves toward the task by incorporating ideals we have already covered within this book.

Say Aloud: **I Will Work on PATIENCE!!! I Will Endure!**

August

"

My LIFE is a Journey!

"

Life is a journey—it's as exciting a roller-coaster ride as you admit it to be! Your experiences demonstrate your fight to create the life you desire to have. There is no such thing as sitting back and waiting on something to happen, so get up and CREATE a profitable journey through life! Chin up, back straight, head high as you walk this road! Fearlessly embark on your journey with a smile on your face and the world at your feet! Try your courage! Use your ambition to achieve your dreams!

Be happy with the pathways that have led you through life. While others are taking life hard, be HAPPY with the life you lead! Embrace life! Don't fear it. Live NOW before it's too late—life, at the prospect of death, has a way of drastically changing things. You may not get the opportunity to try again, so change your approach NOW! You have NOTHING to fear! Don't be afraid of your journey through life!

Live your life EXACTLY as you want! DO IT NOW!

The best day of your life is the one on which
you decide your life is your own. No apologies or excuses.
No one to lean on, rely on, or blame.
The gift is yours—it is an amazing journey—and you alone
are responsible for the quality of it.
This is the day your life really begins.

BOB MOAWAD

August

" I Will Live in the PRESENT! "

If you're anything like me, you spend entirely too much time focusing on the future! You can hardly enjoy the current moment or appreciate wonders of the past for being largely engrossed in what *may* occur. People like us think we have it all figured out! We think we know what will happen such that we either try too hard to change what may not even occur OR we fatefully dismiss valuable experiences thinking we already know the outcome. What a stress-filled life! *Sigh.* Life doesn't have to be as hard as we make it! Que sera, sera: What will be, will be. Exhale and leave it at that!

Sometimes, the best thing we ever do with the future is to leave it exactly where it is! To bring the future into the present isn't good at all. It is worse than a person who won't let go of the past. What sense does it make to hold onto something that has yet to occur? None!

We miss out on much when we don't have our feet firmly placed in the present. We are wandering within wondering minds, steadily drifting from what lies ahead to what lies beneath—we completely miss the here and now! Live in the now! Life happens in the present.

Affirmation Journal
- ★ What aspect of my *past* causes my mind to wander?
- ★ What aspect of my *future* causes my mind to wander?
- ★ What changes can I make to fully embrace the present?

August

> ## Hope in the Future Gives Me POWER in the Present!

Dreams of our futures are what guide the actions of today. The picture we have implanted within our minds must be powerful enough to compel us to action within any given moment. Dreams of our futures must also instill within us the courage and disposition to proactively see our goals through to the end. This is called POWER in the present.

Hope is a precursor to power. Without power, we charge, we try, we fight and we get discouraged. We try, try and try again. Then, we get a glimpse of progress—a tiny little breakthrough that keeps us pressing toward to the end. That's HOPE! With bright, vivid details of our future, hope is easily accessed on a regular basis. This is why vision building is so important! Vision boards are a visual display of our dreams—a daily reminder of *why* we're doing it so we can stay supercharged and focused on our goals.

Today's To-Do's...
- ★ **Create a visual reminder of what you will have in life.**
- ★ **Place your visual within plain sight for daily reminders.**
- ★ **Grow your hope in the future. Gain power in the present.**

Hope smiles from the threshold of the year to come,
Whispering 'it will be happier'...

ALFRED TENNYSON

August

"

Everything in Due Time...

"

Pause for a few minutes.

Stop to think back on all that you have accomplished up until now. Remember the stops along your path where you had to make long- and short-term sacrifices for the sake of *overall* goals. As much as it hurt you to make those forfeitures, you did it knowing that there was *greater* in store for you. You knew that you had to wait in those moments in order to receive the BEST that was to come within your future!

Delayed gratification hurts. With repetition, deferring gratification can get downright UGLY, but when you have DREAMS that are bigger than your britches, momentary lack of satisfaction leads to longevity in your final outcome.

ALL that you want in life will come to you in due time! The wait will require extreme patience, diligence and tenacity in maintaining the goal even with no sign of its materialization. Be patient and content in your waiting knowing that your patient sacrifice is worth the HUGE reward you will have in the end!

Say Aloud: **Everything in Due Time... I Wait in Contentment!**

Affirmation Journal
- ★ **What aspect of my *past* causes my mind to wander?**
- ★ **What aspect of my *future* causes m**

August

"
Every New Day Brings Me CLOSER to My DREAMS!
"

No matter the endeavor in life, we all seek to find success. Many of us would like success to be an escalator ride to the top when we already realize that it is NOT!!! Some people even imagine that all we have to do is climb the stones—many, many stones—to the top of the pyramid. I disagree!

The terms of success are different depending on who you ask. For some, success is linked to personal life. For others, success is linked to professional life. All in all, success is a healthy combination of both.

Any level of success within any arena means that you will leave others behind. THAT, my friends, is when you start climbing the ladder, and who has a problem with *that*?! NOT I! Regardless of your brand of success, seeing it through will take dedication and planning. Arrival at the top of the pyramid consists of a roller-coaster ADVENTURE through rough terrain, flatlands and deep doodoo where you'll encounter lions, and tigers and BEARS!!! OH MY! When you arrive at your destination, it will be worth every mountain you moved out of your way to get exactly where you were meant to be. **Kudos to Your Success!**

Failure is the condiment that gives success its flavor.

TRUMAN CAPOTE

August 7

> ## I Will Accomplish ALL That I DESIRE To!

Put your plans in plain sight and TACKLE them with COURAGE! Don't allow fear to detour you from walking PROGRESSIVELY along your personal path of GREATNESS! Encourage yourself! Don't be defeated by temporary obstacles or other challenges that stand in your way!

Understand that your goals aren't the same as the people around you. Your destiny isn't the same as those around you. Your FAITH isn't the same, so stop comparing yourself, your actions and your behaviors to those around you—*you* are not *them*! YOU are willing to make sacrifices and YOU will make them often! YOU are willing to lose sleep, to go the extra mile and to take risks that no other person will! YOU will accomplish ALL that you desire to, so every single sacrifice that you've made up until now and all the many sacrifices that YOU will make are already worth it!

Celebrate your future accomplishments! Be proud of how far you've come. Know that every step you take now is leading you on a path toward GREATNESS, so BE GREAT.

Don't be afraid!

Say Aloud: I Will Accomplish All That I Desire To!

August

" I Will Value My EXPERIENCES! "

Experiences are the building blocks of the lives we dream of. By yielding to our experiences—new and old, bad and good—we accept the paths that we've been on since day one. This leads us to our desired end. We not only take in past experiences, but we also learn to create valuable experiences that lead to profitable futures.

The value in experience lies in submission. We miss experiences each time we try to modify them. We take the life out of experience when we apply our personal preference to that which is greater than us. Without requiring each new experience to be accommodating to us, we should acclimate ourselves to the new environment and thus increase our personal awareness.

Submit yourself to each experience. Don't make the experience submit itself to you.

Say Aloud: **I Will Value My Experiences.**

You are the sum total of everything you've ever seen, heard, eaten, smelled, been told, forgot—it's all there. Everything influences each of us, and because of that I try to make sure that my experiences are positive.

MAYA ANGELOU

August

> ## I Am Destined for GREATNESS!

If you don't know where you're going in life, you'll end up going nowhere in life.

Find a destination in life, love and the pursuit of happiness. Take whatever roads that you *must* to get there *in one piece*! When life presents chaos, this is what you must do:

**Don't STOP!
GET IT! GET IT!**

Without a destination, you will quickly end up nowhere, so find your dream and GET TO IT! You're as great as you SHOW yourself to be, so commit to practices that align with your lofty goals for a profitable future. Make sacrifices now that position you for GREATNESS! All of the effort you put in NOW will readily present itself in the bright future that you're destined for. Start now!

Affirmation Journal
- ★ **Based on my current actions, what am I destined for?**
- ★ **How can I adjust myself to be destined for GREATNESS?**
- ★ **How can I show my worthiness to have a GREAT future?**

Say Aloud: **I Am Destined for GREATNESS!**

August

"

I Am Preparing NOW for My BRIGHT Future!

"

In preparation for the future that is outlaid before you, you have some unique decisions to make:

Affirmation Journal
- ★ *Who* do I want to be when I grow up?
- ★ *What* do I want to be when I grow up?
- ★ *Where* do I want to be when I grow up?
- ★ *How* do I want people to perceive me?
- ★ *Why* do I want these things? What is my reason?
- ★ What is my purpose?
- ★ What am I doing to get there?

Think very carefully on your responses to these questions. Commit to yourself and to the plans you have, but make room for profitable growth. As often as you need to, note your updates to these responses.

In line with your goals, life will begin to align itself with YOU! GET READY! Recite your plans out loud often and share them with your mentors who will guide you along. Prepare to live the BEST life. Prepare to be the BEST you!!!

Don't be careful what you wish for—BE READY!
God answers even the SILENT prayers, so...
PREPARE YOURSELF!

D NICOLE

August 11

> ## My Life is An ADVENTURE!

Life is an adventure—it's not some well-paved course that leads to nice little places within a *Pleasantville*-type setting. Your steps outline a path that is perfect only for YOU! The journey that you take is an adventure specific only to YOU! The path that you've been on leads right to YOUR unique destiny. Take charge of it! This is YOUR life! Piece it together as you will. Put together all missing pieces and discard those that no longer fit. Travel this road of life to your chosen destination, but don't do it without enjoying what you find along the way! Partake in ALL that life has to offer by appreciating every ounce of joy that it affords you. In this manner, you will honor the good times in life as well as the bad times understanding that a unique combination of *both* is required to make your adventure worthwhile.

Don't let bad times get you down. Press forward—look backward only to appreciate how far you've come! Revisit any noteworthy negative situations and deal with them to take your life back! Take your heart back! Take control of your life and WIN! You deserve it!

Life is an adventure!

Enjoy the experience for ALL that it is worth!

Say Aloud: My Life is an Adventure! I LOVE My Experiences!

August

"

I Am in HIGH ANTICIPATION of My BRIGHT Future!

"

What does your future look like? Do you know? By your lifestyle—and primarily by your thoughts—what type of future have you built for yourself? What are you *do*ing to prepare yourself for the life you've planned?

Don't create goals without creating plans. Infuse your plans with vision! SEE the end *before* you arrive there! Meditate on the things you dream about to inspire a dogged work ethic. Make your vision SO clear that it builds your anticipation of the goals you work toward. You will need an additional push along the way, so remind yourself to stay positive! Cultivate a positive attitude where you *always* give your BEST! Mold your thinking PURPORTEDLY! Shape it with *clear* intent in *high* anticipation of your BRIGHT future!

Affirmation Journal

- ★ **What does my future look like?**
- ★ **What do my thoughts mostly consist of?**
- ★ **By my thoughts, what type of future have I built?**
- ★ **Why am I in high anticipation of my bright future?**

If you have a positive attitude
and constantly strive to give your best effort,
eventually you will overcome your immediate problems
and find you are ready for greater challenges.

PAT RILEY

August 13

" I Will Stand FIRM! "

In all that you grow through, be CONSTANTLY reminded that your story is still being told. There is still more growing for you to do! You *can't* give up now!!! Stand firm! Be steadfast in your decisions no matter how life appears! Center yourself and renew your focus so your feelings don't get the best of you.

Stand with your head high, your chest out and your feet FIRMLY placed in each step that you take! Tackle your goals with tenacity unmatched by others and be encouraged by each accomplishment you celebrate along the way.

Your firm resolution will be based on the strength of your goals so find goals that affirm both your dreams and the future you've planned for yourself. Rest assured knowing that you will achieve ALL that you have set your sights set upon.

Do what it takes to get there!

Say Aloud: **I Will Stand Firm! I Will Not Give Up!**

Affirmation Journal

- ★ **What life situations require me to be more resolute?**
- ★ **How would a firm resolve benefit me in these areas?**
- ★ **What must I do to fortify a firm resolve?**
- ★ **How can I counteract feelings of defeat during growth processes?**

August

I Am FOCUSED!

Say Aloud: **I Am Focused! I Am Disciplined in My Efforts!**

When you first embark on new journeys in life, it seems so easy to get distracted or discouraged. When old journeys get rough, you tragically face temporary defeat where you want to throw your hands up and be done with it all! You *want* to quit, but...

> You will NOT give up!
> You will NOT give in!
> **YOU are FOCUSED!**

Be disciplined in your efforts and stay focused! Limit the number of distractions in your life by dropping any FLUFF that stands in the way of your goals. Allow yourself enough downtime to be revived but enough structure to work twice as hard as anyone else during your working hours.

Say Aloud: **I Am Focused! I Am Disciplined in My Efforts!**

Discipline is remembering what you want.

DAVID CAMPBELL

August 15

> **I Will NEVER Quit!!!**

Some days, you just want to cry. Some days, life just downright HURTS! Some days, all of the effort that you've put in, everything you've endured, and the small results that you may or may not gain in the end, just don't seem worth it.

Some days, you really just want to throw in the towel!

But, that's just *some* days. Think about all of the good days you've had! Think about all the times you made yourself proud even when you had nothing show for it. Recall the moments when you encouraged yourself through tough times, you withstood circumstances *(and people)* that tested your limits, but you're still kicking! You're STILL pushing!!!

While life continually tests the limits of your enduring patience, you will find—time and time again—that you are NOT a quitter. YOU are anything BUT that! YOU are a survivor! YOU are a winner! You've overcome insurmountable challenges in life. You didn't give up *then* and you definitely won't give up *now*!

Say Aloud: **I Will Never Quit! I Will Not Give Up on Myself!**

Affirmation Journal

- ★ **What life situations caused me to consider quitting?**
- ★ **When I did not quit, what has been the result?**
- ★ **What have I learned from those situations specifically?**
- ★ **Overall, what can I learn about not quitting?**

August

" I Am HOPEFUL! "

Hope is all you need in the midst of sorrow, let down, hurt, pain and defeat. Hope is that little BIG power that keeps you pushing through until the end. So long as you're alive, you have NOT reached your end! Keep fighting! Keep pushing! Keep HOPING! You are only at the beginning of your journey because every new day grants you a fresh batch of hope to further inspire your intentions.

To kindle the passion of hope, create actions that inspire new hope! Partake in activities that push you to hopeful patience. Your built up tenacity will refine the character of the hope within you. Find resilience in bold hope. Against all odds, continually be optimistic about your pursuits. In hope, don't EVER forget why you started in the first place!

Say Aloud: **I Am Hopeful! I Will Positively Impact My World!**

Affirmation Journal
- ★ **Why is it important to be hopeful?**
- ★ **How has hope altered my decisions in the past?**
- ★ **How can hope positively impact my future?**

But I have found that in the simple act of living with hope, and in the daily effort to have a positive impact in the world, the days I do have are made all the more meaningful and precious. And for that I am grateful.

ELIZABETH EDWARDS

August 17

> ## I Will NOT Give Up!

You will always WIN if you don't quit!
Don't EVER give up!

If you take concerted action in passionate pursuit of your purpose, you will **ALWAYS** WIN! DON'T **EVER** GIVE UP, and don't ever discount your own POWER within the struggle! There is POWER in weakness! YOU have power in weakness! By your WEAKNESS, the God within you is made STRONG! Tap into ALL of the power that you need!

Don't Give Up!

For everything that you're seeking to become, you MUST be willing to give up all that you've ever been! Don't dwell on what you've lost or what you will have to give up to reach your goals. Be forever willing to make hard sacrifices in order to achieve your dreams, and whatever you do:

DON'T GIVE UP!

Say Aloud: **I Will Not Give Up! I Will Sacrifice for My Dream!**

Affirmation Journal
- ★ What do my dreams mean to me?
- ★ What does my purpose mean to me?
- ★ Why is it important that I don't give up on these things?
- ★ What WILL happen if I don't give up on myself?

August

> **I Will NOT Let Fear Get the Best of ME!**

Life is passing some of you by simply because you won't use what you've already been given! Too many of you walk around missing every single opportunity simply because you won't STAND UP and *DO* what it takes to claim the victory you desire!

You are afraid. You are ashamed. You feel unworthy!

"It's too hard." "It's too tough." "It's not for me." "I don't want it,"—when really, you *do* want it!

Why are you letting life pass you by? Why is it good enough for others to obtain what YOU want? Why is this OK?

IT IS **NOT** OK! Fear is **NOT** OK! Quit allowing your hopes, dreams and wishes to be overshadowed by fear! Don't let preoccupation with fear cause you to miss out on enjoyment in life! YOU have the power to control your situation. YOU have power to control your MIND! REMOVE THE FEAR! Work through the fear of defeat.

There isn't a man or woman in this world who is fearless, but if judged by actions, many seem desperately unafraid!

No evil propensity of the human heart is so powerful that it may not be subdued by discipline.

SENECA

August 19

> ## I Am GROWING!

Growth takes time. It doesn't happen over night. We all realize this, however, we don't always accept and appreciate growth as we should. We don't take advantage of the many opportunities we have to ponder over our progress, our accomplishments and the lives created as a result of the notable growth that we've experienced.

Through our developments, life molds and shapes us. It trains and teaches us to be better despite situations and circumstances. There is nothing to be saddened by as we relive the hardships of life. We learn to accept them, to take them as the very unique set of events that were required to find us within the now profitable frameworks of our current lives.

We benefit on a grand scale by overcoming. We learn who we are, how best to interact with the world and how to have the BEST future we can. We live. We laugh. We love, and we learn. This is all a part of growth.

Say Aloud: I Am Growing! I Am Proud of My Progress!

Affirmation Journal
- ★ What are the most important areas that I have grown in?
- ★ Which areas am I looking forward to growing more in?
- ★ Why is patience so essential to growth?
- ★ How can I maintain my patience during growth periods?

August

"

I Am UNDERSTANDING!

"

We are so impatient with ourselves at times. More than that, we are often very impatient with others. There isn't a single *perfect* human on this earth. While we better ourselves, learning to understand others is top priority. Increased understanding of others helps us develop a deeper connection with ourselves as we gain more knowledge of general human nature.

Say Aloud: **I Am Understanding!**

Patience is a goal that involves being understanding. Instead of getting entirely caught up in the details of what another person does incorrectly, take that energy and do better when YOU are in the same position they are in. If you see poor parents, be a better parent. If you see poor bosses, be a better boss. Poor friends? Be a better one! If someone has wronged you, take the initiative to personally do better across the board! Use your hurt feelings to inspire you to treat others with even more respect. Seek to understand others so that you can better understand yourself.

Any fool can know.
The point is to understand.

ALBERT EINSTEIN

August 21

> ## The BEST Things Come to Those Who WAIT!

Patience is a virtue that comes about through much turmoil, consistency and delayed gratification. Often, when considering patience, we don't do so with positive thoughts in mind. Patience seems dreadful, and it *is* dreadful if we journey through lessons of travail without great spirits and calm countenance. Waiting should be experienced in joy, in peace and in understanding. All things cannot come to us as soon as we ask for, need for or want them—there would be no opportunity for learning and no subsequent growth. The *good*ness found in patience is that we are poised for great gain along the way. More than that which we are waiting for, through patience we also obtain character building advancements that pave the way for maturity, courage and faith. We obtain the BEST, not just in what we *receive*, but in what we *learn* while being patient.

Practice waiting well. Wait, not just looking to receive the end result, but wait looking forward to what is gained through the process. Keeping such benefits in mind, it becomes easy to smile and to also maintain a peaceful spirit of joy while waiting.

Affirmation Journal
★ **What am I waiting for?**
★ **What are the BEST things I have gained along the wait?**
★ **What are the benefits of waiting?**

August

> **I Will WAIT
> with a SMILE on My Face
> and JOY in My Heart!**

Joy describes a countenance unmarred by emotional dissonance. Joy is a spiritual concept that trumps literal turmoil. Smiling is indicative of joy, yet you don't have to smile to have joy nor do you have to have joy to smile. You're blessed indeed when you experience them simultaneously. You're blessed even more when you *share* these gifts.

Joy in this instance is to be differentiated from concepts which are character traits or any other temporal responses. Joy is supernatural. It's a divine blessing imparted to you when you place faith and trust in what is greater than yourself. Therefore, joy must be preceded by humility. The pathway to joy creates an awakening whereby you realize that you don't have to control everything all by yourself. God is an ever present help.

Affirmation Journal
- ★ What things have I done that caused others to smile?
- ★ What things have I done that caused me to smile?
- ★ When was the last time I felt like smiling all day long?
- ★ Why don't I smile more?

> *Don't cry because it's over,
> smile because it happened.*
>
> Dr. Seuss

August 23

" I Am on GOD's Time! "

Every individual has a unique reason to be alive. With those predestined mandates comes a set of procedures that must be followed to arrive at the point of completion. Life promises that you will come across your fair share of headache and heart ache. You face your trails best by continuously acknowledging God's plan for your life.

Say Aloud: **I Am on God's time! What is for Me is for Me!**

Each day, honor your experiences by standing firm within them without moving too far into the future or dwelling too long on the past. Own each moment for what it is and what it will be understanding that everything happens for a reason.

Say Aloud: **I Am on God's time! What is for Me is for Me!**

You can't speed up the work of fate or carry out a destiny that isn't your own. Leave your schedules and your life in the hands of The Life Giver understanding that God's hands are capable, loving hands—God has it ALL under control!

Say Aloud: **I Am on God's time! My Life is in His Hands!**

August

I Am NOT Defeated!

The choice to *feel* defeated is ours to make. Even in losing, there is much to be gained if we so choose. In any context, we learn much more from losing than we do from winning. Where, then, is the defeat?

Affirmation Journal
- ★ What losses have I encountered in life?
- ★ What have I won from those experiences?
- ★ What personal resolve keeps me from accepting defeat?

Don't be long burdened with the stress of defeat. Heads shouldn't hang too low at the sign of failure. Experience the feelings without dwelling in negativity for long. Find the lessons that will be gained from the occasion and move forward with increased determination and renewed vision for success! There will be longing, but only in the immediate aftermath of dreams deferred. In little time, you will get back on track. The next time a formidable challenge arises, you will be ready!

Say Aloud: **I Am Not Defeated! I Am Ready for What's Next!**

*The secret of life, though,
is to fall seven times
and to get up eight times.*

Paulo Coelho

August 25

> ## I Will NOT Work in Haste!

Superhumans are only super at their BEST. You can't be your best working in haste. Take the time to conquer your schedule and don't put your goals at the mercy of life or strict timetables. Tasks need proper time to develop, and as they do, you must allow proper time for competent completion. Sometimes, this requires you to slow down. In other cases, you need to stop altogether.

Any project worth seeing through to the end is also worth its due in time, planning and related considerations. Don't allow deadlines to get the best of you in such a way that you are unable to celebrate gains along the way. Don't lose your life by living on the clock so much that you are unable to enjoy the worthy experiences that you've worked so hard to afford yourself.

Without drawing out tasks to unnecessary durations, take your time in completing them.

Learn to breathe. Learn to relax. Do not work in haste.

Say Aloud: **I Will Not Work in Haste!**

August

> ## Patience Builds Character.
> ## Persistence Fortifies It.

While we wait for the things we desire, and while we press through diverse situations, our character is built through our tolerance of obstacles that would otherwise break us. In waiting, our resilience is built up and our souls are strengthened. In waiting, we learn exactly who we are as individuals while also learning about those around us.

Patience is where we confirm and solidify the defining traits of our character. As trials persist and as we persist within them, fortification of our character is built up within us. We learn exactly who we are by way of our tarrying within unfavorable situations in life.

Say Aloud: **Patience Builds Character! Persistence Fortifies It!**

Life isn't intended to break you—it's here to *make* you.

What is life making out of you? Don't allow negativity or foul play to rob you of who you are at your core. Uncover the hidden gems about yourself through patience, and nurture resilience of character, in and out of pain.

Say Aloud: **Patience Builds Character! Persistence Fortifies It!**

It was character that got us out of bed,
commitment that moved us into action
and discipline that enabled us to follow through.

Zig Ziglar

August 27

> ## I Am Worth WAITING For!

Don't allow others to pressure you into making decisions...

YOU are worth waiting for!!!!

When making decisions, don't EVER wait for perfection. Perfection NEVER happens! When making decisions, don't wait for readiness—readiness RARELY happens! While urging yourself toward BOLD progress, prepare for the journey that you're on. As needed, take your time, but don't move *too* slowly!

ALL that *needs* to happen *will* happen in due time! While it is NOT acceptable to sit on your BUTT and *hope* things into happening, it is also not acceptable to force yourself into decisions that aren't your own! Be willing to wait for yourself and make others do the same.

For everything that you are working toward in life, be patient with *yourself*! You can only move as fast as *one day at a time*! Slow down at other times. Take the time to enjoy the progress you've made thus far understanding that your BIG dreams won't happen overnight. Wait for them. They are worth it. YOU are worth it!

Say Aloud: **I Am Worth Waiting For! I Am Worth It!**

August

> ## It WILL Be WORTH it!
> ## I Am Worth IT
> ## !!!

What are your dreams? What are your goals? How big are they? How big are YOU?!

Think back on your life. Think back on EVERYTHING that led you up to this current point. Seriously, take the time to relive your life. I'll give you a few minutes...

Done?

Did you recall your past life and the choices you once made? Did you think back on the headaches you encountered and those that you created? Did you for a second consider that your current life and your future make EVERYTHING that you have been through well worth it? Well... Did you?

Accept that life as you know it is NOT a waste! Life is GREAT! There isn't a *single* experience of yours that can be considered useless. Your struggle is worth it. The pain is worth it. The agony is worth it. YOU are worth it!

Remember that!

Say Aloud: **It Will Be Worth It! *I* Am Worth it!**

If you love what you do and are willing to do what it takes, it's within your reach. And it'll be worth every minute you spend alone at night, thinking and thinking about what it is you want to design or build.
It'll be worth it, I promise.

STEVE WOZNIAK

August 29

"

I Am BETTER Than My PAST!

"

Thinking back on our past lives, it's a TRUE wonder that some of us even made it this far!

Take a minute or so to acknowledge that truth and reflect on who YOU you used to be. Some of you have such *interesting* past lives that you don't even *want* to spend much time thinking about them, so... let us move on! ☺

The past afforded us with the chance to gain what we needed to arrive where we currently are in life. It took a unique combination of trials, upsets, accomplishments, favor, grace and mercy for us to arrive SUCCESSFULLY to now! Now that we are here, let us again move on!

Accept your past for exactly what it was—nothing more, nothing less. Don't dwell on what could've been, what wasn't or what was. Leave the past exactly where it is: BEHIND YOU! Move on into *greater* knowing that you are SO much BETTER than where you once were!

The person you now are can't go back to the person you once were. Your mindset has changed. Your methods have changed. *You* are NEW! Be happy and know that you are PAST the past!

Be present in the present while focusing on your future!

Say Aloud: **I Am Better Than My Past!!! I Have Moved On!**

August

My FUTURE is Worth WAITING For!

For everything in your past that has weighed you down, and for all you currently strive for, understand that the BEST things in life won't come without hard work and much patience. Be PROUD of all you've endured. Your pain and disappointment have developed your character. You are now stronger and tougher because of the tenacity you've developed within.

Continue to build your character with the resolve that your PROSPEROUS future is worth waiting for. Be willing to sacrifice whatever is needed and always be willing to let go of the old to make room for the new! Put in all of the time, work and dedicated effort required for you to create the life that you desire.

Say Aloud: **I Am Patient! My Future is Worth Waiting For!**

Affirmation Journal
- ★ **What things in life have I put much hard work and effort into?**
- ★ **What has been the benefit of my work and patience?**
- ★ **How can past patience encourage future waiting?**

Patience is the companion of wisdom.

SAINT AUGUSTINE

August

> ## I Will SUCCEED!

One of life's BIGGEST secrets is this:

Success is as simple as *deciding* to be successful!

If it's that easy—and really, it IS—why don't you just go ahead and make the decision NOW!!!

Say Aloud: **I WILL Succeed!!!**

Write it. Say it. SCREAM IT if you have to! As a matter of fact, SCREAM it just because!!!! SCREAM IT regularly and let that passion invigorate you! No need to place your passion where it is less profitable. Put ALL of your passion back into YOURSELF—YOU—the person who WILL be successful!

Let NOTHING challenge that resolve. Let no one come in between you and your success! Make the COMMITMENT and STAY there no matter what!!! Don't be easily wavered and STAY positive—no matter what!!!!

You WILL succeed! Make the decision now and COMMIT!

Say Aloud: **I WILL Succeed! I WILL COMMIT!**

The whole secret of a successful life
is to find out what is one's destiny to do,
and then do it.

HENRY FORD

Gentleness

September

"

I Will Work on GENTLENESS!

"

Gentleness is the embodiment of patience, respect and love for oneself. Through gentleness, we start our love lessons with ourselves first so that we best exhibit kindness, generosity and selflessness toward all others. Gentleness, in practice, involves guiding one's *spirit* to flow over into character and behavioral adjustments that create enduring positive change. The foundation by which we strengthen our mental dexterity comes about through gentleness.

Gentleness Affirmation *(Repeat this aloud)*
To be gentle is to rule my spirit well. I will control my passions and contain my strength. Without being pretentious, I will pardon injuries and correct faults. I will be tranquil. I Will Be Gentle!

Gentleness is the focus of September. This month prioritizes the importance of being kind to yourself. You will learn how to employ practices targeted to heal you from the inside out by creating greater appreciation for yourself. This puts you in the best position to have a better appreciation for all others.

Say Aloud: **I Will Work on Gentleness! I Will Be Kind to ME!**

September

"

I Am MERCIFUL!

"

To embark on a journey toward gentleness, we first visit the concept of mercy. The ability to forgive oneself and others is essential to the overall goal of being gentle. We cannot be kind to ourselves without learning to release the mistakes we've personally made. We must be gentle enough with ourselves to be at peace with our decisions whether the outcomes be good or bad. This level of wholeness entails being at peace with ourselves and our environment such that every decision we make is the right one—not because it is the *correct* one, but because through active participation in our lives, we learn from each decision we make. Mercy enables internal peace in adverse situations. In gentleness, learn to be merciful to yourself and also to others.

Say Aloud: **I Am Merciful! I Always Forgive! I Am Gentle!**

Affirmation Journal
* ★ How good am I at showing mercy toward others?
* ★ How good am I at showing mercy toward myself?
* ★ How can I be better at showing mercy?

Throughout life people will make you mad, disrespect you and treat you bad. Let God deal with the things they do, cause hate in your heart will consume you too.

WILL SMITH

September

> ## I Will CHERISH Life's Lessons!

To get some things right in your life, *some* things have to go WRONG! To get yourself shifted into the posture you should be in, life presents you with diverse situations that cause you to introspectively reflect. Outstanding gentleness means meeting problems with the optimistic understanding that they ALL work together for your good.

There's no need to hurry through situations without getting the value that is to be gained out of them. The knowledge that there is always a lesson to be learned places you in the position of pupil wherein you accept that you can't merely *rush* through situations without mastering everything that is to be acquired from them. Some situations require nothing from you outside of your presence, yet you may opt to turn them into what they are not: DRAMA! Don't make mountains out of molehills.

In peaceful practice, gain all that you can from each problem you face so you won't have to repeat the lesson. If there must be repetition, you'll face the issue again fully aware of how to respond and completely vested in any benefits available to you in each situation.

Affirmation Journal
- ★ How can I be more optimistic about life's struggles?
- ★ How can I find the value in life's lessons *during* them?
- ★ How can I be less dramatic in life?

September

"

I Am CENTERED!

"

To be centered is to live within a realm of peace based on personal equilibrium. Centered lives are conscientious lives that exist within wholeness, clarity and wisdom. The resulting balance enables one to be fully vested with *self* without enabling external factors to jeopardize a calm center. When enduring change, centered individuals more aptly respond to negativity since their resolve is less emotional and more stable.

Affirmation Journal
- ★ What does it mean to be centered?
- ★ What would a centered life look like for me?
- ★ How is a centered life better than my current life?
- ★ What long term impact can I look forward to as a result of being centered?

Say Aloud: I Am Centered! My Mind is Balanced!

*The cyclone derives its powers from a calm center.
So does a person.*

NORMAN VINCENT PEALE

September

" My SKILLS Are POWERFUL! "

The skills that you've been endowed with have the power to move MOUNTAINS! Your skills provide you with the power to build dreams out of NOTHING and to reach goals in a manner that only *you* can.

Be proud of what you have and use your skills to the MAXIMUM! Kindle your own desire and further your dreams by understanding the power of your skills! Move your passions forward by being thankful for your talents and be diligent in your utilization of them. Invest in your skills by gaining all that you can through learning from others, through further educating yourself and also through putting your skills into practice.

Affirmation Journal
- ★ **What skills do I possess?**
- ★ **How do I use what I have been given?**
- ★ **How can my skills empower me?**
- ★ **How can I use my skills to bolster my bright future?**
- ★ **What mountains have I moved by way of my skills?**
- ★ **What mountains am I looking forward to moving using my skills?**

Say Aloud: **My Skills Are Powerful! I Put Them Into Practice!**

September

"

My AFFIRMATIONS Are POWERFUL!

"

Affirmations aren't about repeating some rehearsed line of statements simply because your coach told you to. State your affirmations in PASSION with belief and ferocity that matches the weight of your PURPOSE! While empty statements get you nowhere, they *are* a decent *starting* point if you can find no other suitable arrangement. State your affirmations with CLEAR conviction. Be BOLD in your statements! BELIEVE in what you are saying. Look yourself in the mirror and loudly declare:

THIS IS MY AFFIRMATION! I AM POWERFUL!

Take control of your life by taking control of your mind! Declare to YOURSELF that you WILL have the life you desire! You WILL change your thoughts! You WILL change your actions! You WILL change your posture!

Speak to yourself! LISTEN to the things you say just as your soul listens. Reconstruct your mind by way of your affirmations. Alter your behaviors to follow suit and watch your life begin to flourish IMMEDIATELY!

Say Aloud: **My Affirmations Are Powerful! *I* Am Powerful!**

You have power over your mind—not outside events. Realize this, and you will find strength.

MARCUS AURELIUS

September

"I Will Speak NO Evil!"

We are all limited in our judgments. Each of us is assessing life based on our personal connection with it—a connection that can't totally quantify or qualify the behaviors, actions, thoughts and feelings of any beings other than ourselves. We hardly have a thorough understanding of our *own* behaviors, actions, thoughts and feelings on most days! Some of us intend to speak LIFE yet there is bitterness and defeat oozing out of our pores! With all the positivity we seek to bestow upon others, let's not forget that our premier mission is SELF first so that we BEST serve others.

Be positive! Recite positive affirmations to yourself as often as needed in order to change negative thought processes. Allow yourself enough alone time to meditate on solving problems versus allowing them. Combat negativity in thought with audible positive affirmations and statements that alter the negativity flowing through your system.

Prevent negative statements from escaping your lips!

Today's To-Do's...
- ★ Let NO negative statements escape your lips.
- ★ Let NO negative communication come from you.
- ★ Physically rewrite all negative written communication that you have sent recently sent.
- ★ Mentally, then verbally, restate all negative communications to make them positive.

September

My WORDS Are POWERFUL!

As we view the world, words offer explanation. Through words, we find direction, meaning and fulfillment. Through words, we find self-expression—words help us to become one with self. Words move us to action. Words guide us in fulfilling our visions as they aid in expressing our verbal connections with the world.

Words are POWERFUL!

Words are powerful even when they don't leave our lips. When words find themselves trapped in thought, they repeat in our minds over and over again and become all the more strengthened through repetition.

Guarding our hearts and minds compels us to guarded thought. When thoughts are controlled in silence, let words speak and direct what you think. Let the power of words overcome the control of thought. SPEAK what you *want*! SAY what you *need* aloud and allow your being to hear ALL that you desire. Overcome burdensome thoughts with POWERFUL words that affirm your destiny and kindle the passion of your desires!

The most courageous act is still to think for yourself. Aloud.

Coco Chanel

September

" I Am in Touch with MYSELF! "

Connecting with yourself means learning to understand your personal responses and individual frameworks. It means learning to gauge exactly what it is that makes you quirk. Self responsibility means learning yourself *first*. Afterward, you're able to proactively interface with others from the basis of your personal understanding of self.

For example, *when you are stressed, how does your body respond?* Exhaustion could cause your productivity to slow, and your body may ache for reasons you don't understand. Your chest may begin to hurt. Your heart may begin to race and your back just wants to scream! *How do you know that you are stressed during times when you are just too busy to take a break and pay attention to yourself?* You may attempt to block out the realization that there *is* problem. You carry on with work as normal, yet as the aches of your body become progressively worse, there is no way for you to continue to ignore the signs. *How can you be proactive about such situations without taking your stress out on those around you?*

Stop living as if you are invincible. Take the time to learn how life bothers you and address those issues from within. When problems arise, don't always look outside of yourself for the cause and solution. Look within.

Say Aloud: **I Am In Touch with Myself! I Know Who I Am!**

September

I Will Create a Place of PEACE in My Life!

Peace in life isn't something we just fall into, it is something that we must consciously create. Practices of peace must be constant if we are to see and reap the benefits of their presence. To feel peace on the inside, we must create peace within while allowing our internal wholeness and security to flow outwardly into our environment.

Peaceful practices start with taking time to oneself on a daily basis. These moments could be used to reflect, to read or to write. They could include things like relaxing, exercising or enjoying your favorite activities. As long as this time goes uninterrupted by external irritants, you have successfully created a place of peace in your life. Practice this on a daily basis doing what you can to minimize interruptions.

Today's To-Do's...
★ **List at least 10 peaceful practices to add to your routine!**
★ **Incorporate at least 1 daily for no less than 15 minutes.**
★ **Increase this duration over time.**
★ **Practice peace often, making regular modifications.**

Say Aloud: I Will Create a Place of Peace in My Life!

Find a place inside where there's joy,
and the joy will burn out the pain.

JOSEPH CAMPBELL

September 11

"I Will RESPECT Myself!"

Self-respect is all about pride. It is about appreciating and loving yourself enough to make decisions reflective of how highly you esteem yourself. Self-respect is about honoring yourself through your actions, behaviors and also by the type of effort you put into appeasing yourself. Self-respect is about love. It's about being the total measure of love in all you're willing to give to show thanks for who you are.

We show our level of self-respect by the decisions we make, by the engagements we have, by the challenges that we take on and by the challenges that we disregard. Demonstrations of self-respect are apparent in how we carry ourselves, in how we treat others and in how we handle our passions.

Affirmation Journal
- ★ How do I show respect for myself?
- ★ In what areas can I show more respect for myself?
- ★ How does my self-respect impact how others view me?
- ★ How does my self-respect impact my decisions?

Say Aloud: I Will Respect Myself! I Take Pride in Who I Am!

September

"

I Will CHERISH Myself!

"

Frightfully, many of us rarely, if EVER, take the time we need to cherish ourselves—not to *treat* ourselves, but to truly CHERISH ourselves. Life should NEVER happen for us in a such a way that we're left without time to cherish the #1 person in our lives. Any life that shows signs of this is simply an UNFIT life! Creating the BEST life means making and *taking* the time needed to truly cherish who we are.

We must appreciate ourselves! We must show ourselves how much *we* appreciate *us*. (*This is a great practice to share with our mates!*) We spend ENTIRELY too much time waiting on others to do for us things we don't even make the time to do for ourselves—THEN we have the audacity to get upset with the *other* person! **WOW!** What an unhealthy imbalance!

Cherish who you are! Cherish your calling! Cherish the indispensable qualities that only YOU possess! Of *all* you have to give, what is *any* of it if YOU don't take the time to appreciate it?

I've come to believe that each of us has a personal calling that's as unique as a fingerprint—and that the best way to succeed is to discover what you love and then find a way to offer it to others in the form of service, working hard, and also allowing the energy of the universe to lead you.

OPRAH WINFREY

September 13

"I Will HONOR Myself!"

Honor yourself! Always always ALWAYS honor yourself! Put MUCH thought into where you're headed in life and also into exactly what is needed for you to get there! Make whatever decisions that are needed for you to achieve what you conceive. Show yourself honor by *preparing* your way for greatness! Couple your skills and talents with actions and truths that make success REALITY for you!

You are too valuable for your potential to be taken lightly! You are too brilliant not to see and DO great things, so honor yourself! SURROUND yourself with people who are going places! Rub shoulders with the BEST—people who inspire you to do better!

Affirmation Journal
- ★ How do I show honor for myself?
- ★ In what areas can I show more honor for myself?
- ★ How does honor for myself impact how others see me?
- ★ How does my honor for myself impact my decisions?

Say Aloud: **I Will Honor Myself! I Will Make Success a Reality!**

September

> ## I Will RESPECT My DREAM!

Dreams aren't meant to be deferred. The fact that you have a dream means that you should do everything within your power to address it. Appreciate the fact that you have vision enough to dream, and RESPECT your dream! Trust the vision that you have and quickly align yourself with it. The effort will require mental focus to maintain a clear and positive mind. Timely discipline will also be required for you to live your dreams.

Respect your dream by matching it with worthwhile actions. Find good company that will help you harness the energy residing within. Begin to note your progress.

The journey that you are on is a unique one. Understanding that EVERYTHING happens for a reason, get the most from every interaction. No matter what you do, be sure that your actions are never in vain.

Say Aloud: **I Will Respect My Dream! I Trust in My Dreams!**

Trust in dreams,
for in them is hidden the gate to eternity.

KHALIL GIBRAN

September 15

> ## I Will RESPECT My VISION!

As children, we learn to imagine. As children, we learn to DREAM! When we become older, we sometimes forget to use those same practices to picture lifestyles beyond our wildest dreams and to envision that which lies just beyond our reach. We can't appreciate lofty goals when we don't dream. We can't respect great gains when we have no vision.

Develop the vision that you have by *making* it your reality. Write down the things that you see within your mind and create clear cut plans. Give yourself deadlines for completion of tasks. Build your visions with boards, journals and other methods of writing your vision and making it plain. Do exactly what is needed to honor your vision. Don't make things more complicated than they have to be. Respect your vision by validating it with action. Take command of the efforts of your mind by taking ACTION to see your dreams come to pass.

Say Aloud: **I Will Respect My Vision! I Will Develop It More!**

Affirmation Journal
- ★ **What is my vision?**
- ★ **How can I show that I respect my vision?**
- ★ **How can I ensure that others see my vision?**
- ★ **How can I ensure that others respect my vision?**
- ★ **Why is respect of vision important?**

September

"

I Will RESPECT My IDEAS!

"

The value of ideas is endless. Every man-made advancement in technology, science and resources was developed after the spark of an idea.

Respect your ideas! Put value into that which determines your destiny. Being that ideas are of priceless value, put considerable effort into not just respecting your ideas, but also into *creating* valuable ideas. Take the time to daydream! Daydream regularly so that you guide your thoughts toward the good. Plan out how life is *supposed* to look for you on a DAILY basis!

Don't let fear block your faith and keep you from daydreaming. Don't let the ill-informed bias of another person dictate YOUR financial future or happiness. Fears imposed on you by OTHERS and their LIMITED beliefs is just as harmful as your own limiting fears and faulty belief systems.

Respect the ideas that come to your mind. Value them by growing them through research, goal-setting and modeling.

Say Aloud: **I Will Respect My Ideas! I Will Not Limit Myself!**

*Be less curious about people
and more curious about ideas.*

MARIE CURIE

September 17

"I Will RESPECT My THOUGHTS!"

Your thoughts aren't meant to be taken in vain. They come to YOU for a reason. Pay attention to them! Evaluate them. VALUE them. Respect your thoughts!

In line with greater spiritual awareness, you'll find yourself having mental connections that are deeper than those of others. Be thankful for the depth of your intuition and begin to act on the thoughts that come to you. Don't brush them off as unimportant muck never to be evaluated. Ponder on your thoughts. For the thoughts that you don't understand, ask questions. Conduct your own research to help you understand the depth of your increased intuitiveness. Position yourself to hear and to learn more about life by way of your thoughts.

To-Do's...
- ★ **Begin to make record of your intense thoughts.**
- ★ **Record the thoughts that come to you the most and note the dates when they occur.**
- ★ **Draw connections on how your thoughts readily apply to your life.**
- ★ **Guide your thoughts by deepening your mental awareness.**
- ★ **Guide your actions by respecting your thoughts.**

Say Aloud: I Will Respect My Thoughts! I Will Pay Attention!

September

> ## I Will RESPECT My VOICE!

The next time you find life pressing again, seek to impress yourself and positively EXPRESS yourself. Don't hold it in! Somebody needs to hear it. YOU need to hear it! Release the power of your voice by stating your declarations out loud! Release the power of your PURPOSE by not being afraid of your own voice!

Use your voice for empowerment—in both truth and wisdom—for the betterment of humanity. Speak good things out of your mouth, never evil. Your voice deserves that level of respect. YOU control the goodness of your voice and the goodness of your LIFE through how you use your voice.

For all negativity ever spoken to or *through* you, counteract it by releasing a constant stream of positivity from your mouth. Use your voice to optimize the pleasant power of your life!

Say Aloud: **I Will Respect My Voice! I Will Speak LIFE!!!**

Don't let the noise of others' opinions drown out your own inner voice.

STEVE JOBS

September

"I Will Not Fear ME!"

The easiest thing to be fearful of is yourself. That which we have the most knowledge of, the most command over, the most power to change is the very same thing that we find most unruly and messy! We are fearful of getting to know ourselves! Such knowledge requires shutting everyone else out and spending quiet time with ourselves long enough to be captain of our own ship! Personal awareness means being more introspective, being more accountable and being more patient. *And who wants to do that?!* HA! ☺

After getting over the *initial* hurdles of getting to know yourself, learning to love yourself and learning to love *on* yourself, you'll come to the BLISSFUL conclusion that you should've started last year!!! Self-love is the MOST valuable gift we give to ourselves—it's a gift that we spread with others relentlessly, throughout all eternity. Self-love erases fear of self because it removes doubt, pity and shame while creating great pride, dignity and tolerance.

Say Aloud: **I Will Not Fear ME! I Will Not Fear ME!**

Affirmation Journal
- ★ **What does it mean to fear myself?**
- ★ **How does it feel to fear myself?**
- ★ **How can my fear impact passionate pursuit of purpose?**

September

"

I Will LISTEN to Myself!

"

We hear best in silence.

Silence is when it's best to listen, so be sure that you create the proper environment to hear yourself. Listen also to the world around you to find life's answers to your pointed questions. To have command over yourself, you must listen to yourself.

To-Do's...

- ★ To listen to yourself, first accept, love and respect yourself. Focus on those things at all times.
- ★ Honor yourself by devoting worthwhile time to those tasks. You deserve it!
- ★ While completing practices of self-love, begin to ask pointed questions of yourself and let life show you the answers.
- ★ Journal your thoughts, questions and answers to guide your progression toward self-awareness.
- ★ Journal to release any pent up emotion.
- ★ When journaling, be guided by nothing more than the composition box. Empty yourself of *whatever* is needed.

He who cannot command himself should obey.
And many can command themselves,
but much is still lacking before they can obey themselves.

FRIEDRICH NIETZSCHE

September 21

> ## I Will Speak LIFE into Myself!

Positivism is GREAT, but what is positivism if you're not positive with YOURSELF! You can do all of the motivating and speaking *and* encouraging in the world, but it means NOTHING if you can't motivate, encourage and speak life to yourself!

Believe in yourself even if no one else does. Prove naysayers wrong! Prove *yourself* wrong! If you're down-talking and bad-mouthing yourself, that behavior has got to STOP! **NOW!!!** Don't use another sentence or negative word to put yourself down!

Speak positive affirmations out loud to yourself daily. That's what this book is all about! It isn't enough to simply repeat the affirmations in your mind. Make a practice of LOUDLY reaffirming yourself regularly to make positive self-talk part of your daily life!

Today's To-Do's...
★ List 3 positive reflections that you need to repeat to yourself daily.
★ Write them down in 3 places where you will see them daily.
★ Each time you see them, recite them out loud.
★ Update the reflections as needed.

Say Aloud: I Will Speak Life into Myself! I Will Be Positive!

September

> ## I Am AWARE!

Successful navigation through life mandates that we happily balance mental components with emotional ones while always prioritizing the spiritual. Understanding that our whole hearts consist of more than just emotion, we open ourselves up to spiritual concepts, and in turn, we are able to touch our souls.

Although it should be, self-awareness isn't a widely visited concept. Self-awareness is where we gain knowledge of our own capabilities including the internal power that we have to change life into EXACTLY what we will make it. Introspection is the way we begin.

Today's To-Do's...
- ★ **Reflect on the gains and losses that you've had.**
- ★ **Practice being intuitive enough to find the value in each.**

Say Aloud: **I Am Aware! I Find Value in My Own Power!**

I am the captain of my soul.

NELSON MANDELA

September 23

I Am PROGRESSIVE!

We put SO much time—wasted time—in endeavoring to change others when we should really put spare time into changing *ourselves*! When we change *our* postures, we change *our* lives! That's called PROGRESSION!

We live under the impression that EVERYONE should be just like us! Everyone should do as we do, think as we think and even PRAY as we pray!

"Let us—EVERYBODY—do the SAME thing," seems to be the overly opinionated faulty motto at times.

STOP THAT! Put ALL the spare time you have into bettering YOURSELF! If you're going to develop a lofty assessment of *anyone*, compose it regarding YOURSELF! Realize that you're not perfect—neither is anyone else. Put your efforts into simply doing the best YOU can with what YOU have! Don't waste time judging others when the best way you can help them is by being a progressive example!

You can change a person's life by simply providing unconditional love. More notably, you'll change your own life by simply embarking on such a journey. Be progressive enough to focus your energies in self-correction. In doing this, you'll find that you have little time to critique others.

Say Aloud: I Am Progressive! Progress Starts from Within!

September

I Am FULL of POSITIVE ENERGY!

Negative mindsets are completely limiting. As much as they limit us, they also limit those around us if we can't find ways to support, encourage or simply interact with the people in our environment. We get NOTHING accomplished when everything we see is negative. We get NOTHING accomplished when our viewpoints, our engagements and our behaviors are counteractive. By feeding into negativity, we create more of it.

Stop the cycle by releasing your positive energy. Kindle the flames of positive passion by altering your take on life. Your perspective within negative situations doesn't actually *have* to be negative. Put a positive spin on EVERY situation you encounter! Learn to shift your mindset IMMEDIATELY in every situation that doesn't sit well with you so that you can continually release positive energy into your life and into the lives of those around you. There is limited value in negativity so limit your perspective to one that is optimistically positive. Be positive and positive will be.

Say Aloud: **I Am Full of Positive Energy!**

Positive anything is better than negative nothing.

Elbert Hubbard

September

> ## I Am in Touch with My FEELINGS!

The problem with relationships is that, all too often, we don't allow people to relate to us. We keep them from connecting with us. We give them a mostly happy, seemingly positive, fairly upbeat shell of haphazardly tucked away emotions. This is not to say that we aren't being honest with them. In most cases, we're just not *sharing* with them. We're vulnerable without transparency.

We have taught ourselves to keep feelings where we think they're most secure: *within*. We keep our feelings where we think they're most respected: *with us*. We keep our feelings where we think they require no acknowledgment: *withheld*. Suppressing feelings in such a way interferes with our desire to lead full, rewarding lives.

Coach yourself to wholly embrace life by fully experiencing the emotions within. Being in touch with your feelings doesn't mean that you're *emotional*. It means that you won't encounter life void of the sense of feeling.

Empty lives contain little emotion. Full lives handle emotion within a manageable framework.

Affirmation Journal
- ★ Am I in touch with my feelings?
- ★ Which feelings do I allow? Which feelings do I block?
- ★ What is the difference?

September

" I Will Rule My Spirit BETTER! "

SO! We are becoming *one* with the feelings! We are feeling *all* the emotions! We are letting it *all* in. Woosah! Woosah! *In* come the feelings. *In* come the emotions. *In* come the memories and judgments and *Woosaaahhh*! **Woosah**! STOP!

How in the WORLD is it possible to be *one* with the feelings without being *emotional*?! We do that by ruling our spirit well! We can't let every little thing that comes our way, or every little—or BIG—emotion that we feel, wreck pure HAVOC on our souls! By becoming one with self, we face ourselves and others without being broken and without acting out of character.

No emotion that you feel will cause you to act out character once you learn how to manage your own spirit. Knowledge that you have control over nothing other than yourself places you in the BEST position to do just that!

Affirmation Journal
- ★ How well do I rule my spirit?
- ★ How can I rule my spirit better?
- ★ How can I change my life by ruling my spirit well?

*I am, indeed, a king,
because I know how to rule myself.*

PIETRO ARETINO

September 27

"

I Am RICH in PASSION!

"

Passion is our vulnerable expression of emotional energies. The fact that we are blessed with feeling means that each of our emotions should be expressed, yet feelings are exactly what we are afraid of because of the passionate vulnerabilities they open us to.

Don't be afraid of *feeling*! If you're going to love, love HARD. If you're upset, cry! In moderation, crying actually helps much more than it hurts. You have to learn not to be fearful of your emotions. Emotions are the BEST, most CLEAR sign of self-expression. If you're afraid of crying, you're afraid of love—don't be fearful of that which you long for the most! Be RICH in passion! Become ONE with the emotion! WORK IT!

There is absolutely NOTHING wrong with being passionate. The problem lies in displaying passion in nonproductive, outrageous ways. Express passion in favorable ways such as writing, exploring or exercising. Take the time to read if you need. Whatever you do, use your riches in passion for good. Never use passion in rage, anger or bitterness. As it relates to your goals, pursue them with all the emotional passion that they deserve. Be emotionally connected to the things you pursue. You'll find that this passion will help you GREATLY during times when you're discouraged or when sacrifices have to be made.

If you're going to be rich in anything, be rich in passion!

September

> ## I Will Keep the Fire of Passion BURNING for My Dream!

You don't lose sleep over it?! You don't dream about it?! You don't go out of your way for it?! I daresay: It's no PASSION of yours! It's not a friend, not a lover and not a GOAL of yours!!! Your COMMITMENT to a thing is *wholly* demonstrated by how you adjust your LIFE to make room for it. Made no adjustments? IT'S **NOT** LOVE!!! You'll lose sleep for jobs that you don't like and for tests that you *still* fail!!! HA!

So, I ask...

**What would you SACRIFICE
to see your DREAMS come true?**

...to see your PLANS come to pass? Nothing? Then again, I say to YOU, my friend, it's no goal of yours!

> *"Wide eyes lie open in the morning of night
> to see the best visions come to light."*
> — D NICOLE

Say Aloud: **I Keep the Fire of Passion Burning for My Dream!**

> *Hold fast to dreams,
> For if dreams die
> Life is a broken-winged bird,
> That cannot fly.*

LANGSTON HUGHES

September

" I Will Control My PASSION! "

People who present themselves as our adversaries are often perplexed, and sometimes further enraged, by our resolute peace during their expressive chaos. They want us to alter our fine character by being as disagreeable as they are in any given moment. They want us to get visibly outside of our comfort zone in a battle of irrationality. What they don't understand is that we have EVERYTHING to lose and NOTHING to gain by relinquishing complete control of ourselves to an unworthy opponent. They also mistakenly assume that peace amidst passion is a comfortable process—it is not—yet it is better to win in *peace* than to battle in passion!

Affirmation Journal
- ★ When was the last time I acted out of negative passion?
- ★ What was the result?
- ★ How do I now control my passion?
- ★ What has been the result?
- ★ Why is it always best to control my passion?

Say Aloud: I Will Control My Passion! I Am Full of Peace!

September

" I LOVE ME!!! "

Dr. Danetra Quarterman, my corporate mentor, would often chide, "**Look out for #1! Always look out for #1! Who is #1?**"

Keep yourself as your #1 priority! How can you *best* serve without *first* being whole and happy within? Healthy love for oneself is critical to living the BEST life! Self-love is an indispensable attribute that is needed to appreciate ALL that life offers. We must first love ourselves to fairly welcome and reciprocate the love of others.

In serving ourselves first, we learn to embrace selfless service to others. Wholeness allows internal love and appreciation to spill over with gracious abundance to a world in need. Other starting points for love threaten to leave #1 out of the equation—we unwittingly exclude ourselves from the love we seek. Until we love ourselves wholly, we can never fully *appreciate* love; we will have a hard time *discerning* love; and we will be too engrossed with *giving* love that we'll be unaware when love finds itself standing at our own front door.

Say Aloud: **I Love Me! I Am #1! I Will Always Look Out for #1!**

You are your best thing.

TONI MORRISON

Humility

October 1

> **I Will Work on HUMILITY!**

Our lives don't exist simply for the betterment of ourselves. By the same token, the people around us have MUCH to bring into our lives if we position ourselves to receive their blessed abundance.

In this season, we shift our focal point to people. We focus on being respectable humans as we coexist alongside others. Repositioning ourselves for growth requires *constant* concentration on humility. Humility affords us with a disposition best suited for giving and receiving—activities that increase our awareness of charitable equity within all humanity.

Humility Affirmation *(Repeat this aloud)*
Through humility, I have the courage to be selfless—I think of myself less. Humility shows my bravery, reverence and wisdom. I confront fear and doubt while refraining from despair. Humility is how I teach in love by faithfulness.

October highlights the importance of humility within our lives by showing the roles we must take on *for* ourselves *toward* others. In humbly serving others, we morally sharpen ourselves while increasing our personal and professional value, our vitality and our longevity.

Say Aloud: **I Will Work on Humility! I Will Increase My Value!**

October

"

I Will SACRIFICE!

"

Changes often come through much rigor and strife, the combination of which could be quickly summed up as sacrifice. Changes are often seen as sacrifice because adjustments aren't always wanted or even *needed* at times. Life is all about sacrifice—it's about making constant credible changes on a progressive continuum toward GREATNESS!

Success in life *requires* change—constant change—change that mandates humble sacrifice to see its reward. If you are to see the end results that you dream of, sacrifice should be constant and comfortable enough for you to remove any negative response that you have toward it. In fact, you should WELCOME sacrifice! Sacrificing means that you're humbly asserting yourself toward compelling growth.

Affirmation Journal
- ★ How do I feel about making sacrifices for myself?
- ★ How often do I practice making sacrifices for myself?
- ★ How do my lifelong sacrifices play into my future?

Say Aloud: **I Will Sacrifice! Sacrifice Makes Me Better!**

Sacrifice is a part of life. It's supposed to be.
It's not something to regret. It's something to aspire to.

MITCH ALBOM

October

"
I Will Not Fear OPPORTUNITY!
"

Opportunity abounds in life. Like love, and God, opportunity is everywhere and in ALL things. Opportunity is yours to find, yet you will NEVER be able to see opportunity through blinders of fear!

Affirmation Journal
- ★ How do I feel about opportunity?
- ★ How do I feel about fear?
- ★ How does fear impact opportunities that come my way?

Fear is stifling! It stands in the way of success based on your inability to see opportunity. You can't *see* what you can't *see*! Goals, and the attainment of dreams, ride on your ability to take advantage of opportunities that come your way daily. Ambitions can't be limited only to what you can create for yourself. You must be willing to see opportunity in *all* things and also be ambitious enough to subsequently create the life that you desire using the advancements presented to you. You can't see GRAND levels of success if you succumb to the boundaries of fear. The magnitude of your goals must always trump that of your fears!

Create goals that are powerful! Don't let fear impede your progress!

Say Aloud: I Will Not Fear Opportunity! I Will Not Fear!!!

October

> ## I Will Not Be ASHAMED!

Success can't be had without failure, and you can't learn from failure without embracing it. If you can't accept your mistakes, you can't learn from them, and if you can't learn, you can't teach. In that way, you make no progress at all!

Say Aloud: **I Will Not Be Ashamed! I Will Hold My Head High!**

People are more afraid of losing than they are of winning. The fear of losing is so great that people don't even *try*, so they lose EVERY single time! There is no success without much failure! Success isn't found by what is gained in the end—success is found along the path toward attainment:

> *"You know, Charlie Brown,*
> *they say we learn more from losing than from winning."*
> —LINUS VAN PELT

Failure is nothing to be ashamed of, so fail FORWARD with your head held HIGH and with the world at your feet! Be PROUD of the progress you've made understanding that failure is to be expected, AND appreciated, along the way!

> *A man should never be ashamed to own*
> *that he has been in the wrong,*
> *which is but saying in other words*
> *that he is wiser today than he was yesterday.*
>
> ALEXANDER POPE

October

"
I Am LISTENING!
"

Good listening is a skill very difficult to come by. Therefore, it's also difficult to master. Interestingly, there are a number of highly esteemed traits of success that could stand in the way of maintaining a productive listening ear. If you aren't proactive about keeping your ears meek and attentive, traits such as independence, decisiveness, prowess and more, could stand in the way of more effortless success found through acute listening.

Listening is a never-ending process—it NEVER stops. Listening involves much more than just your ears, so be proactive in listening even when you aren't *hearing* what is being said.

Exceptional listening requires full mental, emotional and spiritual participation which includes the involvement of your senses, your experiences and your personal awareness.

Affirmation Journal
★ How effective am I at listening?
★ How can I be better at listening?
★ Why is it important for me to become a better listener?

Say Aloud: I Am Listening! I Listen with My Senses and Skills!

October

"

I Am a LEADER!

"

YOU Are a LEADER!

You are a trailblazer! Once you realize the extent of your POWER as a tastemaker, channel that energy into profitable endeavors that further drive progressive enterprise! Let your leadership skill be evident in ALL that your hands touch! Let your thoughts, dreams and visions inspire others to *be* and to *do* their BEST!

Say Aloud: **I Am a Leader! I Inspire Others to *Be* the BEST!**

It's EXCITING to be an inspiration, a role model, a mentor, a leader, an exhorter or a COACH! It's EXCITING to help others achieve goals, dreams and business success!!! Find out what makes YOU excited about being a leader and do THAT! Do it richly and lovingly, with pride, and in competence. Be excited about imparting your knowledge to others using actionable means. No matter how far your progress as a leader, always, always, **ALWAYS** remain COMPLETELY humble!

The challenge of leadership is to be strong, but not rude;
be kind, but not weak; be bold, but not bully;
be thoughtful, but not lazy; be humble, but not timid;
be proud, but not arrogant;
have humor, but without folly.

JIM ROHN

October 7

I Will Be a GREAT Example!

Great leadership is found in great stewardship—the BEST leaders lead *themselves* first! They show command of leadership through how they purportedly guide their own lives. True leaders don't have to be formally asked to take positions of leadership—they default to head roles without specific instruction to do so. The lifestyle of a leader demonstrates fitness for authoritative roles through influential stewardship.

Affirmation Journal
★ How great of an example am I?
★ What does my lifestyle exemplify to others?
★ How do I show leadership within my example?

Let your lifestyle lead others onto *right* paths. Be a worthy example of success, perseverance and happiness in the face of all opportunity. Be humble in your efforts and in your presentation of yourself while being BOLD enough to inspire compelling courage within others. Don't be afraid to show the world what you're made of! Be a fine example. Lead with an upright lifestyle that boasts wholeness.

Say Aloud: **I Will Be a Great Example! I Will *Show* Leadership!**

October

> ## I Am a TEACHER!

Most people are masters of *telling*. They are masters of directing. They have ALL the best advice to give because they know what EVERYONE else is doing *wrong*. There are entirely too many people who are unafraid to share these unsolicited, misguided opinions. This means trouble!

Instead of freely *telling* so much, be a master of *showing*. The GREAT examples that you find in life are those who are masters of *doing*. They are the people who you never have to *ask* what they are doing—anything that they do is always very readily apparent, without question. Be one of those. Be the type of person who doesn't just *talk*—be a person who *does*. Teach others by the way that you *live*. Teach others by the way that you *show*. Teach others by the way that you DO.

You are a teacher!

Affirmation Journal
- **Am I a master of *telling* OR Am I a master of *doing*?**
- **How well do I teach others by my own actions?**
- **How can I be better at teaching by example?**

Say Aloud: **I Am a Teacher! I Teach By Showing and Doing!**

The mediocre teacher tells. The good teacher explains.
The superior teacher demonstrates.
The great teacher inspires.

WILLIAM ARTHUR WARD

October

"My Life is An EXAMPLE!"

Is your life a good example to others? Are you proud of all you have to offer? Do you share your gifts with others regardless of their willingness to receive? How great are you at stewardship?

These questions, and others, will help you measure your level of unspoken leadership within your circles. If you're unafraid to be who you are, and if you readily show yourself as an effective manager of *yourself*, you're already in place to effectively lead and guide others. Your example of goodness is already apparent through the way that you guide your own actions.

Shared life experiences benefit others who might someday decide to partake in similar journeys as yours. Even without someone else taking the exact route as yours, your personal courage motivates them to be great in their individual aspirations, so how great of an example are you?

Affirmation Journal
- ★ What type of example do others see in me?
- ★ How great am I at stewardship?
- ★ How can I become a better example?

Say Aloud: My Life is An Example! I Share Life with Others!

October

" I Will PRACTICE What I Teach! "

When viewing your life, others learn from your example. If you demonstrate positive traits, positivity is what they gain. If you demonstrate negative traits, negativity is what they gain. Through simply observing your life, there are those within your environment who eventually become pupils of what you have to teach. Through your teachings, you express your take on life based on your personal experience on a number of topics. Using various methods, you deliver to them what you have to give in the form of solicited and unsolicited advice.

Ask yourself, **"In all of my advising, am I *learning*? Am I making use of the teachings that I dole out to others?"**

Are you? Are you using what you have on yourself first? Is all of your teaching falling—lost on your own deaf ears?

To be a GREAT leader, lead by example—practice what you teach. Don't be so big on advising that you forget to test theories on yourself first. You are your own best pupil!

Say Aloud: **I Will Practice What I Teach and Lead By Example!**

The way to get started is to quit talking and begin doing.

WALT DISNEY COMPANY

October

" I Am THANKFUL for Support! "

The best support you EVER receive is the support you didn't ask for! Support—no matter the shape, size or format—should always be sincerely appreciated and equally rendered as much as possible. Don't support only those who support your or only those who you *want* to support. Put pride to the side and support others because it's the RIGHT thing to do!

Sometimes, great support seems as hard to come by as great workers. *(This is especially true if you'd like that support to be great workers!* ☺*)* Support, through *any* means, is ALWAYS to be praised and acknowledged! Be thankful for all that's been afforded to you by way of friends, family members, associates and even strangers who've gone the extra mile to help you! Show them how grateful you are and welcome their support well into the future.

Say Aloud: **I Am Thankful for Support!**

Many times, you don't *have* support because you don't *see* support in all of the many ways that it presents itself. Don't overlook what's already being readily given to you. You may be looking in the wrong places for what you already have in sincere abundance! Be humble and be grateful for what you have. Thank others for supporting you!

October

> **I Will Not Fear GREATNESS!**

The entrepreneurially minded will NEVER be content with working on someone else's job! Leaders don't remain followers for long. Those aiming for GREATNESS feel anxious amidst mediocrity. Whatever *your* brand of courage,

DO NOT FEAR!!!

Don't fear the GREATNESS within you, and don't fear the greatness of those around you! Let NOTHING about success intimidate you—be MOTIVATED by it! Be encouraged by progress and by new ways of thinking! Don't settle for mediocrity! Don't pick up mediocre habits and accept them as yours. Rid yourself of self-imposed limits, and be *free* in the knowledge that you're as GREAT as you *think* yourself to be!

Affirmation Journal
- ★ How great am I? How great can I be?
- ★ What scares me about greatness?
- ★ What are my self-imposed limits?

Say Aloud: I Will Not Fear Greatness! I *AM* GREATNESS!

Have no fear of perfection—you'll never reach it.

Salvador Dalí

October 13

I Will HONOR My Friends!

Friends are lifelong companions. Whether close to them in distance or in emotion, friends are lifelong support systems. They are the people you talk to when you tire of talking to yourself. When friends aren't around, you miss their presence because you enjoy having someone to share your life with—your life feels empty without them.

Through honoring friends, you show them the love and appreciation that you have for them. As much as they mean to you, friends should ALWAYS be reminded of the joy they bring! Friendships are your practice field for self-expression, communication and healthy display of feelings. In consideration of all they do for you, your friends should KNOW that they are one of the highlights of your life! This should be evident through how you honor and respect them.

Affirmation Journal
- ★ How well do I respect my friends?
- ★ How do I show my friends that I appreciate and admire them?
- ★ What can I do regularly to show honor to my friends?

Appreciation for your friends should go without saying. This isn't to say that appreciation shouldn't be shown.

Honor your friends—*show* them your love!

October

"
I Will CHERISH Friendship!
"

Friends are the brothers and sisters that you have the grand fortune of choosing! They are your saving grace, your sounding board, your sidekicks and your BRAINS—friends are partners! Friends are one of the most cherished accomplishments you will ever have in life, yet you don't always let 'em know!

Friends are your reminder that you made it—they help you celebrate all that you are and all that you will come to be! Friends keep you honest. They help you live the BEST life! When life doesn't go as planned, friends are there to help you clean up the mess and move forward with dignity!

What would you do without friends?! You might've stayed out of some trouble if it weren't for your friends, but that would give you less stories to tell and far less laughs to share!

Remember ALL that your friends have been for you.

Cherish the joy that they bring into your life!

Affirmation Journal
- ★ **What do my friends mean to me?**
- ★ **How have my friends added to the joy of my life?**

Don't walk behind me; I may not lead.
Don't walk in front of me; I may not follow.
Just walk beside me and be my friend.

ALBERT CAMUS

October

15

> **I Will HONOR My Family!**

Families are your lifelong support system. Whether you want them to or not, they stick by you through thick and thin. Through your family, you find your initial identity. You formulate your foundational outlook on life based on familial interactions. There is much about your internal and external make-up that you owe directly to your family. Your family is the great foundational measure through which you assess your past and launch your future. For this and more, show them honor.

Your family is honored in how you carry yourself and by how you serve your community and others. You honor your family through your values and exhibitions of solid moral character. Honor toward your family is shown through awareness of family history, linkages and continued connections to loved ones. You honor your family by raising a family of your own that you can be proud of as you share stories passed down through the generations to come.

Say Aloud: I Will Honor My Family!

Affirmation Journal
- ★ Why is it important to honor my family?
- ★ In what ways do I show honor to my family?
- ★ How can I be better about honoring my family?

October

I Will CHERISH Family!

Cherish your family because of your personal make up. Your family helps to mold and shape you into who you are as an individual. They are your listening ears who serve as mirrors into your soul. Many fantastic things can be said about your family and what each individual member is for you. In gratitude, cherish your family for being your first friends and for being the most dependable builders of your character.

Families best teach most things you know about the world!

Today's To-Do's...

- ★ List the 10 family members that you most cherish.
- ★ Through the remainder of this month, contact each of these family members.
- ★ Let each of them know *exactly* what they mean to you.
- ★ RECOMMENDATION: Compose a hand-written letter to be delivered to each of them. Mail the letters.
- ★ Include an envelop and postage within each letter in hopes that your family members write to you in return.

Say Aloud: I Will Cherish My Family!

*When everything goes to hell,
the people who stand by you without flinching—
they are your family.*

JIM BUTCHER

October 17

"
I Will CHERISH Others!
"

You don't have to grow through the same experiences as others to value what they've been through. You don't have to encounter the same situations as others to accept their lives. All you need is respect for them as human beings in order to appreciate what others have to offer. The value in others can easily be assessed by a simple review of your own life. Despite language, societal and racial barriers, *everyone* shares similar experiences through generations cross culturally.

Appreciation for another comes from a deep-seated respect for *yourself*. You may not wear the same clothes, have the same lifestyle or even speak the same tongue, but each person shares some similar life experience as you. You don't have to walk a mile in another's shoes to know their pain— your own feet hurt much the same. *Everyone* feels emotions. *Everyone* has pains, and *everyone* seeks love!

Cherish the people around you—not because of what they have to give. Cherish them simply for who they are.

Say Aloud: I Will Cherish Others! I Respect Their Experience!

October

"
I Will CHERISH Diversity!
"

Life presents an ENDLESS spectrum of creativity in the variety of diversification that you are blessed to behold! Through color, culture and creed you have the grand fortune of learning in a number of ways by intermingling your unique frameworks with the diversity of others.

Diversity broadens the horizons of all participants through the platform of inclusion. Newness is welcomed and accepted with the goal of blended growth. Lack of diversity imposes limits on all since there is no new gain in old insights without a varied vantage points. Rules, because of the limits they create, commonly stifle creative variety, diversity of thought and diversity of approach. In diversity, everyone brings their own voice, their own thought process and their own methodology to the table.

There are no rules within diversity, so it is LIMITLESS—without walls, without structure and without boundaries. This makes the possibilities ENDLESS!

Say Aloud: I Will Cherish Diversity!

Christian, Jew, Muslim, shaman, Zoroastrian, stone, ground, mountain, river, each has a secret way of being with the mystery, unique and not to be judged.

RUMI

October

"

I Will Seek Out Others for Constructive Feedback!

"

When requesting feedback for growth, it's wise to ask not only those closest to you, but also those who challenge you—both currently and within your chosen future.

One aspect of my certification to become a Life Coach Trainer required that I petition others for feedback. I received GREAT feedback! It was ALL positive! I had to delve deeper to find feedback that would help me to solidify the great output that I was already receiving. I asked for specifics that would help me to *improve*: **Actionable Feedback!**

Regularly Request Feedback from At Least Five Others

- ★ If you are married or dating, ask your mate.
- ★ If you are a parent, ask your child(ren).
- ★ If you are an entrepreneur, ask a new client and an old client. Ask your worst—yes, WORST—and best clients.
- ★ If you are a student, ask a teacher. If you are a college student, ask someone in the field you aspire to.
- ★ Ask someone who has known you for your entire life, and ask someone you just met.
- ★ Ask someone you haven't spoken to in a while.
- ★ If you have joined a new organization, ask the founding members and the newest members.
- ★ Finally, and most importantly, always, always, ALWAYS ask someone who intimidates you.

You never quite know how you're perceived until you ask! This then empowers you to raise the bar to the next level!

October

"
I Will HONOR My Mentors!
"

Mentoring is easily one of the most exciting opportunities in the world! Who wouldn't want to *lovingly* impart EXPERTISE about life, love and the pursuit of happiness to an eager listening ear for an extended period of time?! **EXACTLY!** EVERYONE wants this cherished opportunity, so for ALL who have been blessed to carry the title *mentor*:

KUDOS TO YOU for A Job Well Done!!!

Mentors are EVERYTHING! You confide in them. You learn from them, and you LOVE them for being cherished models in life! Mentors make you better! They willingly show you the ropes and commonly enable you to skip some steps where you might otherwise slip up. Mentors make life a tad bit easier because they support you when you fall and they encourage you where you lack—they help you to believe in yourself! What has your mentor done for you lately? Thank them for it ALL! Honor them however you can!

Affirmation Journal
- ★ How have my mentors helped me over the years?
- ★ How do I honor my mentors?

*I am not a teacher,
but an awakener.*

ROBERT FROST

October 21

" I Will Value SELF-EXAMINATION! "

In putting yourself in the BEST position to move forward within the realms of GREATNESS, it's always in your best interest to not only quiet yourself enough to *listen* to others, but to also go to necessary lengths to continuously solicit the *feedback* of others. The hope is that you come across actionable input that propels you to *be* and to *do* better as an individual and also as a leader within your respective roles and communities.

Without proper input from all relevant sources, self-examinations are lacking. Soul-searching self-examination have benefits that will far exceed the common thoughts you have about yourself no matter their frequency. Introspection requires time, adequate input and willingness to break the molds in order to find viable resolutions. Profitable self-examination is an unceasing process. New information is readily applied to find further insight while building onto foundations that have already laid over time.

Affirmation Journal
- ★ When did I last conduct a thorough self-examination?
- ★ What factors should I consider during introspection?
- ★ How frequently will I commit to self-examination?

Say Aloud: **I Will Value Constant Self-Examination!**

October

> **I Will HUMBLE Myself!**

"We *have* not because we *ask* not!"

That is a fact! The most basic things you could EVER ask for are often just immediately beyond your awareness *or* they are beyond your acceptance. Many times, you can *see* exactly what you desire—you perceive it, yet you are blind to asking and even more blind to receiving! You limit yourself by your own lack of humility, acceptance and appreciation!

GET OUT OF YOUR OWN WAY!!!!

Sometimes, you have NOTHING because you ask NOTHING of those right beside you!

Affirmation Journal
- ★ What am I standing in the way of?
- ★ What am I asking for without being humble to receive?

Be a master of giving and receiving! Be a master of *getting out of your own way* long enough to get what you've desired all along. BE HUMBLE!

Humble yourself enough to do something that makes you proud!

A great man is always willing to be little.

RALPH WALDO EMERSON

October 23

" I Will HONOR My Parents! "

To honor your parents is to accept them for who *they* are and to also appreciate them for who *you* are. Honor your parents—not simply in thanks for what they've done for you but also in acknowledgment for their help in shaping you into the individual that you've become. Thank them through your efforts, in your successes and with the recognition that you were created as a product of their own personal encounters with life.

In love, and with sincere gratitude for your life, always embrace the utmost joy in consideration of showing your parents the honor due them. Whether they be good or bad parents, rich or poor parents, alive or with you no more, parents are to you a great many things. They are life-givers, and for this, you owe them your ALL.

Affirmation Journal
- ★ **In what ways do I show honor to my parents?**
- ★ **Why do my parents deserve honor?**
- ★ **How could I better show honor to my parents?**

Say Aloud: **I Will Honor My Parents!**

October

" I Will Look to Others for HELP! "

No one ever said that success is a journey to be taken alone! Don't be afraid to ask for help! Find at least one person around you, whom you respect—a person who silently motivates you—and ask that person for HELP!!! If you can't find someone to depend on, you will NOT succeed because at the very least, you must *first* be able to depend on yourself!

Don't make the foul decision to be invariably self-sufficient. You *may* believe that self-sufficiency is a prided characteristic of culture, race, gender, generation and related groups. While independence *is* a grand trait to possess, being too self-reliant can produce stagnancy, stubbornness and pride. Without the inclusion of outside input, you will find yourself backed up against a wall not knowing *how* to ask for help when you *need* it MOST! *(TRUST ME on this one!!!)* In other instances, you will ask for help and have absolutely NO clue how to use it! Make a commitment NOW to learn the value in asking for and *receiving* help!!!

Say Aloud: **I Will Look to Others for Help! I Will Receive Well!**

It is unwise to be too sure of one's own wisdom.
It is healthy to be reminded that the strongest might weaken
and the wisest might err.

MAHATMA GANDHI

October

"

I Will LISTEN!

"

Many people suffer greatly from the disease of closing out the thoughts and ideas of others *and* also from feeling the need to constantly vocalize our own. Everyone wants to do ALL the talking—no one wants to stop and listen.

One main component of listening is that you must first learn to quiet yourself so that you're in the best position to fully hear and comprehend. This isn't to say that you shouldn't vocalize your interests—beyond simply expressing ourselves, you must exercise wisdom in timing and presentation of feedback.

Self-empowerment involves more than just *self*. It requires the inclusion of people and processes within our environment. Others may have very valuable things to express to you, so don't be afraid to seek out, *and* respect, the input of another. Without listening to those around you and paying attention to your environment, you won't be readily able to position yourself for greatest impact.

Affirmation Journal
- ★ In what areas of my life can I stand to do more listening?
- ★ Besides people, what other things should I listen to?
- ★ How can I learn to quiet myself and listen better?

Say Aloud: **I Will Change! I Will Listen and Maximize Impact!**

October

" I Will LISTEN with My WHOLE Heart! "

Listening isn't a characteristic that should ever be taken lightly because it's your looking glass into the world. You listen with your ears, your eyes and the rest of your senses. Anyone seeking to be a grossly effective listener learns to also listen with their heart.

Bringing your heart into the equation makes use of the listening senses all the more impactful. When you listen with your heart, you not only listen to hear, but you listen to lead and impact change within *any* situation. Pure hearts are the best listeners, so it's recommended that you listen to *understand* versus merely listening to *respond*. Pure listening ears should be impartial and without judgment, seeking nothing more than clarity and understanding. Come from a place of openness, integrity and wisdom as you tend to the thoughts of others.

Affirmation Journal
★ What does it mean to listen with my heart?
★ What can I gain from life by listening more thoroughly?

Say Aloud: **I Will Listen Thoroughly, with My Whole Heart!**

The best listeners listen between the lines.

NINA MALKIN

October 27

"I Will Consistently Support an Entrepreneur!"

Many lack the desire and good sense needed to consistently support others in joy and humility. Some wrongly feel that others must be *deserving* of support or that they must *do* something widely "impressive" for support to be justified. Don't sit on the sidelines justifying your own lack of action! Non-supportive people are all too ready to lend a listening ear when other people fail because of... YOU GUESSED IT: Lack of Support! **What a world!**

Entrepreneurs DESERVE your support! Entrepreneurs DESERVE for you to show how proud you are of them for boldly venturing out on their own. They deserve it, not because someone says so, but because they NEED it!

Just the same as anyone else, courageous people need to be reminded that someone cares! They need pats on the back the same as anyone else, if not MORE so! It gets lonely at the top! That's a fact.

Don't allow the entrepreneurs around you to feel lonely. Show them just how proud you are by supporting them through whatever means you can.

Affirmation Journal
- ★ Which entrepreneurs within my network make me proud? Do they know that I am proud of them?
- ★ How have I shown them my support in the past?
- ★ How can I regularly show them my support in the future?

October

“

I Will Consistently Support a Worthy Cause!

”

Ever-changing attitudes dictate the persons, products and platforms that people will—and will not—support. If people won't support each other, what then, will they do? How will they encourage not only the person or platform in question, but how will this behavior encourage more leaders to venture out with their own products and platforms?

Support others because their causes deserve it! Their courage deserves it. *They* deserve it and *you* deserve it! Your measures of support have far-reaching implications for the future of society, for your communities and for your family. Furthermore, the support you show to others facilitates lasting feelings of goodness within.

Who have you supported lately?

Affirmation Journal
- ★ **What worthy cause have I supported lately? Why?**
- ★ **What worthy cause would I like to support? Why?**
- ★ **What do my personal contributions do for these causes?**
- ★ **What do my contributions to these causes do for me?**

Say Aloud: **I Will Consistently Support a Worthy Cause!**

When I do good, I feel good.
When I do bad, I feel bad.
That's my religion.

ABRAHAM LINCOLN

October 29

" I Will CHERISH Growth! "

Life gives you hurdles. Life gives you *many* hurdles. With these hurdles come pain, loss and disappointment. You *will* cry at times—it hurts, but you live to see another day!

Unfortunately, you might sometimes find yourself repeating the same experiences multiple times. You miss the message anytime our pain is too unbearable for you to self-reflect. You miss the message when you work *around* situations instead of working *through* them. You miss the message each time you deny the existence of a problem and your role within its solution *and* cause.

Don't continue to miss messages. Take ownership of issues and face them HEAD-ON!

Though the hurt and burdens are yours to bear, there is growth potential within each and every moment. Cherish that growth! You face HUGE frustration if you find yourself repeating the toughest lessons. Your happiness isn't worth losing because of your lack of actionable awareness, so be present in EVERY moment! Look forward to the growth that even pain can bring.

Say Aloud: **I Will Cherish Growth! I Will Be Actionably Aware!**

October

" I Will Be BETTER! "

Say Aloud: **I Will Be Better! I Will Make Personal Progress!**

Some people LOVE to join in the ebb and flow of political debates and social movements. Some LOVE to passionately participate in the *current* current events! People throw around lofty statements regarding what needs to be done to do *this* and changed about *that* within our world, within our society or even within our dying solar system!!! Some people take joy in fighting for, or *against*, movements that have absolutely NOTHING to do with them! **NOTHING!**

The BEST place to start movements for social betterment is *within*! If YOU want to change something, start first with *yourself*! Don't sit back and wait for a willing example of progressive stewardship—be your own example! While you may not always be able to immediately evoke change in life, you *will* always be able to aggressively change yourself!

Say Aloud: **I Will Be Better! I Will Change NOW!**

Change Your Posture! Change Your LIFE!

Don't wish it were easier.
Wish you were better.

JIM ROHN

October 31

"

I Will Be HUMBLE!

"

You can travel many places in life yet you go NOWHERE if you travel without humility. You could accomplish a great number of goals yet you accomplish NOTHING without humility. You may transcend awareness of varied thought yet you know NOTHING without humility.

Do you gain *anything* out of this world if humility doesn't accompany you along the way? What have you gained without humility as the reward? NOTHING!

You are NOTHING without humility in your firm grasp!

Never place yourself above anyone but *yourself*! You are only better than the person that YOU were yesterday. Aspire to be as great as YOUR fullest potential—once you arrive at the top, consider yourself above no one. Keep yourself mentally aware of the process that you underwent to embrace the life that you have. Remember the most humbling experiences of your life, and let those be remind you of your humanity—of your kinship with those who are still on their own personal journey to greatness.

Say Aloud: **I Will Be Humble! I Will Reach FULL Potential!**

On the highest throne in the world,
we still sit only on our own bottom.

MICHEL DE MONTAIGNE

Kindness

November 1

"

I Will Work on KINDNESS!

"

Kindness is an expression of goodness toward others. It's a showing of high regard for people you come in contact with.

Kindness Affirmation *(Repeat this aloud)*
To be kind is to act for the good of other people at all times. Through kindness and respect, I show myself useful and fit. I adapt myself in servitude and sweetness, exhibiting compassion and sympathy with no sign of abrasiveness.

To the beautiful people who cross your path, may you fill their days with many many hugs and kisses, much fun, laughter and boatloads of AWESOMENESS! Words alone can't always sufficiently express how much people mean to you, but you can let them know you're thankful through random acts of kindness.

November is focused on kindness and your displays of gentleness and tenderheartedness toward others. We review methods of kindness which enable you to go even further in your aim to be a model of kindness.

Say Aloud: **I Will Work on Kindness! I Will Be Kind!**

November

"

I Will CHANGE My ATTITUDE!

"

Face it—life can be tough!!! You face so many battles and so many circumstances that can break you down if you encounter them with the wrong attitude. As you grow and evolve, so too do your attitudes. Attitudes are a reflection of your experiences. They show progressive evolution toward a more positive direction.

It's always said that if you want something you've never had, you must do things you've never done. As you drift away from former friends as you *grow* your separate ways, you should also be drifting FAR away from your former SELF! With everything around you constantly changing, how can you possibly stay the same?

Say Aloud: **I Will Change My Attitude! I Will Change My Life!**

A renewed attitude comes with renewed focus, a renewed mentality and abundance of new hope! Life looks MUCH brighter once the viewing lens is changed.

Your attitude is like a box of crayons that color your world. Constantly color your picture gray, and your picture will always be bleak. Try adding some bright colors to the picture by including humor, and your picture begins to lighten up.

ALLEN KLEIN

November

"

I Will LISTEN to Others!

"

Within the world, there exists the illogical idea that a person's status, position, role or *lack* of status, position or role removes their right to an opinion. Au contraire! The fact that a person does *not* hold a certain role MANDATES their right to an opinion! Why? This is a DEMOCRACY!!! Opinions are STANDARD! Your very own LIFE is a democracy being that it is SO governed by the popular opinion—albeit the popular opinion may rightfully be your *own*!!! ☺

Don't readily dismiss the input of other individuals. Considering the fact that a person cares enough about you to even *share* their input shows their concern, their thought and their simple acknowledgment of your presence within their lives. *You should be grateful!* The people who care the MOST are likely identical to the ones who *talk* the most. Learn to listen! As freely as you volunteer and impart your own "wisdom" to others, be as apt to hear what others have to say to you in return! Admittedly, all of the feedback that you receive may not be applicable—that's perfectly fine within this context! Today's affirmation is about the basis of *listening* moreso than proper application technique!

Make a practice of listening to understand versus merely listening to respond.

Say Aloud: I Will Listen to Others! I Will Listen to Understand!

November

" I Will Be PEACEFUL! "

Peace in your life is a concept that you must be proactive about. You can't sit around and *wait* for peace to find you! You have to CREATE peace in *every* moment and *every* second of *every* day!

Being peaceful means coming from a place of balance and wholeness. It means existing in a framework where all is well *within* you no matter what is happening *around* you. Since you can't control your outside environment, you must constantly arm yourself with the ability to stay calm on the *inside*.

Peace is your safety net. Peace is your sanity when all else has gone COMPLETELY insane. Prioritize peace in life. Without it, you will soon find that the rest of life's luxuries amount to little without peace as their constant companion.

Be peaceful! No matter what life brings your way, commit yourself to peaceful resolve.

Say Aloud: **I Will Be Peaceful!**

*Circumstances are beyond human control,
but our conduct is in our own power.*

BENJAMIN DISRAELI

November

"I Will Be a Better FRIEND!"

Being a better friend means learning to listen when your friends aren't audibly speaking. It means learning to see what isn't readily obvious. It means being more for them than you'd have them to be for you. The BEST friends are those who are selfless—those who don't allow limitations of the title to keep them from showing brotherly or sisterly love to all who are accepted as kindred spirits. Operation within the role of *friend* is a privilege that should never be taken lightly.

Friendship is a great honor to bestow and behold. Friends are the sisters and brothers that you get to choose. Readily embrace them as such by happily welcoming friends into your world.

Appreciation for friendship is best shown by returning the favor. People sometimes make the mistake of letting misunderstandings, distance or other insignificant factors interfere with the progression of friendships. Great friends are one of the most valued treasures on earth, so it is in your best interest to forgive and forget all wrongdoings in situations that are worthy of continuation. Friends add so much value to your life that *letting go* shouldn't always be as easy as you make it. The same goes for you—*walking away* from friends shouldn't be an easy thing to do. Sometimes, you just need to tough it out. In some friendships, you need to commit as a sister or a brother rather than just as a friend.

November

"

I Will Let My Light SHINE!

"

My personal meditation, prayer and relaxation practices often involve candles. For me, candles represent peace, reverence and adoration. Candles are a representation of shine, brilliance and light. During any of the aforementioned processes, I am reminded to let my light shine, and no matter what I am *growing* through, this reminder brings me peace.

I recommend this process for *anyone* struggling with *anything*. Just light a candle. No need to watch it. Go about your day and *see* GOD move!!!

Candles are regularly lit at various times for various reasons. Going forward, light candles for yourself remembering that you've been given something to share with others. Your light is a gift to the world. It should be shared at all times possible—even when you don't feel like it! Whenever you can, **SHINE YOUR LIGHT!**

Know that YOU are a gift to the world. YOU are in GOD's hands. Be a ready representation of God's grace by letting your light so shine!

Say Aloud: **I Will Let My Light Shine! I Embody God's Grace!**

Keep your face to the sunshine and you cannot see a shadow.

HELEN KELLER

November

"I Will RESPECT My Partner!"

Too many relationships come together without respect. People exist within fiery frameworks where there is no mutual honor, loyalty or high regard for the other party involved. This is **COMPLETELY** unacceptable! Of all that you owe any other human being—especially those with whom you've chosen to share your lives—respect is MOST vital. A standard of respect creates the foundation for all other positive attributes to be appropriately developed and sustained.

Your engagements are a direct reflection of how you view yourself. If you decide to withhold honor, loyalty and respect from yourself, be responsible enough not to involve the unsuspecting in your own damaging exploits.

Respecting your partner means exhibiting timeless love and honor that is free from limitations. The decisions you make regarding them shouldn't feel like sacrifices. You should be more than happy to take EVERY opportunity to ensure your partner knows that you appreciate them and their love.

Affirmation Journal
- ★ In what areas am I lacking respect *from* my partner?
- ★ In what areas am I lacking respect *for* my partner?
- ★ In what ways can I show more respect for my partner?
- ★ How can I implement necessary changes?

November

> **I Will SMILE!**

Smiles are blessings. Laughter is a gift. Why not share the JOY of those pleasantries with others? Each time that you do, you are not only blessing others by sharing your gift but you are also honoring God. You reap what you sow, so sharing something as simple as a smile gains you happiness—a shared moment of internal joy!

Each of your engagements presents you with the opportunity to share various gifts of happiness with those around you. You can effortlessly change your environments by always wearing a smile on your face and by leaving laughter upon lips.

Thinking positive is not just about altering your thoughts. Positive thinking is inclusive of your actions, your deeds and your behaviors. You must *be* and also *do* positive within your life. If we can't first change your thoughts, you can always adjust your behaviors and *behave* things into existence.

Happiness and laughter first start with a smile.

Focus today on trailblazing with your smile!

Say Aloud: I Will Smile! I Will Laugh! I Will Be Happy!

I've got nothing to do today but smile.

PAUL SIMON

November

" I Will RESPECT Others! "

Respect for another human being isn't *optional*.

Respect is REQUIRED!!!

Existence alongside others is just cause for you to esteem them as highly as you esteem yourself. You should regard yourself *so* highly that your respect for all others is readily apparent. In happiness, show your respect for others by way of admiration, honor and patience.

Affirmation Journal
- **In what ways do I show respect for others?**
- **In what ways am I lacking in showing respect for others?**
- **What will it take for me to better respect others?**

Self-respect spills over into general respect for all mankind. Value yourself highly enough that your own esteem compels you to treat others with the utmost regard. If ever you become weary, stop in the moment and remind yourself that no one is worth you losing your self-respect over. Continually grow in love for yourself and bountifully apply the same to others.

Say Aloud: **I Will Respect Myself! I Will Respect Others!**

November

"I Will SERVE!"

Service starts with humility. It's about honoring others with your assistance, your time and your resources. Service is about giving back while paying it forward. Your community deserves your services for all that it has taught you and allowed you to be. Acts of service demonstrate gratitude. What better way to show thanks than to help out?

This world deserves your services for all that it has been for you. Locally, you can join or create programs within your community that promote service, unity and betterment. Personally, you can mentor, volunteer and support those within your social environments. Professionally, you have the opportunity to participate in the efforts of your workforce to create friendly, profitable and knowledgeable work environments.

Affirmation Journal
- ★ How do I serve?
- ★ How will I serve better/more in the future?
- ★ What does my act of service do for others?

Say Aloud: **I Will Serve! I Will Give Back to Others!**

True humility is not thinking less of yourself;
it is thinking of yourself less.

C.S. LEWIS

November

" I Will Be USEFUL to Others! "

Having a fear of commitment is synonymous with having fear of SELF! Most people don't commit because they don't want to be counted on by others. They don't want to have anyone depending on their performance, which may not always be *great* at any given time. Instead of committing, they choose the lesser evil: being elusive and noncommittal. These fears are rarely, if EVER, about anyone other than *self*.

In order for YOU to be useful to others, remove the fears associated with commitment. There is no failure in commitment—there is only growth. Your life is fruitless if you don't share what you've been given. It's your job to plant seeds that grow into lifelong harvest for the benefit of all.

Being useful to others is as simple as using what we've been given.

What have YOU been given?

Affirmation Journal
- ★ **What do I have that is useful to others?**
- ★ **How do I give using what I have?**
- ★ **How does my usefulness help me in return?**

Say Aloud: I Will Be Useful to Others! I Use What I Have!

November

" I Will Be a RESOURCE for Others! "

In all of your giving and serving and helping, you will find that the BEST thing you can EVER be to others is a resource. You don't have to be the person with ALL of the answers, but if people know that in you they have an invaluable treasure, they will want to connect with you both personally and professionally time and time again!

Resourcefulness is a timeless skill. By being proficient you not only service the needs of others, but you are well fit to obtain exactly what you need for *yourself*! Such adeptness takes you FAR in life as others will quickly see how shrewd you are based on your tenacious approach to EVERYTHING! You will be an inspiration who is well supported by all who are blessed to crossed your path!

Affirmation Journal
★ How resourceful am I?
★ How have others viewed me as a resource?
★ How do I use my resourcefulness to my own benefit?

Say Aloud: **I Will Be a Resource for Others!**

*A man of words and not of deeds
is like a garden full of weeds.*

ENGLISH PROVERB

November 13

> ## I LEAD!!!

You are a leader! You are reading this book, so you already lead! **GREAT JOB!** Being the leader that you are, always be mindful to stay leadership-focused despite life. Don't ever allow life to get the upper hand in such a way that you fall from the good graces of your role as a leader! Followers follow because of the values consistent with leadership. These values include wisdom, ACTION, **CONSISTENCY**...

Pride yourself on always upholding values demonstrative of your inherent role as a leader. This doesn't mean you need to be superhuman! Show the REALITY of your humanity by being true to who you are and by leading first through example. The BEST leaders demonstrate resilience. While life is happening to everyone else, the example of the leader illustrates malleability—the ability to BOUNCE BACK!

Life doesn't quit—leaders don't either, so BE **CONSISTENT**! Be STRONG and courageous! Don't shake at every little sign of trouble. Be wise in your approach and methodical in your movements. Don't be hurried but make pointed progress with clear intent.

Say Aloud: **I Am Wise! I Take Action! I Am Consistent! I Lead!**

November

"

I TEACH!!!

"

You impart knowledge to others by teaching them the lessons that you've learned. The knowledge that you've acquired is shared with others to increase their own intelligence in any subject matter.

Words are typically thought of as the primary method used to teach *yet* there are a great many lessons taught using no words at all.

Understanding that teaching isn't limited to words, embrace teaching using various means. Recognize that others gain from you based on your lifestyle, your mistakes, your character and your decisions. People learn more from you based on these factors than they learn by simply hearing your words, so what are you teaching?

Affirmation Journal
- ★ **What are others learning through my example?**
- ★ **What are others learning through my words?**
- ★ **Are these messages similar OR are there mixed signals?**

Say Aloud: **I Teach! My Life is *the* Example of My Teaching!**

Preach the Gospel at all times,
and when necessary, use words.

FRANCIS OF ASSISI

November 15

"

I Am SHARING!

"

In charity and benevolence, show your favor toward others; in humility, provide gifts of time, talent and resources with the world around you; by way of your lifestyle, impart the growth that you've been blessed to experience. *This* is how you share.

Sharing is the pathway toward positivity in a world ripe with negativity! Sharing is great inspiration to all who receive its reward! Sharing is a means of support and encouragement, often unsolicited yet always available when needed.

You are purposed to share. Your life conditions you to be a recipient of sharing, so relish the opportunity to *return* the favor! When you share, you show that others have been MORE for you than you have sometimes been for yourself even in the smallest things.

Random and repeat acts of kindness show the epitome of the sharer's soul! Endeavor to touch MANY souls in the same manner that many have touched YOURS!

Say Aloud: **I Am Sharing! I Am *Showing* Kindness!**

November

" I DO!!! "

What are you doing with your time? What are you doing with your life? What are you doing with all that you've been given? Are you taking actions that will change your life? Are you taking actions that will change your community?

Goals and dreams are nothing if you do nothing to achieve them. High regard and respect is nothing if you do nothing to show it. You must be a DOer! SHOW through your ACTIONS! If you take no action, what are you showing? What are you showing to *yourself* and what are you showing to others?

*Do*ers don't ask for permission—they take action! Instead of tip-toeing through your life looking for permission to take charge, COMMAND control by taking action to create the life you deserve! Be a *DOER*!

Affirmation Journal
- ★ **What am I doing with my time?**
- ★ **What am I doing with my life?**
- ★ **What am I doing with all that I have been given?**

*If you're not making mistakes,
then you're not doing anything.
I'm positive that a doer makes mistakes.*

JOHN WOODEN

November 17

"

I Will Give!

"

The MOST helpful people in life are those who are givers! Givers increase your potential by providing you with resources not otherwise at your disposal. They help you see that the world is even more beautiful than you once viewed it. Giving people cause you to be humble, grateful and... well, you learn to become a giver yourself!

Today's To-Do's...
- ★ Give thanks to those who have helped you along the way.
- ★ List out 10 people who have sown into you in the past.
- ★ For each of them, fulfill a "random" act of kindness.

The act of giving solidifies the goal of kindness. Giving is a tangible means of showing kindness and supporting others. Humility results from awareness of the desire to move the passions of others forward as you simultaneously position *yourself* for forward mobility. Through giving, you also honor and thank those who have helped to pave the way for you in life.

Affirmation Journal
- ★ Who have I supported through my giving?
- ★ How have my gifts benefited others?
- ★ How do my gifts benefit me?

Say Aloud: I Will Give! I Gift Others with My Support!

November

My Life is a GIFT!

Life is a gift to be cherished and shared with those around you! The secrets of your life are unlocked with each opportunity you take to share more of yourself in deed and truth. You provide awakening for the souls of others when you expand yourself through giving. As you use our own gifts of light, you take the stand for others to do the same!

Embrace the gifts that God has given you. Embrace your LIFE! Understand that you are not here by mistake. Your life urges you to a higher calling through which you will fulfill your ultimate path. On the way toward that deeper meaning, challenge yourself to remove the bounds of fear so that you may expand beyond your wildest dreams!

Life is a gift!

What are you doing with yours?

Affirmation Journal
- ★ How am I sharing the gift of my life with myself?
- ★ How am I sharing the gift of my life with others?
- ★ How am I sharing the gift of my life with God?

Say Aloud: My Life is a Gift!

Do not be afraid; our fate
Cannot be taken from us; it is a gift.

DANTE ALIGHIERI

November

" I Am SUPPORTIVE! "

Our society could stand to make GREAT gains in the area of support. Individually, each of us could stand to do the same!

Support is how you demonstrate advocacy for a particular person, product or platform. It's a way to honor and encourage gains made for the betterment of individual communities and of society as a whole. By being supportive, you not only endorse those with the courage to branch out, but you also increase awareness of steps necessary to back others who are doing the same.

Say Aloud: I Am Supportive! I Will *Show* Support to Others!

Always be willing to provide services and contributions to those who are setting the stage for change. This includes those within your immediate environment and also those with global scale. Support is shown in many ways and humble support isn't guided by personal gains for any contributions of time, effort or commitment, so don't support others based on whether they support you. Support your fellowman in the same manner that you would have him or her support you—in *true* humility and kindness.

Affirmation Journal
- ★ How supportive am I of others?
- ★ How supportive am I of myself?
- ★ In what ways will I show support in the future?

November

"

I Will Not Be a CRITIC!

"

With all that you learn in life, these lessons are less about making firm assessments and more about learning how to best navigate within in a dynamic world.

All too often, many people voluntarily take the fruitless opportunity to place themselves within the role of critic. Insufficient details viewed from misinformed eyes are seemingly enough to make far-reaching judgments that consequently limit realization of objective viewpoints. These invalid critiques keep *everyone* from the goals of respect and diversity. Since it stifles interactions, poor judgment prevents diversity, unity, growth and creativity. People end up existing alone yet humans are inadequately equipped to traverse life alone.

Learn how to exist in this world without judging others. If you assess anyone at all, assess only yourself. Be your own governing authority where *facts* are the basis of your claims.

Say Aloud: **I Will Not Be a Critic! I Will Not Judge Others!**

The ability to observe without evaluating is the highest form of intelligence.

JIDDU KRISHNAMURTI

November 21

"

I Will MENTOR!

"

Mentoring presents you with the opportunity to give back to your respective community. Through mentoring you're able to pave the way for other bright individuals to access resources that may or may not have been shared with you. In seeing goodness in those around you, your hope should always be toward their betterment. Join top talent on their paths by offering them the advantage of mentorship whereby you instill values and skill-sets that will propel them into their BEST future! *You just can't pass up GREAT talent!*

Relish the opportunity to mentor a deserving individual! As much as they benefit from what is gained from *you*, you benefit all the more by what you gain from *them*!

After parenting, mentoring is the next BEST thing! ☺

It doesn't matter your race, age, occupation, religion, creed... **EVERYONE** is a prime candidate to mentor another individual! Informally, you already silently mentor based on your lifestyle, so take your stewardship to the next level and FORMALLY invite someone to be your mentee! Share with them the same knowledge you *wish* was shared with you!

Help another soul along on their journey throughout life!

Say Aloud: **I Will Mentor! I Will Pay It Forward!**

November

"

I Will Speak LIFE!

"

Of all the words that escape your lips on any given day, how much of what you say is actually positive? How often can you count on yourself to verbalize affirming statements throughout the course of a single day? Think about it! Are you the Negative Nancy, Debbie Downer or Petty Patty of your group? Maybe you're a Melancholy Michael, Sickening Sam or Billy the Bully. If you are: **STOP!!!!**

NO ONE wants to be around you with all of your *constant* negativity!!! If you're honest with yourself, you realize that YOU don't even want to be around you! QUIT with all of the negative talk and be more positive in your life! Don't settle for just THINKING positive, but DO positive, BE positive and SPEAK positively! SAY ALOUD the things that you WILL achieve in life and stop always waiting around for someone else to encourage you or pat you on the back! DIY!

DO IT YOURSELF!!!!

In ALL that you *do* and in all that you *say* today, let it portray your path toward POSITIVISM! **SPEAK LIFE!!!**

> *Few things in the world are more powerful*
> *than a positive push.*
> *A smile. A world of optimism and hope.*
> *A 'you can do it' when things are tough.*
>
> RICHARD M. DEVOS

November 23

"

I Will SHARE!

"

Life is too short to disregard expressing thoughts of love, care, and concern. If there's someone that you love or someone that you miss, do what it takes to let them know!

All too often, people miss moments to show and to share in gratitude for others. Some people are *quick* to think that no one loves them and that no one cares.

BE the love that you want to receive! *Show* others the same acts of kindness, generosity and appreciation that you would want them to show you. Love and kindness toward others should never be about whether they will, or will not, show that same measure to you in return. Be kind *just because*! Be kind because it's the RIGHT thing to do and because random acts of kindness make you, the giver, feel just as good as the recipient!

Be random today!
SHARE!

Affirmation Journal
- ★ When was the last time I shared my love for a friend?
- ★ How often do I share my appreciation for others?
- ★ Who, in my life, needs to know that I care about them?

Say Aloud: I Will Share! I Will Show Others Loving Kindness!

November

" I Will Spread GOOD CONTAGION! "

During speaking engagements, I explain to participants that I SPEAK with **exclamation points**!!! I even use considerable exclamation points within my written communication! Exclamation points are a tenant of my personality! The more exclamation points I *use*, the more exclamation points I *feel*!

Imagine how people perceive you, and your life, when you use exclamation points. Of course, you can't bank *wholly* on perception here, but OH THE **JOY** when *perception* of exclamation points becomes *reality* for you! Ohhhhh… You have LIVED at that point!

The world (i.e. **LIFE!**) could present you with trial upon trial, yet trials are only trials if you *view* them as such. Think about it! The goal, then, is to change your way of *thinking*. The more you *view* life as positive, the more positive life will BE!

Bring JOY to your life and also to the lives of others. A person always has good things to say about those who helped them laugh, smile and LIVE! Spread good contagion!

> *I do believe we're all connected.*
> *I do believe in positive energy.*
> *I do believe in the power of prayer.*
> *I do believe in putting good out into the world.*
> *And I believe in taking care of each other.*
>
> HARVEY FIERSTEIN

November

"

I SHOW!

"

Kindness is the practice of doing unto others as you would have them do unto you. It involves practices of sacrifice, humility and peace, in love. The best role that you can take in kindness is that of the leader, the giver, the *do*er. *Show* kindness to others and kindness will be received back to you! Believe the best of others and let your leadership show them how to do the same. Be the BEST example you can be in showing character that is resilient, refined and REMARKABLE. Without being haughty, give others a reason to *be* and to *do* better for themselves by seeing *your* fine example.

Say Aloud: **I Am a Leader! I Am a Giver! I Am a Doer! I *Show*!**

In your demonstrations of kindness, be a model of diplomacy. Let your humility speak VOLUMES by how you show random acts of kindness as much as you possibly can. Without having an expectation of ANYTHING, show others the same amount of kindness, generosity and love as you would like to receive from them in return.

Affirmation Journal
- ★ How can I show that I believe the best of myself?
- ★ How can I show that I believe the best of others?
- ★ How can I show that I am a model of leadership?

November

> ## I Am a VESSEL!

Don't be under the impression that your life exits only for you—it doesn't. Don't think that every lesson that you learn is only for you—it isn't. Don't think that you are here only to help yourself—you aren't! Get it? Got it?! GOOD!

Life is SO much bigger than who you are and what you can accomplish by your own right. Life is composed of self PLUS every little thing, big thing, seen and unseen, real or fake thing that comes within your awareness—that includes people. Don't make the mistake of living as if the things you experience exist only for your own personal growth. Some of what you experience happens for everyone else BUT you! Ever consider that?! You've existed in someone's life at some point simply because of what *you* had to offer *them*! The experience existed for you *solely* because of what you were in the moment for another human being. Let that simmer.

Life exists for you to guide yourself. It also exists for you to guide others to be better. Be the vessel that you were created to be. Be all things to all people. Teach and let them learn.

Say Aloud: **I Am a Vessel! My Life Exists for Others Too!**

My religion is very simple.
My religion is kindness.

DALAI LAMA XIV

November

> ## I SHARE!

Sharing is Caring!

It's true! Sharing *is* caring. The contributions that you invest into others are a telltale sign of your care and concern for them. Sharing isn't limited to direct gifts of time, money or other physical means of giving—you share through your lifestyle, your character and through expressions of goodness shown within your interactions.

In being resourceful, share the information you have at your disposal and give others the knowledge that you've received. In being gifted in various skill-sets, share your gifts as a volunteer, teacher or business owner while giving back your talents as goods or services. In being committed to acts of kindness, share through mentoring, helping and bettering *yourself* so that you may give back to your community the value that was once given to you.

Commit to sharing *all* that you have to give. Don't limit your engagement with life by not sharing who you are with the ENTIRE world! Deeper meaning and solid connections are found when you share. Sharing opens the door for growth, both internally and outwardly into the world.

What will YOU share?

Affirmation Journal

★ **What additional growth could be seen within my world if I learned to share more?**

November

"

I Will Serve My COMMUNITY Better!

"

Community service makes the world go 'round! Without serving your immediate community *first*, you truly miss the **ULTIMATE MISSION** of individualistic service to all humanity. Service and community go hand in hand. They act right alongside unity, pride and resolution. Of all that ails the world, humanity would find FERVENT resolve should people venture to place their efforts *directly* into the communities where they reside. Anytime you look around your own environment and think, "Something's missing!", *that* is the exact moment that you should follow up with an action-prone brainstorm targeted to fix whatever is broken— provide whatever is missing. You can't be disappointed by what you don't endeavor to change.

The feeling of disappointment is a **Call to ACTION**:

DO Something About It!!!

Complaints are impractical when you can *always* be a FACILITATOR of change.

Instead of simply *talking*, start serving!

Say Aloud: **I Will Serve My Community Better!!!**

The best index to a person's character is how he treats people who can't do him any good, and how he treats people who can't fight back.

ABIGAIL VAN BUREN

November 29

" I WILL GO GREEN! "

Socially, responsibilities are boundless. You have a duty to serve your community through efforts that will change society, and in turn, impact the world.

What are YOU doing to impact lasting change within your environment?

The Go Green cause has been developed to prolong use of resources within the environment. Practices have been implemented that will extend the lifespan of natural resources so that they may be useful to future generations. Help these initiatives by recycling goods that are able to be reused. Re-purpose items and make a commitment to be more mindful when using resources. By increasing awareness on the topic, you learn that there are a great many ways to Go Green green in practice.

Going Green starts with a mindset to lead a less wasteful life. As you become more socially responsible and supportive toward just causes, you also challenge others to do the same.

How are YOU going green?

Say Aloud: **I Will Go Green! I Challenge *Others* to Go Green!**

November

"

I Will Be KIND!

"

As a child, one of the first skills that you are taught is kindness. You learn how to share and how to be aware of your playmates with the hope of developing into an adult who readily embraces fellowship and friendship.

Kindness, in all of its golden simplicity, is the easiest—yet sometimes most difficult—of all traits. Kindness is all too often based on your mood in any given moment which means your ability to *fulfill* acts of kindness flexes numerous times within any given day. Exhibitions of kindness shouldn't rest so heavily on your moods. If you are to change your moods to be more positive, acts of kindness are a GREAT place to start! By showing others positivity, you reap the same happiness that you graciously sow.

Don't ever let a sour mood detour you from doing something kind for another. No matter what is done to you, share love by being kind to everyone you come in contact with. The rewards of your good nature will be evidenced by your pure heart, your gentle spirit and by the lasting calm that will encircle your life. Let your kindness speak for you!

Be nice.
And if you can't do that, just don't be mean.

RICHELLE E. GOODRICH

12 Love

December 1

> ## I Will Work on LOVE!

People make love such a sticky issue! *Such* a tricky topic! Love is an *in-your-FACE-even-when-you-turn-your-BACK-to-it* topic—*especially* when turning your back to love is an outcry of your YEARNING for that which seemingly cannot be obtained! There are SO many misunderstandings in love—so many tried and true, untried and untrue conspicuous conceptions of this "thing" that humans so readily, so consistently, chase after. Equally, people very readily and very consistently SQUANDER any promising steps in the direction of the lifelong goal of love.

Why is that? That's **NOT** love! Love rejoices in righteousness and truth. Love believes BEST of everyone. Love is sacrificial, humble, mannerly, proper and selfless! Love takes **NO** account of wrong! Love is EASY (*once you get out of the way!!!*)!

Learn to LOVE and learn to love HARD!

Love Affirmation *(Repeat this aloud)*
True love addresses my will, not my emotion. I will love by choice, without exception and with no expectation. My love will be a strong, enduring, unfailing and unconditional, desire and exhibition of goodwill toward myself and others.

Say Aloud: **I Will Work on LOVE! I Will Love and Love *Hard*!**

December

> **I Will Be LOVING!**

How does one become more loving? **Just Do It!** You can't spend time *trying* to figure it out, and you definitely can't wait on others to take the lead! YOU are the love you seek! *Do unto others as you would have them do unto you*! This method works WONDERS in your outlook on life and in how your guide yourself. It causes you to exhibit much more self-control, more leniency, more patience, understanding and all of the characteristics that have been covered in this book. You gain it all simply by using yourself as the guiding keystone. In turn, you become more loving toward others!

Affirmation Journal
- **What is my guiding principle for showing love?**
- **How has that guiding principle helped me love?**
- **In what areas of my life can I be more loving?**

Don't *try* to be loving. **Just Do It!** Tasks dependent upon *attempts* to complete them are as good as those gone UNDONE!

Stop *trying*. Start DOING. *Be* **LOVING!**

Love doesn't mean anything if you're not willing to make a commitment, and you have to think not only about what you want, but about what (s)he wants. Not just now, but in the future.

NICHOLAS SPARKS

December

"

I Will CHERISH My Heritage!

"

Value your heritage. Put stock in where you come from to see great strides illustrated by where you are going. Stories aren't told if not imbued with the history that produces them. You are nothing without your past. You are incomplete without clarity, and the substance upon which your stories are based is found within your bloodline.

You can't separate yourself from that which molded and shaped you into your current state. What becomes of your legacy without someone to pass your story from one generation to the next? What becomes of legacies of your forefathers without stories that are cherished and shared?

Existence isn't grounded in the present—it is founded upon ages and ages of families who came before you to pave the way for *your* greatness. Don't take their stories lightly. Don't take their lives lightly. In finding deeper connection with yourself, you are more than remiss if you leave out the paths of your heritage.

Cherish your heritage. Add definition to your legacy.

Affirmation Journal
- ★ **What do I know about my heritage?**
- ★ **What would I like to find out about my heritage?**
- ★ **Where will I start?**

Say Aloud: **I Will Cherish My Heritage and Define My Legacy!**

December

" I Will Nurture POSITIVE Relationships! "

Relationships come and go—the good ones and the bad ones. They come. They go. All of the relationships that you are blessed with don't come to last a lifetime. Your unions with others serve various purposes—some serve as examples, some as teachers and some as testers. No matter the relationships you find yourself in, ALWAYS seek to maintain those that bring good into your life.

The value of positive relationships is immeasurable. Gains made through those who bear fruits of positivity are too limitless to count. For that reason, maintenance of these relationships is wise. Positive relationships increase long-term happiness, so be bold in fighting for relationships where the brilliance seems endless. Release what is negative. Maintain that which brings joy!

Affirmation Journal
- ★ What types of positive relationships do I maintain?
- ★ How do I nurture those relationships?
- ★ How do I handle negative relationships in a manner that will increase my happiness?

Let us be grateful to the people who make us happy;
they are the charming gardeners
who make our souls blossom.

MARCEL PROUST

December

"
I Will CHERISH My Parents!
"

No matter whether you have good ones, great ones *or* if they are downright HORRIBLE, your parents are a gift.

Say Aloud: **Parents are a Gift! I Will Cherish My Parents!**

If asked, you could surely recount a slew of misdeeds faced at the hands of your parents. You could feel, for whatever reason, that your parents are to blame for any and all injustices you faced prior to adulthood. Even still, there is *much* wisdom, ownership and PEACE in acknowledging that everything your parents were—and everything that they were not—comes to make up everything that you *are* and everything that you will *become*!

This awakening deserves reflection.

At this point, some of you could stop reading this book ENTIRELY because in the above statements you have obtained all that you EVER needed! You're nearly done reading though, so how about we just carry on? ☺

Parents have a tough job, and some parents just will NOT get it right! The brilliance of it is that ALL of the chaos and celebration that defines your experience with your parents is to be cherished for all that it made YOU! Your development required a great many things—some hurtful and harmful, some happy and heavenly. This combination created the perfect YOU, so cherish your parents. YOU are their gift!

December

"
I Will Make My PARENTS Proud!
"

From infamous macaroni pictures planted on the fridge until the pasta fell off, to the things brought home from school that you can't *quite* make out, children ALWAYS endeavor to make their mommies and daddies proud! As a child, you LIVE for the days that you would make your parents proud and GREAT parents were always most eager to share their children's successes with the rest of WORLD! Who knew this wouldn't change once you transitioned into adulthood? There is STILL that twang of happiness in knowing you make your parents smile, not to mention the unrehearsed mental back-flips you do when they publicly acknowledge their pride. The pride of your parents makes you happy!

Affirmation Journal
★ How do I feel to know that I make my parents proud?
★ When was the last time I made my parents proud?
★ What has made my parents *most* proud of me?

Parents live for successes of their children. Parents thrive on the joys and accomplishments of their babies. As a fully grown adult baby, you will continually make them proud!

> *Parents were the only ones obligated to love you;*
> *from the rest of the world you had to earn it.*
>
> ANN BRASHARES

December

"

I Will Be a Better SIBLING!

"

Your siblings don't choose you, and you don't choose them, but you can bet your butt that YOU have the BEST of the bunch because the siblings that you have are **YOURS**!!! They are the pick of the litter chosen especially for YOU—with your brilliant self!

As brilliant as you are, have you ever taken your siblings for granted? Have you ever been less for your siblings than you were for others who don't fill such an important role in your life? How is it that you can be better to others than you are to your very own siblings? Though you have your reasons—endless, endless reasons—make the commitment right now—this very moment—to do better by your siblings!

Be a better sibling and watch that same betterment be reciprocated within your environment. Take whatever steps you can RIGHT NOW to treat your siblings better! Tell them all of the good things that you've never shared. Tell them all of the good things that they need to hear! Tell them all of the good things that you need to get off of your chest, and GO AHEAD: **Be a Better Sibling!**

Affirmation Journal
- ★ **How can I be a better sibling?**
- ★ **What would I like to share verbally with my sibling(s)?**
- ★ **What experiences would I like to share with my sibling(s)?** *(Consider the past and future.)*

December

> **I Will CHERISH Sweet Memories!**

Your life is the culmination of memories that you've created and those that you have shared. Memories last a lifetime while all else fades away. Memories are what matter. They are an illustration of all you have experienced. Memories contain your joys, your sorrows, your progress and your pain. They stay to remind you of your gains and losses—of the lessons that you've learned—and for that, they should always be cherished and never left behind.

Affirmation Journal
- ★ **What sweet memories do I have?**
- ★ **What sweet memories have I shared with others?**
- ★ **What sweet memories have I created for others?**

Your legacy lives in memories—it shouldn't die there. All that you have to share should be expressed in the best manner possible so that you have the opportunity to create even more memories while allowing your legacy to live on.

Look for every chance to create new experiences and cherish the sweet memories that you have.

*What matters in life is not what happens to you
but what you remember and how you remember it.*

GABRIEL GARCÍA MÁRQUEZ

December

"

I Am Full of GRACE!

"

If you chose it to be so, your life could be filled with much aggression. As a passionate being, you could create aggression in even the *simplest* of situations based solely on your disposition. Through grace, with love for yourself primarily, you learn to temper emotional exhibitions. You learn that all is not won in rage or anger. Supposed gains acquired in negativity are short-lived once you learn that the methods leave long-term consequences of madness.

Wisdom employs the practice of grace. Learned individuals know that it is better to tiptoe lightly through discord and leave in wholeness than to foolishly stomp around in vain fits of rage and return to a life in shambles.

Be graceful in your demonstrations of passion. Mind your manners *and* your pulse rate! Spare yourself any and all drama by maintaining a peaceful spirit. Just. Breathe.

The grace that you exemplify can only gain you blessings in the end. In grace, there is peace, strength, and wisdom, notwithstanding all of the value gained in stewardship. The resulting fortune of such a spirit will be seen in all you do.

Huge gains are to be had for all who are models of grace!

Affirmation Journal
- ★ Why is gracefulness an indispensable quality to have?
- ★ How can I show myself to be a model of grace?
- ★ What are some situations where I can be more graceful?

December

"

I Am FORGIVING!

"

A forgiving individual is a graceful individual. A forgiving individual is peaceful, gentle and good. A forgiving individual is a human first. EVERY human makes mistakes. Repeated mistakes turn into bad habits, and... well, humans have bad habits!

Being forgiving means that you love past mistakes that others have made. You love enough not to dwell on painful memories or negative reminders of hurt you endured at the hands of others or other hurt you've placed upon yourself.

Don't be predisposed to hanging onto pain for the sake of having a poor story to tell. LET PAIN GO! Let anger go! Learn to forgive, and don't battle in rage. Don't allow any other person to gain control of your emotions in a negative way. Don't excuse your own poor behavior by justifying negative actions! Be accountable to yourself while maintaining a spirit of peace, and **BE FORGIVING**!

Don't hold onto negativity at all! Let it go IMMEDIATELY. Spare yourself the agony of a heart in turmoil. FORGIVE!

Say Aloud: **I Am Forgiving! I Do Not Hold On! I Let Go!!!**

The best fighter is never angry.

LAO TZU

December

> ## I Am FORGIVABLE!

Accept the truth about YOU—you make mistakes. Everyone does! Mistakes are part of what makes you human.

Owning up to mistakes and moving past them is done through awareness, acknowledgment and accountability. Without patience though, mistakes begin to haunt you. Poor decisions become lifelong demons that turn into generational baggage—hurt caused to numerous individuals simply because YOU did not forgive *yourself*.

Forgiveness is as simple as love. **JUST DO IT!** Like love, forgiveness is only as complicated as you make it! The love that you have for yourself warrants your own forgiveness. Know that you are worth it. YOU are worth forgiveness. YOU are worth moving on. YOU are worth letting go of past mistakes. Your future happiness depends on it!

No matter what you have done, YOU ARE FORGIVABLE!

Say Aloud: **I AM FORGIVABLE! I Have Forgiven Myself!**

Forgive yourself! God has already forgiven you. Now, give others the opportunity to forgive you! Write a letter. Send a message. Humbly explain your position and request their forgiveness. That is all you have to do!

No matter what you have done, YOU ARE FORGIVABLE!

December

" I AM WORTHY!!! "

Self-worth is the image that you create of yourself. Feelings of self-worth impact every single action that you take, every single engagement that you make and every single experience that you gain from life. Positive self-image isn't only essential to livelihood, it is REQUIRED for success! The goals you create and those that you accomplish are based on your feelings of self-worth. You can't achieve anything greater than what your self-worth allows you to!

It is up to you to *constantly* declare: **I AM WORTHY!!!**

Remove any notion of the thoughts, feelings and fears of others from the assessment of YOUR worth. Your value is as great as YOU believe it is! Don't let any other person determine how YOU feel about YOURSELF! **Don't give people control over YOU!!!** You have ALL of the power, control and knowledge that you need to CONSTANTLY declare: **I AM WORTHY!!!**

Say Aloud: **I Am Worthy! I Am WORTHY! I AM WORTHY!!!**

Everything that happens to you
is a reflection of what you believe about yourself.
We cannot outperform our level of self-esteem.
We cannot draw to ourselves more than
we think we are worth.

IYANLA VANZANT

December 13

"
I Am LEADING!
"

There are leaders, and there are followers. Everyone reading *this* book is a leader because you have taken the time to enlighten yourself! Not only will you enlighten yourself, but you will also take the steps necessary to *be* and to *do* better.

Way to lead! Kudos to you!!!

Leading isn't about being the head of the pack, having a title or receiving recognition. Leading is about being a great steward. If the best thing that you can steward is yourself, you have chosen the ONLY starting point! KUDOS AGAIN!

Leadership is grounded in ACTION. Leaders don't wait and watch without taking action. Leaders don't leave the fun to everyone else while they sit in a cushy, plush chair. Leaders get off their butts! Leaders take the wheel! Leaders make the charge!

Are you leading? Is life passing you by while you wait on it to be perfect? Will you have more regrets under your belt than learning opportunities? Ask yourself: **Am I leading?**

Affirmation Journal
- **What internal qualities make me a leader?**
- **How do I outwardly demonstrate that I am a leader?**
- **How can I be a better leader?**

Say Aloud: **I Am Leading! I Enlighten Myself *and* Others!**

December

"I Am LOVING!"

Do you put your BEST foot forward in love opportunities? Do you demonstrate that you are an individual *willing* to share in love? Whether they be friend or foe, how do you treat people who come in contact with you? **Are you loving?**

We all know SO many people who are *yearning* for love, hoping for love, praying for love, fighting for love, fighting *in* love—people LOST, trying to FIND love—people lost, trying to find that which they can CREATE!!!

Don't get lost trying to find what you already *are*!

Be Love.

Be Loving.

Affirmation Journal
- ★ How do I make and take the BEST love opportunities?
- ★ How do I demonstrate my willingness to share in love?
- ★ How do I treat the people that come in contact with me, whether they be friend or foe?
- ★ How do I show that I am loving?

Say Aloud: **I Am Loving! I Love Myself *and* Others!**

...because I thought I was in love.
And when you think you're in love, you are willing to stick it out and make it work until it is love.

BECCA FITZPATRICK

December 15

"

I Am LOVABLE!

"

Ask yourself: **Am I lovable?** EVERYONE is *able* to be loved!
Ask yourself: **Am I lovable? Do I *allow* myself to be loved?**

Allowance of love is an entirely different matter altogether! Consideration of whether you *accept* love takes into account the limits that you place on others, the limits that you place on yourself and more importantly, it calls into question the limits that you place on LOVE!

Any individual missing love from their life is simply not *allowing* love into their life. Love is everywhere and in all things! In situations where love seems hard to find, dig DEEP! Love is EVERYONE and in ALL things because love exists *within* everyone!!!

Find love within yourself and spread that outwardly into the WORLD! Always love others as you would have them love you. Always love others as you already love yourself! Self-love is where all other love flows from, so love yourself with GREAT love!

Affirmation Journal
- ★ **How lovable am I?**
- ★ **How well do I love myself?**
- ★ **How well do I allow myself to be loved by others?**

Say Aloud: **I Am Lovable! I Allow *and* Accept Love!**

December

"

I Am RICH in Love!

"

Love, as an act, is a matter of *how* you do it versus *if* you do it. That being a fact, it goes without question that you should impose NO governance on the capacity of love. The goal is not to control love or to limit love—you should love without concern, without question and with MUCH conviction. You should love without struggle, against all opposition. You love because without the joy of *it*, life just isn't enough!

You become for others what you seek for *yourself*! To *feel* richness in love, you *show* richness in love! Show love unto others as you would have them show love unto you!

Affirmation Journal
* How do I behave regarding love?
* How do I limit love?
* How do I show richness in love?

Say Aloud: **I Am Rich in Love! I *Show* the Love That I Seek!**

'Did I offer peace today?
Did I bring a smile to someone's face?
Did I say words of healing? Did I let go of my anger and resentment? Did I forgive? Did I love?'
These are the real questions.
I must trust that the little bit of love that I sow now will be many fruits, here in this world and the life to come.

HENRI NOUWEN

December 17

"

My Life is a BLESSING!

"

Life, in and of itself, is a blessing! Life is the most palpable blessing you will EVER receive. There are so many things that you could be, but to be ALIVE, is the *finest* accomplishment of them all! ☺

Say Aloud: **My Life is a Blessing!**

With all of your wins and losses, successes and failures, the blessing of life itself warrants *much* acknowledgment and appreciation. Don't focus your time on too many objects that will never be as essential to you as life itself.

Say Aloud: **My Life is a Blessing!**

Through the activities that you partake in and by the way that you live your life, you MUST exhibit gratitude for the gift of life. There is no better way to demonstrate your gratefulness than by living life to the fullest, *giving* your best and by *getting* the best out of EVERY moment!

Say Aloud: **My Life is a Blessing!**

Affirmation Journal
- ★ How do I personally KNOW that my life is a blessing?
- ★ How has my life been a blessing to others specifically?
- ★ How can I ensure that I will always appreciate my life?

December

I Will Bring JOY to Lives of Others!

Happiness is my goal. The core trait of *joy* is what I desire above ALL else in the world. Lucky me, the pursuit of happiness involves standard components and my prioritization of *joy* finds me in possession of other noteworthy traits along the way. A prioritization of joy also finds me in the BEST place to bring that same joy into the lives of others!

It's easy to find the people who value happiness and joy! They are the people you find smiling and laughing and taking the BEST from EACH adventure! They are the people who view life as an adventure versus those who view it as a countdown until the clock runs out. **OUCH!**

Don't be one of those people who are simply "here" feeling as though they have no purpose and no enjoyment to take out of any experience. Bring the BEST *to* life! GET the BEST *from* life!

Affirmation Journal
- ★ **What do I bring to life?**
- ★ **What do I get from life?**
- ★ **What do I bring to the lives of others?**

*The best way to cheer yourself
is to try to cheer someone else up.*

MARK TWAIN

December 19

"I Want to Feel God's Love!"

Love—without all of its man-made complexities—is a profoundly simple concept. Love becomes complicated when you put humanistic logic behind a commodity that can't be fully conceptualized within the limits of the brain, therefore making your attainment of it all the more... intangible. Don't make love something that it is not with all of your negative opinions, faulty logic and nonessential reasons for not being able to freely give, and freely receive, a gift that never left and always was: Love.

Love always is. Love always was. Love will always be.

God always is. God always was. God will always be.

God is love. God never leaves. Your desire to love anyone or receive love from anyone is unequivocally your desire to feel and receive God's love—the gift that always is. It is your attempt at connecting with God—God always is. Any lack in love consists of man-made constructs that interfere with the love connection for which you yearn.

The BIGGEST mistake is that you seek a love in people that is *only* found in God. Feeling God's love is to feel a love free of enmity, strife and judgment. God's love is love in the only form that *always* exists. God's love is love without blemish. To desire the feeling of God's love is to simply desire God. God. Is. Love. No need to desire what is already there. The key is to *accept* Him. God is as real as your mind allows Him to be, so too, is pure love. Love is as real as you allow it be.

December

> **I Want to Love Like God Loves!**

Say Aloud:

I've learned many things in love and war. I've learned to enjoy the experience and to never miss a moment. There are still lessons to be loved and learned. I am learning to love and learning to love hard. I am learning to love without recompense, to love without thinking, to love without knowing, and learning to love while *showing*. As wholeheartedly as I can, I am learning to love in the same manner that I *want* to be loved in return.

I want to love. I want to love hard. I want to love without warning, without expectation and without exception—I want to love without ceasing! LOVE WITHOUT A LIMIT! I want a love without walls—a no holds barred kinda love.

I want to love with as much of my heart as I can stand to give: Love when it hurts; Love through the hurt; Love where love is welcome and definitely where it is missed.

I want to love like God loves and reflect the love of God!

The great thing to remember is that though our feelings come and go God's love for us does not.

C.S. Lewis

December 21

> ## I Will LOVE Others BETTER!

In my lifetime, I have yet to come across a person without acceptance issues. I have yet to come across a person without friendship issues. I have yet to come across a person without family issues, life issues—past, present, and future issues— ALL of which are LOVE issues.

Can you believe that?! Really! Can you?

Of all of the love issues you are plagued with, you make a choice every single day to hang onto those issues, many of which would be resolved through the simple act of communication.

You make love more complex than it has to be!

Practice getting out of your own way. Do what is needed to resolve the present love issues you have so that you can live a better, more healthy and stress-free life. Love others better. Do that by sharing! Express your love issues in productive ways so that you can move forward in an abundance of love!

Affirmation Journal
★ What are my love issues?
★ What are the most pressing issues that need resolving?
★ How will my resolution of these issues change my life?

Say Aloud: I Will Lead a Love-Filled Life! I Will Have a Life FREE of the Confines I Place Around and Within My Walls!

December

" I Will Speak LIFE into OTHERS! "

You take so much away from others when you fail to empower them. You take so much away from yourself when you fail to feel empowered enough to do so. Lack of communication, faith and effort is causes you to miss the boat! You can't afford to fear yourself and what you have to bring to the table.

The words that you have to impart are your gift to share with the world. The goal is to SPEAK LIFE into most anyone you come in contact with. There is *always* an opportunity to lift someone up. There is *always* an opportunity to share a kind word, a smile. There is *always* an opportunity to give, to share and to support. Don't shy away from your God-given MANDATE to BE GREAT!

SPEAK LIFE into others EVERY chance you get!

Affirmation Journal
- ★ **What do I want others to feel after interaction with me?**
- ★ **What *do* others feel after our interaction?** *(Ask a few.)*
- ★ **How can I SPEAK LIFE into others?**
- ★ **How can I be better?**

> *Correction does much,*
> *but encouragement does more.*
>
> JOHANN WOLFGANG VON GOETHE

December 23

> **I Have MANY Loving FRIENDS!**

Tabulation of the amount of friends you have in life would be a daunting process should you choose to undertake such a task. Friends come in all shapes, sizes, creeds and nationalities. Your acknowledgment of whether persons are friends to you never takes into consideration a person's simple *desire* to befriend you. Whether you accept their friendship or not, imagine calculating the MASS number of people who would LOVE to be your friend—now, this *is* assuming that you *are* a great person. If you're a horrible person, ehhhh... not so much! ☺

Friends can never *truly* be your friends unless you *let* them. You limit the gains that can be made in productive friendships when you get in the way of it. Try getting out the way for a bit. Open up your eyes to see the love that already SURROUNDS you by way of your friends.

Your friends can only be as loving as you *allow* them to be.

Affirmation Journal
- ★ How loving do I allow my friends to be?
- ★ Who desires to be my friend?
- ★ How might I be getting in the way of friendship?
- ★ What type of limits might I have put on my friends?

Say Aloud: **I Have Many Loving Friends! I Accept Friendship!**

December

"

I Am BLESSED By My FRIENDS!

"

In the same way that God is SO much bigger than the confines of any single religion, your friends are MUCH bigger than ANY limits you would put on a fitting definition for their roles in your life! Friends bring much more to you than you could ever quantify—their sole existence being to increase the joy and experiences you have with life. Friends are everything for you here on earth that you can't be for yourself. The blessings that come along with friendship are too numerous to count! Without friends in your life, what would you do with the enjoyment of it? How could you share all that life offers you?

Friends help you navigate. They help you to explore various destinations, and they give you something to come back to. Friends remind you of home—of all that you've come to be in life. Friends keep you aware of your truest identity. They are your mirror of self-reflection.

Affirmation Journal
- ★ How have my friends blessed my life?
- ★ How can I show my appreciation for friendship?

*A friend is someone who knows all about you
and still loves you.*

ELBERT HUBBARD

December 25

> ## I Will OPEN My Heart!

Closed mouths don't get fed. What happens with closed hearts? The tricky thing about closed hearts is that sometimes you don't always know that they're closed!

Everyone has been fated with the experience of feeling ways that can't be understood, for having feelings that offer no explanation, or *not* feeling a way that they SHOULD feel! *That one is the WORST!!!*

Opening your own heart has to be something that you're proactive about. Don't put things out of mind simply because they're out of your sight. Don't put things out of mind because they cause you too much pain. Don't put things out of mind because you're worried about interfering with another person's life. Opening up is about YOUR heart. It's about saving YOUR soul. Once you embrace saving grace for yourself, the awakening will readily spill over into those around you.

Being introspective, responsible and accountable means healing in places you dare not visit! It means checking spots, opening doors, and getting to the bottom of feelings you may not even be aware of.

While you can't be faulted for what you're unaware of within yourself, you *can* open your heart to whatever comes within your awareness: good, bad, ugly or hidden!

Say Aloud: I Will Open My Heart! I Will Be More Aware!

December

"
I Will LISTEN to My Heart!
"

Because people have brains, they feel FORCED to use them! HA! People feel compelled to substantiate that which defies logic: feelings. Once feelings become involved, ineffective handling of the negative ones makes emotions altogether unbearable. Some people decide that they're better off dealing with **no** emotion at all rather than suffering with misuse of any negative emotions.

Choose a different option for yourself personally! Give YOURSELF more credit! Give your HEART more credit! Contrary to common belief, your heart is designed to carry burdens MUCH worse than what you *think* it is capable of. Mental capacity likes to limit even what your mind can withstand, but that's just logic speaking! If the heart had a position in the matter, it would say, "Minds withstand little suffrage, and hearts bear it ALL!"

Listen to your heart! Be open with the things that you feel and know that it is absolutely OK to *feel*. THEN, go on to express pain in a productive manner! Be patient with yourself and others. Impatience is the result of blocking passion within your heart, so listen to your heart.

To handle yourself, use your head;
to handle others, use your heart.

ELEANOR ROOSEVELT

December 27

"
I Will Show Others the BEST Love!
"

Showing others love can be a daunting task when you make it about them and not about you. Egos have a need to qualify the love you feel and show for others. Minds try to justify what you will and will not do by inadequate measures of whether others deserve your love or not. Don't incorrectly assume that people can *earn* your love while never acknowledging the fact that you are often undeserving of theirs.

This is YOUR life! Take control of your life *and* your love! Get out of life, and love, exactly what you want. Better yet, TAKE out of life exactly what you DEMAND! Those demands can't be at the mercy of your feelings, emotions, love, lust, perception or any other faulty judgment of a biased view of reality. Love can't be limited to that—to thoughts, to the ebb and flow of misunderstood feelings, or limited to the comings and goings of emotionally unstable humans with equally faulty views of *reality*.

Get outside of yourself and take your love to the next level.

Say Aloud: **I Will Show Others the BEST Love!**

I will remove my negative judgments from each love transaction that I make! I will purge myself of unclean beliefs and hindrances that stifle my ability to love in its purest form.

I Will Show Others the BEST Love!

December

"

Sharing LOVE is Always the Best Course of ACTION!

"

Many people limit love and provide biased love thinking that the love they share is for those that they share it with. In actuality, everyone loves for *themselves*! YOU love *others* because it makes *you* feel good, *yet* you walk through life thinking that keeping love to yourself is helping you and hurting someone else. That is NOT true! In limiting love, you are hurting yourself! You don't realize the damage that is done when harboring thoughts of negativity and feelings of *dis-ease*. LET THOSE THINGS **GO**!!! **Your healing is in *sharing* love!** Love enough to clear your heart of the muck of hostility!

Be selfish about your love and watch your love expand! Try loving because of the good feeling that it gives YOU! Loving in this manner removes the hindrances that are found when thinking that others don't deserve or appreciate your love. Do *you* deserve and appreciate your love? If so, share the love that you have to give and make *yourself* feel GREAT! By doing this, you will begin to effortlessly remove those love struggles that have kept you backed up and you will begin to love again! Do it for YOU! Do it for LOVE!

Love is that condition in which
the happiness of another person is essential to your own.

ROBERT A. HEINLEIN

December 29

I Am WILLING!

True healing exists in love. True soul-changing, mind-blowing, problem-solving breakthroughs are found in love. Whatever you are looking for in life can be found in love. Love first starts with self. When you love yourself, you tell the world that you are ready and willing to embrace ALL that it has to offer. The master shift is in learning that abundant self-love readily welcomes love from wherever else it may come. This means that you love others in humility, with reverence and appreciation for their desire to share the blessing of love with you.

Love can't be fully embraced without your awareness of it in *all* things and in *all* people. For any mishandling of love that you have experienced in your past, be willing to take your love to the next level by letting go of whatever may be holding you back. Release people, release habits and release judgments that are keeping you from the goal of love. Be willing to do whatever it takes to find the healing that you need in love. Clean out the closets of darkness and get to the bottom of the filth that remains in your life! If that means having conversations, have them! If that means journaling, do it! Be willing! Be willing to LOVE!

Affirmation Journal
- ★ **What do I need to do in order to fully embrace love?**
- ★ **What *am* I *willing* to do in order to fully embrace love?**

December

"

I Will TRUST!

"

You learn to trust others by learning to trust yourself. Trust in another person is not based upon your misguided beliefs regarding whether they will mess up or not. Humans aren't perfect. You shouldn't expect them to be! Awareness of this reality allows you to *breathe*. Beyond acknowledging the humanity of others, you must also accept imperfection within *yourself*! *Breathe*, again.

Acknowledgment of facts of fallibility within oneself and others doesn't mean that you simply go along with injustices done to yourself and others. It simply means that you can move on *after* the fact without holding on to things or people that are opposed to your goals of progressiveness and peace.

Healthy foundations of trust are found in first trusting *yourself*. Be the best that YOU can be—all else will follow. Set the standard for the trust that you would like to bestow upon others. By being the best and brightest example of trust that you can, expect to receive nothing less but the best in others and be able to quickly discard anything that doesn't measure up to the standard that you've created.

Of all forms of caution,
caution in love is perhaps the most fatal to true happiness.

BERTRAND RUSSELL

December 31

> ## I Will LOVE!

It makes no sense to have a brain and not think. By the same token, it makes no sense to have the capacity to love and not utilize it—when you love, *then* you exist. The ultimate resolution of any year, and the ultimate success in life, is to love! Ending this year with a BANG means committing to just that—LOVE, always, and in *all* ways.

Love like it is the air you need to breathe. Love simply because you need love to *believe*. You know that love exists, so seek it out unceasingly. Love without just cause and for no good reason! Just LOVE! Love because you *have* to. Teach your children and those around you that life is NOTHING if not for love.

Of all that you could accomplish and obtain, it is truly all for naught without love to share its reward. Learn to love with great love. The humble practice of love teaches you to change *yourself*. In changing yourself, you are best positioned to change the WORLD.

Change Your Posture! Change Your LIFE!

Not all of us can do great things.
But we can do small things with great love.

MOTHER TERESA

There's More!

Additional reader-only content including worksheets, workbooks, writing prompts and journals can be found at www.Change-Your-Posture.com. Visit us for resources on this book and others within the Change Your Posture series.

I would LOVE to personally connect with you!
Attn: Coach D Nicole!
Sh'Shares NETWORK
1601-1 N Main St 13202
Jacksonville, FL 32206

www.Change-Your-Posture.com
www.CoachDNicole.com
www.ShShares.com

Send book praise and reading group pictures to:
SHINE@Change-Your-Posture.com

It is my sincere prayer that you were blessed by the contents of this book. I look forward to securing our connection well into the future!
Thank you for your GREATNESS!

Coach D Nicole is a very charming and spirited first-class professional who is passionate about encouraging, supporting and coaching others within their personal lives and business endeavors. As a transformational life coach, she is most loved for her wit, boisterous personality, direct and upfront coaching style, and generous, authentic smile!

www.ingramcontent.com/pod-product-compliance
Lightning Source LLC
Chambersburg PA
CBHW052008070526
44584CB00016B/1666